The Arnold and Caroline Rose Monograph Series
of the American Sociological Association

From student to nurse

Other books in the series

J. Milton Yinger, Kiyoshi Ikeda, Frank Laycock, and Stephen J. Cutler: *Middle Start: An Experiment in the Educational Enrichment of Young Adolescents*

James A. Geschwender: *Class, Race, and Worker Insurgency: The League of Revolutionary Black Workers*

Paul Ritterband: *Education, Employment, and Migration: Israel in Comparative Perspective*

John Low-Beer: *Protest and Participation: The New Working Class in Italy*

Orrin E. Klapp: *Opening and Closing: Strategies of Information Adaptation in Society*

Rita James Simon: *Continuity and Change: A Study of Two Ethnic Communities in Israel*

Marshall B. Clinard: *Cities with Little Crime: The Case of Switzerland*

Steven T. Bossert: *Tasks and Social Relationships in Classrooms: A Study of Instructional Organization and Its Consequences*

Richard E. Johnson: *Juvenile Delinquency and Its Origins: An Integrated Theoretical Approach*

David R. Heise: *Understanding Events: Affect and the Construction of Social Action*

Volumes previously published by the American Sociological Association

Michael Schwartz and Sheldon Stryker: *Deviance, Selves and Others*

Robert M. Hauser: *Socioeconomic Background and Educational Performance*

Morris Rosenberg and Roberta G. Simmons: *Black and White Self-Esteem: The Urban School Child*

Chad Gordon: *Looking Ahead: Self-Conceptions: Race and Family as Determinants of Adolescent Orientation to Achievement*

Anthony M. Orum: *Black Students in Protest: A Study of the Origins of the Black Student Movement*

Ruth M. Gasson, Archibald O. Haller, and William H. Sewell: *Attitudes and Facilitation in the Attainment of Status*

Sheila R. Klatzky: *Patterns of Contact with Relatives*

Herman Turk: *Interorganizational Activation in Urban Communities: Deductions from the Concept of System*

John DeLamater: *The Study of Political Commitment*

Alan C. Kerckhoff: *Ambition and Attainment: A Study of Four Samples of American Boys*

Scott McNall: *The Greek Peasant*

Lowell L. Hargens: *Patterns of Scientific Research: A Comparative Analysis of Research in Three Scientific Fields*

Charles Hirschman: *Ethnic Stratification in Peninsular Malaysia*

From student to nurse
A longitudinal study of socialization

Ida Harper Simpson
Professor of Sociology
Duke University

with

Kurt W. Back
Professor of Sociology
Duke University

Thelma Ingles
Professor Emeritus of Sociology
Rockefeller University

Alan C. Kerckhoff
Professor of Sociology
Duke University

John C. McKinney
Professor of Sociology
Duke University

Cambridge University Press

Cambridge
London   New York   Melbourne

Published by the Syndics of the Cambridge University Press
The Pitt Building, Trumpington Street, Cambridge CB2 1RP
32 East 57th Street, New York, NY 10022, USA
296 Beaconsfield Parade, Middle Park, Melbourne 3206, Australia

© Cambridge University Press 1979

First published 1979

Printed in the United States of America
Typeset by Telecki Publishing Services, Malverne, NY 11565
Printed and bound by The Murray Printing Co., Westford, Mass.

Library of Congress Cataloging in Publication Data

Simpson, Ida Harper.

From student to nurse.

(The Arnold and Caroline Rose monograph series
of the American Sociological Association)
Bibliography: p.

1. Nursing students – United States – Longitudinal studies.
2. Nursing – Study and teaching.
3. Professional socialization – Longitudinal Studies.
I. Back, Kurt W. II. Title.
III. Series: The Arnold and Caroline Rose
monograph series in sociology.
RT79.S55   301.5   78–31933
ISBN 0 521 22683 X   hard covers
ISBN 0 521 29616 1   paperback

Contents

Tables

Prologue

The 1950s were a time when nurses questioned what their role was and tried to determine what it should be. Their uncertainty grew with the growth of new nursing functions. Some new functions were brought on by the ascendancy of large, technologically oriented hospitals, and others by the expansion of nursing outside hospitals. Patient care was increasingly implemented through large complicated machinery requiring precise procedures. Nurses feared that these technological procedures were making physical care a distinct, isolated function and that the person of the patient was often left uncared for.

Along with the increased visibility and centrality of physical care, nursing took on new functions brought on by the bureaucratization of hospitals. Hospital nursing functions were divided along lines of skill and parceled out as distinct tasks to separate occupations; most prominent were practical nurses and attendants. Nursing took on added responsibility for assigning, coordinating, and keeping account of the work of the ancillary nursing occupations. These new functions turned nurses into administrators working with hospital personnel who stood between them and patients.

At the same time that administrative and clerical responsibilities were being added to nurses' work within hospitals, nursing work outside hospitals grew. Nursing was becoming internally divided by place of work. Nursing education, public-health nursing, and psychiatric nursing emerged as strong components of nursing, supplying far more than their proportionate shares of leaders. But most nurses still worked in hospitals. Leaders felt that hospital nurses should uphold high ideals of nursing and provide care directed to the whole patient, not just physical care.

To find out what nurses were doing in order to determine what their functions should be, the American Nurses' Association voted in 1950 to sponsor five years of research. The research was spread over at least thirty-four projects done mainly by sociologists, whose findings were synthesized by Everett C. Hughes, Helen MacGill Hughes, and Irwin Deutscher in *Twenty Thousand Nurses Tell Their Story*. The main finding about nursing work was that "bedside care is no longer the principal occupation of the nurse and the higher the nurse rises in the hospital hierarchy . . . the less does she see of the patient" (Hughes et al., 1958: 131). The care of the person of the patient – bedside or touch tasks – was increasingly left to ancillary nursing personnel.

Nurses had long known that their work was orienting them away from direct-patient care and were already endorsing research that they hoped would give clues on how to refocus the attention of nurses on the patients themselves. They saw the answer in a redesign of nursing-education curricula. Here again, interests of nursing leaders met those of sociologists. The rapid growth of professions that could be entered only through prolonged education gave increased visibility to recruitment and socialization into professions. Nursing-school curricula concentrated on skill training and basic theory; little place was given to the systematic inculcation of the common values of nursing. Sociologists argued that if nurses were to become "professional" in the sense of serving patients and upholding the ideals of nursing, students must learn values and incorporate them into their tasks. This was the view of professional socialization current among sociologists in the 1950s.

Nursing educators endorsed research on the socialization of nursing students, hoping to learn how students became professional nurses. The research to be reported in this book was one of the projects started in the late 1950s. Members of the Duke University Department of Sociology and School of Nursing joined together in 1958 and initiated a project to follow successive cohorts of students through their education and into the first year of nursing practice. The project was funded the following year by USPHS. Observations of students were to run through 1964. It was the belief of the sociologists and nursing educators on the project that professional socialization was crucial in implementing the objectives of a profession. The sociologists saw socialization occurring through group influences. We felt that to learn what these were and how they transmitted values would serve nursing well. With the knowledge in hand, nursing educators could supplement their dominant concern with curriculum by taking fuller account of the group processes in order to instill common values centered on patient care.

A longitudinal study of six years' duration invariably risks running much longer than initially planned. Data analysis extends beyond data collection; and during the longer period of study, matters do not stand still. Researchers are also involved in other studies that are compacted in time and hold the researchers' attention better than the longitudinal study. Staff turnover complicates a longtime project. For these reasons and for others unrelated to the research, more than ten years passed from the beginning of the project before an analysis of data was undertaken. In the meantime, works had been published that challenged our view that socialization was as complete or occurred as smoothly as we had conceived it to. Findings on socialization were disparate, and we felt that a fuller understanding of the state of the field was necessary if we were to understand the reasons for the disparities. Time continued to pass, and our data on the nursing school and its students became increasingly dated. Nursing education was changing and, even more, women were changing. In view of all this, the objective of the monograph was shifted from the narrow question that had guided the research operation to a broader concern. We decided to address some issues that were now apparent in the field, using the data on the socialization of nurses. On settling down to analyzing data and writing, we reread two seminal works, *Boys in White* (Becker et al., 1961) and *The Student-Physician* (Merton et al., 1957). On rereading the two books together, we did not find them as opposing as Becker et al. had stated. They spoke to different issues, and the findings of one could not contradict the other's conclusions. Both were crucial in a study of professional socialization. This realization redirected the research emphasis to try to bring together the contributions of the two. The aim was to develop a model that would deal with issues treated by each and would also deal with other questions revealed by a study of the literature and not raised in earlier research.

Acknowledgments

From Student to Nurse uses data from a longitudinal study entitled "The Professionalization Process in Nursing," that was funded by the United States Public Health Service (NU00028). John C. McKinney was project director, and he and Kurt W. Back administered the research operation. The initial research team consisted of them and Alan C. Kerckhoff and me from the Department of Sociology and Thelma Ingles from the School of Nursing of Duke University. This group developed nascent ideas into an ongoing research project. Many people worked on the project at one time or another. They included James C. Kimberly, Carleton Guptill, Joy Gold Haralick, Alfred Dean, Kenneth Miller, and Richard Warnecke. Their contributions to the collection and processing of data used in this study are gratefully appreciated.

The Duke School of Nursing was an unofficial but approving sponsor. Under the leadership of Dean Ann M. Jacobansky, the administration, faculty, students, and their parents welcomed the investigation. They hoped the study would benefit nursing. They cooperated fully in the research, but they are in no way responsible for this study's findings or conclusions.

The research reported in this book owes much to many people. Joanna Morris, Jeanette Harper, and Robert Jackson did computer work, and Sharon Sandomirsky Poss and Richard T. Campbell gave statistical and computer advice. Valerie Hawkins typed an earlier draft and Jean Brenner the final one. Bob and Frank Simpson proofread tables.

The book benefited substantially from comments on earlier drafts by Howard S. Becker, Samuel Bloom, Glen H. Elder, Jr., Norval D. Glenn, and Robin M. Williams, Jr. Their criticisms and suggestions made this a better book. Richard L. Simpson read drafts attentively. His critical judgment and editorial help were invaluable.

Ida Harper Simpson

Durham, North Carolina
February, 1979

PART I

Professional socialization: theory and research problems

1. Professional socialization: perspectives and issues

Professional schools are charged with educating students to be skilled and committed workers who will faithfully do the work of their professions. In essence, their charge is to socialize students. But do they succeed? This monograph addresses that question in a study of socialization of student nurses. It begins by assessing the field of occupational socialization, which is divided in its answer. Until the publication of *Boys in White* (Becker et al., 1961), it was commonly assumed that professional schools socialized students for professional roles. *Boys in White*, which studied the educational experiences of medical students at the University of Kansas, challenged this assumption. It did so by taking issue with the findings of *The Student-Physician* (Merton et al., 1957), which reported research on the socialization of medical students at Cornell, Pennsylvania, and Western Reserve. The two books established different perspectives on occupational socialization. The perspective identified with *The Student-Physician* we call the *induction approach*, and that with *Boys in White*, the *reaction approach*. The induction approach, focusing on professional education itself, corresponds roughly to what Olesen and Whittaker (1970) call *assimilation* and other writers have called the *normative approach*. The reaction approach, centered on motivation, identities, and commitments, corresponds to what has been called the *situational approach* to professional education (Bloom, 1965:152–73; Elliott, 1972:76–93).

These different perspectives on occupational socialization are unlike different approaches in some other fields of inquiry in which different perspectives correspond to different theories of the same phenomena. The latter look at the same things but explain them differently. For example, different perspectives on delinquency offer different explanations of the same delinquent behavior (e.g., Hirschi, 1969). In contrast, the induction and reaction approaches to occupational socialization do not deal with the same phenomena. They study different *dependent* variables. But their separate subject matters are called by the same glo-

3

Table 1-1. *Differing elements of representative studies using the induction and reaction models*

Models and studies	Conditions	Outcomes
Induction studies		
Merton et al. (1957)	Sustained and growing involvement in a role	Acquisition of attitudes, skills, and behavior patterns of a role
Kadushin (1969)	Participation in activities of a role	Professional self-concept
Reaction studies		
Becker et al. (1961)	Objective options and students' evaluations of situations	Perspectives toward situations, long-range and immediate
Olesen and Whittaker (1968)	Reciprocities in contacts with faculty and in lateral roles	Strategies to deal with existential situations

bal term – socialization. Calling different things by the same global term has obscured their differences and confused their separate contributions.

The induction approach focuses on the acquisition of the professional role by students during professional education; it studies attitudes, values, and outlooks along with the skills and knowledge that constitute the professional role (Merton, 1957:40; Merton et al., 1957:287-8). The reaction approach looks at students but does not view them as acquiring a professional role. It looks at their identities and the commitments that sustain them during their professional education and motivate them to complete it and go on to professional practice. In contrast, the induction approach takes motivation for granted, not a subject of inquiry. The induction perspective sees students as being inducted into a role; the reaction perspective sees them reacting to educational experiences. To illustrate their essential differences, Table 1-1 summarizes how some representative studies view the conditions and outcomes of socialization.

The position this monograph takes is that the two perspectives need not compete. The main variables studied by both are essential aspects of socialization. Studying acquisitions of cognitive sets, apart from motivation to persist in a role, is insufficient as a view of socialization. Looking at motivation to pursue a role apart from the learning of outlooks that inform behavior once it is acquired is also insufficient. Each concern should be included in a model of professional socialization, and it is our objective to develop and apply a model that includes both.

This monograph will not use a global concept of socialization. It will examine dimensions of cognitive learnings and motivations stressed respectively by the two approaches. Including the different dimensions in a single model is not as straightforward as it might seem. The induction and reaction perspectives, in defining socialization and professional education around one or another variable, have raised some critical issues. Until the issues are resolved, they hinder the bringing together of the two perspectives' contributions in one conceptual scheme. The most basic issue is the questioning by the reaction approach of the main assumption of the induction approach: that behaviors learned in one situation are retained in different situations later. Corollary issues flow from this basic issue.

The reaction approach looks at behavior in specific situational contexts and at its variation from one context to another. Abstract norms that might apply across different situations are not its interest. Its proponents doubt that a professional role common to all practice situations is institutionalized or learned.

Another issue between the two approaches pertains to the question, who controls students' behavior? The reaction approach sees students as the main shapers of their own behavior; the induction approach sees faculty as socializing agents.

The induction and reaction perspectives start from opposite assumptions, explicit or implicit, on virtually all questions related to occupational socialization. Because they start with different questions, to use the findings of one approach to answer questions studied by the other only joins the issues that divide research in the field. Studies in one tradition cannot invalidate findings of the other. The position of this monograph is that each has contributed to understanding occupational socialization and their respective contributions need to be recognized and brought together. In this way the issues that confront the field can be dealt with. The model we develop is an attempt to bridge the two perspectives, and we will use it to address empirically the main issues that now have the field at an impasse.

The empirical problem of this monograph is to describe socialization of student nurses. We ask whether the educational program of a nursing school imparts cognitive orientations that persist across status transitions, and whether it develops identities and commitments to nursing that support the transition of the student into the professional role of the nurse. These are the two most essential questions about socialization: the development of cognitive sets and motivations and their persistence from one situation to another.

As we use the term, *occupational socialization* includes the imparting of skills and knowledge to do the work of an occupation, of orientations that inform behavior in a professional role, and of identities and commitments that motivate the person to pursue the occupation. We see socialization occurring during professional education. It adjusts students to their education, but unlike adjustments to specific situations, it persists. Its persistence across status transitions and situational changes is one of its distinguishing features. Another is its generality. The knowledge and skills, orientations, and motivations transcend situational constraints, applying to the occupational role in varied settings. Knowledge and skills may be learned without acquiring orientations or developing an occupational identity and motivations; identities and motivations may be developed without acquiring occupational orientations; or orientations may be acquired without developing motivation to pursue the occupation. But knowledge and skills are prerequisites for acquisition of enduring orientations and motivations; one cannot do the occupation's work without its technical knowledge and skills. Knowledge and orientations are cognitive, informing one how to behave. Identities and motivations relate the person to the occupation. Knowledge, orientations, and motivations are distinct components. Only when all three have developed is a person fully socialized.

The contributions of the induction and reaction perspectives are important to the conceptual model we develop to study the socialization of student nurses. We begin by examining the two perspectives to highlight their contributions and to set forth issues in the field with which our own model must deal. Part I of the book examines the induction and reaction perspectives and develops our conceptual model. Parts II and III apply the model to data from a school of nursing to examine its utility, and Part IV discusses implications of the findings and suggests further refinement.

The induction approach

The seminal work that develops conceptually the induction model of socialization is that by Merton in *The Student-Physician* (1957:3–80). Because of the prominence of Merton's statement and the studies in *The Student-Physician* that draw on it, this approach has been termed the Columbia view of socialization (Gouldner, 1962:207). The induction approach did not begin or end with these studies; it also characterized such earlier studies as Donovan's exploration of the waitress (1920), the saleslady (1929), and the schoolma'am (1938); Dornbusch's (1955) analysis of coast-guard cadet training; and Sutherland's (1937) study of the professional thief, as well as later studies such as those by Sherlock and Morris (1967) and Kadushin (1969).

The induction approach rests on several assumptions: (1) A profession is institutionalized in society and a professional subculture develops around it (Merton, 1957:71). (2) The main repository of this culture is the professional school and its faculty, who are charged by their parent profession with instructing students in the knowledge and skills of professional practice and, through their contact with students, with introducing them to the norms and lore of the profession. (3) The professional school is a subsystem of the larger professional system. Faculty and student roles are tied together through complementary interests. Students look to faculty and accept faculty definitions of professional culture and faculty expectations of how to become professional. (4) Matriculation in a professional school places students in the status of student-professionals; faculty look upon them as professionals in the making – a transitional and developing status – and treat them accordingly (Bloom, 1965:154–5). Given these assumptions, studies employing the induction approach analyze students' experiences as occurring within the context of the professional system and socializing students in professional culture. Socialization is seen as involving the acquisition of attitudes and values along with the skills and behavior patterns that constitute the professional role (Merton, 1957:40; Merton et al., 1957:287–8). Socialization processes include direct learning through didactic teaching and indirect learning through example and sustained involvement with others in the professional subsystem (Merton, 1957:41–2). Students gradually acquire the professional culture through cumulative learning that develops them into "full" professionals.

The induction model takes a professional outcome for granted, though recognizing that it may be incomplete, and sees the problem of socialization as a matter of transmitting professional culture to students who are eager to learn it. The transmission occurs through role relationships in which students learn the expectations of professional roles. The professional culture is implicitly conceived as a coherent cognitive set of knowledge, skills, and norms that can be taught, learned, and carried into professional practice. Socialization can be assessed by observing the growth of orientations that are consistent with the expectations built into student roles. Variations or failures of socialization within a particular school arise from inconsistent expectations of different teachers, from incongruities of classroom teaching and students' experiences in professional role-sets, or from views brought by students to their education that are incompatible with what they are taught.

In the induction model, the development of orientations by a professional school appears to rest on two main conditions of the education program: (1) that definitions of professional roles be upheld by faculty in their teaching and their relations with students and by other significant professional role alters with whom students interact, and (2) the provision of training experiences arranged to enable students to see the connection of the skills they learn to the enactment of the professional role. When these conditions are satisfactorily met, a school can successfully induct students into its profession.

Proponents of the induction approach do not assert, as is sometimes said, that all students in all professional schools become fully socialized into professional roles. Success of socialization depends on the educational program of a school, its fit with the professional culture, and the opportunities it provides for students to assimilate professional-role expectations through experiences that occur within professional-role contexts or can be related to such contexts. Neither does the model assume that the outcome of socialization is to make all professionals like-minded (Dornbusch, 1955:316); or that the norms learned are absolutes with a narrowly constricted range of possible applications and no alternatives (Fox, 1957:235-9; Merton, 1957:76); or that the norms are fully internalized (Merton, 1957:71-9); or that professional practice may not modify the behaviors and values the students have learned (Dornbusch, 1955:321).

The model's most basic tenet is that social learning occurs during professional education – norms are imparted, attitudes are formed to accord with the norms, an appreciation is gained of ends toward which the profession's work is directed – and that these acquisitions develop a professional self constituted by a "more or less consistent set of dispositions which govern . . . behavior in a wide variety of professional . . . situations" (Merton et al., 1957:287). Students build backgrounds of experiences having elements in common with those of the seasoned professionals with whom the students later will join in a community of purpose and common ways of conduct. Students' normative acquisitions, like the knowledge and skills they learn, are carried into professional practice and are used to deal with the role demands of professional work. Proponents of the induction approach, although they have not studied later professional practice, have assumed that the persistence of these norms under varying conditions of professional work is a source of continuance and stability of the profession.

The induction model allows generalization from one socialization situation to another. Processes of induction into occupational groups are presumably the same in essence, though with variations among different programs and occupational roles. This view of induction, however, does not take account of the fact that student-professional roles and professional roles for which students are being trained are embedded in structures of power. Differences in power of the roles may well affect the persistence of what students learn. In its attention to induction, the approach has assumed, not studied, the persistence of student learnings in their work as professionals. Similarly, in its attention to the professional role, the model has assumed but has not systematically studied the student's motivation to pursue the professional role.

The reaction approach

There are variants of the approach we call reaction, but they are alike in viewing professional education with assumptions very different from those of the induction approach. Writings by Becker and Olesen and Whittaker are perhaps the clearest examples of this approach. Studies using the reaction approach do not conceive a professional school as a subsystem of its parent profession (Bloom, 1965:154); instead, they analyze the professional school as an independently organized social unit. Neither do they regard the professional school as a social system with its positions – students and faculty – bound together through mutual and complementary interests and role expectations. Instead, they see students – and probably would see faculty members if they were studied – as separate groups, each distinguished by common objectives and by power to act collectively in furtherance of their objectives. Common objectives arise when individuals hold the same position in a social organization, thus subjecting them to the same contingencies as they seek to realize common goals. Students' common interests are reinforced through long-range career goals and through their being educated as cohorts. Holding interests in common and having their individual situations within the school based on the same organizational forces, students share experiences; their interactions with each other breed common outlooks that bind them together as a student group and provide perspectives from which they view their training. The reaction model assumes that to understand the behavior of individuals, the appropriate units of study are the individuals as they are situated. Their situations may, of course, include membership in a group that shapes their behavior and outlooks.

Followers of the reaction model question the basic assumptions of the induction model. They doubt that a professional role is institutionalized in society (Bucher and Strauss, 1961), that it is regulated by cultural norms shared by its practitioners, and that these norms transcend the social contexts where professional roles are enacted (Freidson, 1970). In addition, they question whether standards upheld by faculty and other role alters are uniform within or across schools of a profession (Bucher and Strauss, 1961). Writers emphasize instead that the schools of a given profession are differently organized and serve different populations (cf. Mumford, 1970). They do not think that even within one school the standards stressed by the faculty are in fact mirrored in student perspectives. They see students' views as adaptive responses to their subordinate position in professional schools, where they are regarded and treated as students, not as junior colleagues (Bloom, 1965:152).

A main difference between the two approaches hinges on the question of social control of behavior, its locus and its effects on the orientations and behavior of the student and the certified professional. The induction model pictures a profession as a solidary system with social control arising from shared outlooks and mutual interests. The professional school is conceived as both a part and an agency of the profession, charged with inducting students into it in a way that ensures its continuous structure and function. Studies of professional education employing the induction approach are grounded on the supposition that students learn norms and values and that as practitioners these norms and values guide them to act in ways consistent with the institutionalized role of the occupation.

The reaction model, in contrast, conceives social control as a matter of power. Behavioral options increase power; contingencies on behavior reduce it. Contingencies are constraints. They arise from demands on students *as* students and from roles in other systems of action (Davis and Olesen, 1963). These constraints bear directly on students to limit their ability to act in accordance with their long-range objectives (Becker et al., 1961) and to achieve a sense of well-being and comfort (Davis and Olesen, 1963; Olesen and Whittaker, 1968). Positions differ in the behavioral options they provide. When individuals change positions, their options change. They may gain or lose power. Changes in constraints and options require new adaptations. Previous ways of dealing with problems, called perspectives by Becker et al. (1961), are unlikely to work because the conditions to which they were adapted have changed. The reaction model sees learning to behave in a status as occurring after, not before, the individual occupies the status. Its exponents do not consider adequate or useful the assumption of the induction model that a professional product is produced during professional education (Olesen and Whittaker, 1968:5–6, 298; Becker et al., 1961: 420).

Proponents of the reaction approach do not deny that students are educated in attitudes besides learning skills and knowledge (Freidson, 1970:88; Becker et al., 1961:425), but they do not think the attitudes and behaviors learned during professional education are the major influences on the behavior of practitioners, whose power and status differ markedly from those of students. This doubt challenges the very significance of studies of professional socialization conceived as the induction of students into professions (Olesen and Whittaker, 1970:179–221). To substantiate this line of argument, Freidson (1970:89) summarizes findings of research on physicians, lawyers, and correctional caseworkers to show that "There is some very persuasive evidence that 'socialization' does not explain some important elements of professional performance half so well as does the organization of the immediate environment." The focus of the reaction approach is on *students,* not on the professional role. Topics studied include the adaptation of students to the demands of the curriculum (Becker et al., 1961) and the emergent identities of students as they act on and react to their professional schooling (Olesen and Whittaker, 1968). Its focus is limited to the here and now, in contrast to the induction model, which assumes a long-term process.

Socialization as continuity of behavior

The basic issue between the two approaches is whether students are socialized for incumbency of a professional role. Do what students learn and their motivation persist? Proponents of both perspectives agree that continuity in an individual's behavior in moving from one position to another is the essence of socialization. Induction-model studies have assumed such continuity across status transitions. They regard continuity as resting on membership in the professional group and acquisition of professional culture. Followers of the reaction approach reject the inculcation of guiding norms and attitudes as an explanation of behavior in future situations, partly because the future is unknown until it is experienced, but more fundamentally because this approach sees behavior as emerging from the transactions between the self and the exigencies of situations. They have suggested three different explanations of continuity.

1. One suggested explanation is structural: *Continuity results from positions' being serially interconnected and having the same essential elements.* "Stabilities in the organization of behavior and of self-regard are inextricably dependent upon stability of social structure" (Becker and Strauss, 1956:263). In addition, a central assumption of writers using this approach is that life does not stand still as individuals change their statuses. When individuals move from one situation to another, the social situations within which they act change. The concept of *career*, then, is used to describe the individual's patterned movement or lack of movement through a social structure. It provides a way to see simultaneously the individual and the situation (Goffman, 1961: 127). In later writings, Becker, who has wrestled with the question of continuity, locates continuity in an individual's career. He has advanced the second and third explanations.

2. Another source of career continuity is *continuity in the life goals and general perspectives that guide the selection and pursuit of a career.* This account may be seen as an alternative to

the induction model's explanation, which stresses the inculcation of norms and attitudes in professional education. Becker sees life goals and long-range perspectives – which are comparable to the inculcation of norms in that they are concepts referring to cognitive phenomena – as informing one's choices at career turning points and one's approaches to action in situations that follow status transitions. Life goals thus give direction to a career.

3. The third explanation of continuity is found in Becker's treatment of motivation: *An individual moves from one position to another because of the gains the move entails.* In these later writings, Becker uses the concepts of goals and motivation to overcome limitations of Becker and Strauss' (1956) earlier account of continuity as simply the lack of change.

We do not see the two perspectives' explanations of continuity as opposing. They involve separate and distinct variables that may be used complementarily. Motivation explains membership in a profession and continuance of a career and fills a gap in the induction model. Inculcation of a professional role involves variables that can be observed to see whether behavior learned as a student is continued as a professional. Both explanations are important in the model we will construct.

Dimensions of socialization

What developments during professional education are necessary if occupational behavior is to exhibit continuity in training and from training to work? We see three requirements:

1. enough cognitive preparation for a person to perform the role,
2. orientations that inform a person's perception of demands of the role and of behavior to meet the demands, and
3. motivation sufficient to make the transition from one situation to another.

These requirements correspond to Brim's (1966: 24–7) outline of socialization as preparing people for roles so they will know what is expected of them, will know how to deal with the expectations, and will desire to practice the expected behavior and pursue the appropriate ends. We propose a three-dimensional conception of socialization based on the three requirements. We call the dimensions *education, orientations,* and *relatedness to the occupation.*

Education is required if one is to know what is expected and how to do it. Studies all too often ignore it as a part of socialization. Orientations provide a frame of reference for perceiving and acting on others' expectations. They are similar to what Becker calls perspectives and to the induction studies' idea of role learning, with the crucial difference that an orientation may be brought into one situation from another. The situation may reinforce and elaborate an orientation's development; or it may instead arrest, redirect, or even uproot it. Whereas the induction studies see socialization as the teaching and learning of roles that fit together to reflect and perpetuate the social structure, we make no such assumption. The orientations we study may vary independently of each other and they may not all be equally learned. Our concept of relatedness to the occupation also refers to a category of variables rather than to a single variable. We shall delineate three, all of which link the person to the occupation in ways that motivate continuance in the occupation.

Professional socialization as a type of adult socialization

Our discussion of socialization studies has deliberately been restricted to professional socialization. Professional socialization is an example of what Wheeler (1966) terms developmental socialization. Other kinds of developmental socialization, as in marriage or in religious and political organizations, may have elements in common with occupational socialization in professional schools, but the routes of entry into these roles differ markedly from entry into professional schools, as Wheeler (1966: 61) shows in his typology of interpersonal settings of socialization agencies. Professional students normally proceed through their programs in well-identified and often cohesive cohorts. Their roles while they are being socialized are structurally tied to future roles in occupational systems. Procedures of entry are very similar among schools that train for different professions, and the transitional exit routes are fixed in the professional marketplace in ways that do not correspond to what happens in other kinds of developmental socialization situations, where there is in fact not usually any expectation of exit from the group or organization doing the socializing – only an expectation of growing identification with it. Professional socialization differs even more markedly from what happens in total institutions charged with resocialization, such as prisons and mental hospitals. People are brought to prisons by force and into mental institutions because they are incapacitated (and also often by force). Not only does the entry procedure differ, but so does the exit, which in the case of resocializing organizations lacks the standardized, serially attached, succeeding status in which the socialized individual can be placed in a rewarding and recognized position, as in professional socialization. For these reasons, we claim no generalizability of our findings beyond professional socialization in professional schools.

Perspectives of this study

Professional knowledge and skill are the essence of the "goods" offered in the labor market of any occupation. Control over this market is the basis of a school's recruitment charge. Any profession devotes substantial effort, time, expense, and equipment to transmitting its knowledge and skills, whose possession defines the profession in the eyes of laymen and practitioners alike. Students' attention is directed to learning factual knowledge and skills that will certify them for work in the occupation. They may complain about these educational requirements, but they accept them or leave the program. Students' complaints represent reactions to tensions generated by the need to conform to program requirements and inform us of constraints within a program (Becker et al., 1961:21; Olesen and Whittaker, 1968), but the complaints are short-lived, changing in frequency and content with progress through the program. They are personal reactions and are not reliable indicators of acquisition of knowledge, occupational orientations, or personal relatedness to the occupational role.

Shifts in occupational orientations and in relatedness of the self to the occupation accompany occupational training. The timing and direction of shifts do not necessarily parallel the faculty's deliberate influence attempts. Indeed, we shall observe shifts that diverge from faculty goals. A professional school program nevertheless inducts students into the occupation, though the induction process may be contrary to the program's objectives. Whatever the outcome of a particular program may be, it makes students similar in important ways to their teachers and to already inducted practitioners. Professional-school experience is a common bond among members of a profession. It may differ substantially among them, but it gives all of them access to the occupation. Its certification for occupational membership may be as important as the preparation it gives.

There is a temptation to view socialization as consisting of discrete slices of time, one after another. To do so is risky, for the observer may think a series of delimited time-bound events adds up to the whole process. Such a procedure may unwittingly overemphasize selected events and reactions to them or it may fail to identify the most significant times when processes are begun and stabilized. Snapshots are static. Even when chronologically arranged, they may obscure the connections that create diachronic patterns. Transition from one status to another, or from one stage of a process to another, generates incongruities and tensions. If looked at in the long range, transitions may seem directional, but the total process is not simply additive or necessarily cumulative.

The course of socialization invariably follows a sequence of entering a school, experiencing its program, and exiting to a career. A major concern of our study will be persistence of responses as students move through the program and exit as practitioners. Movement from one academic year to the next and from school to professional practice changes the students' statuses and introduces them to new situations, but they bring to each situation their experiences of earlier ones. We shall examine socialization in stages paralleling the recruitment process: entering school, going through the academic-year sequence of its program, and leaving as practitioners. But we shall look closely for events and reactions linking the stages to produce continuity in a long-range process. Our focus will be on the development of orientations and relatedness of the self to the occupation, with education seen primarily as the context within which these developments occur. We see development as having occurred when reaction becomes consistent and persists or continues to grow in a given direction. We examine these processes in a study conducted from 1959 through 1965 at the Duke University School of Nursing.

2. Professions and professional education

The issues we have discussed so far pertain directly to the socialization of students. We now need to deal with a related issue: whether a professional role is institutionalized in the marketplace. A social role must be institutionalized in order for students to assume it after they are taught it. In our society, professions have a privileged position that entails institutionalized roles. Their places are secured in large part by professional schools acting as their recruitment agents. The school controls the inflow of labor into its parent profession. It performs three basic tasks. It selects the persons to be admitted to the profession; it educates them in professional knowledge and skills; and it instills appropriate professional orientations. There is no quarrel about the first two recruitment tasks, but the third is an issue in the field. The issue has two sides: whether or not students learn orientations and whether or not a professional role is institutionalized so that orientations learned may be followed later by practitioners in their work. Socialization means preparing people to perform social roles. It cannot occur without an institutionalized role to perform. We assume that the privileged place of a profession is built on its institutionalized role. The role includes orientations that reflect and protect the profession's interests. This chapter will seek to show that the privileged position requires that the professional school instill in its students orientations consistent with the profession's interests in the marketplace.

Professions and professional knowledge

Professions are unique among occupations in their combination of providing highly valued services, having authority to define the nature of the services they provide on the basis of a monopoly of specialized knowledge rather than the possession of capital (as in the case of proprietors), and regulating their own work or controlling its regulation. Traditional professions, of which medicine is the prototype, serve cli-

17

ents directly. Society gives such a profession an exclusive license to its practice and a mandate to define the nature of the practice, including how others are to behave in relation to its work (Hughes, 1958:78). In nonprofessional lines of work, authority rests *not* in the practitioners or in their colleague groups, but in positions in organizations or in resources, such as wealth, which they can use to gain compliance from others. Professionals, in contrast, have authority vested directly in them by the public's homage to the professions' claims to monopolies of the knowledge required by the work and by their certification as having been taught this knowledge. Professional services such as those of lawyers and physicians are of vital importance to clients (Etzioni, 1964:77) so that laymen regard them as matters of deeply moral concern (Hughes, 1958:79–80). The license and mandate that society grants a profession rest, in the eyes of the public, on the compelling nature of the problems with which the profession deals, coupled with the layman's complete dependence on the profession to deal with the problems because of its monopoly of the complex knowledge the solutions demand.

The power and status of professionals are based on the possession of knowledge. From this fact flows the power of the professional school, with its control over the transmission of the knowledge needed for professional certification. It is through the professional school that the profession controls the knowledge basis for its societal power. The power of the professional school over its students, for whom it is the sole route into the profession, puts it into a position to standardize and impart knowledge. In so doing it can mold students' orientations to their later work.

Occupational orientations and market control

To see the concerns around which orientations develop, it is helpful to systematize Hughes's (1958) concepts of license and mandate. License, according to Hughes (1958:79), "consists of allowing and expecting some people to do things which other people are not allowed or expected to do" whereas mandate is the occupation's claim, honored by society, "to define what is proper conduct of others toward the matters concerned with their work" (Hughes, 1958:78). Hughes's usage is broader than the legal concept of occupational license. The license to define and control the work rests on the knowledge base needed to per-

Table 2-1. *Components of recruitment and socialization by a professional school*

Mandate	License	
	Knowledge base	Collegialism
Service	A. Service as performance of tasks that apply specialized knowledge	B. Professional group as definer and guardian of its service domain and developer of related knowledge
Authority	C. Authority based upon and restricted by knowledge	D. Professional group as regulator of professional performance and related social structure

form its function (Goode, 1969) and a self-conscious solidarity that builds proprietary interests in the occupation as a collectivity (Hughes, 1958). The occupation becomes a "community within a community" (Goode, 1957). The mandate not only includes the right to define the profession's relations to others who deal with it, such as clients and other occupational groups, but also sanctions to ensure that others will behave as members of the profession have decided they should. License and mandate give legitimacy to each other.

Table 2-1 cross-classifies two basic elements of societal mandate against two basic elements of license to show the duties of a professional school as the agency of recruitment into its parent profession. The elements of license are knowledge and collegialism. The elements of mandate are service and authority. Knowledge, whether science or lore, is rationally articulated and is codified in books and other impersonal sources so that it can be imparted by formal instruction. A lengthy period of training signifies mastery of the knowledge required for professional certification. Collegialism refers to using one's fellow professionals as the most important reference and validating group for one's occupational behavior (Goode, 1969) and having their legitimacy as arbiters respected, especially by workers in related occupations. In contrast to the elements of license, which are internal to the occupation, those of the mandate relate the occupation to outsiders. Service defines what the occupation does in the marketplace, and authority regulates its relations to recipients of the service and to other occupations.

The four cells resulting from the cross-classification are not alternatives or options. All four are occupational concerns. Any professional school aims to instill knowledge and orientations to ensure that its graduates will meet the obligations of the profession's license and mandate when they become practitioners. The four cells indicate what a school needs to do to recruit new members so they will uphold the corporate interests of the profession. Each cell corresponds to an occupational concern.

Cell A – the convergence of knowledge and service – points to an occupational expectation that a school will redirect students' views of service, if this is necessary, to align their service orientations with their work as professionals. The professional view of service differs from the laity's. Professionals see service as the application of knowledge. Clients see service as the results of the application. They want the best professional help when in need and believe that knowledgeable professionals give the best. Clients expect the professional to know what to do about their conditions and to do those things. The convergence of knowledge and service specifies two important considerations for the delivery of service: knowledge and its application. A school educates its students to serve by emphasizing that they learn the knowledge of the field and master techniques to apply the knowledge to cases. Training and service become one and the same; to serve is to know what to do and to do it.

Cell B indicates that the profession is the guardian as well as the definer of the service it gives. It exercises its guardianship through restrictions on membership in the profession. Because service is the application of knowledge, only those properly trained can serve. Keeping incompetents out of the profession defends service. Defenses are built around every phase of recruitment. Entry is policed by screening applicants for admission and by upholding standards for graduation and professional certification. Educational content is also monitored. The monitoring is done through the accreditation of programs. Accreditation regulates recruitment by controlling curriculum and faculty qualifications. Proper knowledge must be taught so that the occupation's claim over its service domain is maintained. If schools were to be established that taught new approaches in conflict with existing ones, how could current workers defend the service they give? Proper means both that the "right" knowledge is taught and that qualified teachers staff the program. Schools that teach approaches in conflict with existing knowledge would be seen as injurious to service; their graduates would be considered untrained. The accrediting of schools assures that the knowledge base will be fairly standardized and common to all practitioners.

The colleague group also defends service through state and local licensing. It enlists the power of the state to police the occupation's service domain. Persons not trained by official agents of the professions or who fail to meet standards of the school cannot qualify for state certification. Licensing examinations are intended to ensure the minimal level of preparation needed to give service. Licensing protects service by keeping incompetents, quacks, and other pretenders from meddling in the service domain. The expectation that the occupational group acts as guardian of its profession's service establishes a service identity for the profession. The socialization of students to appreciate the colleague group and its associations helps to guard the proprietary rights of the profession. A profession's monopoly over its service requires collegiality.

Cells A and B together embody the profession's views on service. Socialization in occupational perspectives is required because students begin as laymen. The shift in perspectives releases the emergent professional from the emotional burdens imposed by the moral sanctions surrounding the occupation's work. The professional group, not the individual practitioner, has the societal license to define the profession's work, and the public regards the practitioner as someone informed by professional knowledge. The high regard the public holds for professional competence undergirds the profession's mandate. The public honors the profession's right to translate its moral function into specialized work tasks and to accept the social relationships arranged by professionals to perform their specialized work tasks.

The lay view of service reciprocates the professional view, but the two are quite different. Most professional schools interpret their charge generally as the education of students. They set up programs designed to teach knowledge and skills with little explicit attention to ideology. The view is that as students learn the knowledge and skills they are prepared to assume the professional role. But students do not enter the school as empty vessels. They enter with conceptions of the work they want to do. They bring their lay views with them. These lay views give simple and stereotyped definitions of the occupation's work. These stereotyped views of the occupation's work are what students expect to learn to do. Education impresses on the students, however, that service is not as simple as it looks from the lay view. Before students can serve, they must have sufficient knowledge to ascertain the precise nature of the client's problems and devise a course of action, and they must have the skills to perform tasks that yield the service. A sharp distinction between the occupational and the lay views is set up.

The differences between the lay and professional views generate some of the main difficulties and tensions of professional education. The interaction of the two views is inside the person of the student. Accommodation of the views may take various forms and degrees of completeness. Students may lose sight, at least temporarily, of service goals and develop a cynical view adapted to their roles as students trying to clear hurdles. (See Bloom, 1965, for a review of studies on the growth of cynicism among medical students; also Morris and Sherlock, 1971, on dental students.) Or students may try initially "to learn it all" to overcome the feelings of personal vulnerability that come with uncertainty and only in time learn to accommodate to the uncertainty of knowledge and their own abilities (Fox, 1957). The occupational view emphasizes the act of applying knowledge, not its results. When students acquire this view, they are freed from confronting morally results of an application. Whatever the personal accommodation to the student role, the occupation's interest is in students' learning to perceive service in terms of tasks that apply specialized knowledge. The occupation's mandate rests on such a perception.

Cells C and D in Table 2-1 pertain to the occupation's control over its work. Because the profession's mandate rests on its knowledge, its authority (Cell C) is based upon its knowledge. The intersection of knowledge and authority is manifested in professional judgment. A professional seeks to improve the condition of a client and uses professional knowledge to that end. Professional performance consists of solving problems by applying knowledge to cases. The knowledge is general. Problems of clients are usually complex, and even if simple, more than one interpretation of a case is possible because of the generality and abstractness of the knowledge. For these reasons the professional role carries the expectation that clients trust the judgment of professionals. In agreeing to pay a fee for professional advice, clients tacitly promise in advance to follow the advice the professional gives. Trust in the judgment of professionals represents professionals' authority.

Professional education directly and indirectly stresses this knowledge-based authority. Students learn early that as professionals they will be expected to solve problems and make decisions for others. Education builds students' confidence that the decisions they make and the solutions they employ are well founded. Command of knowledge is essential to know what to do, and equally important is the ability to apply the knowledge to particular cases. Judgment requires that the professional be willing to make decisions affecting the welfare of clients. An unavoidable aspect of the decision is the risk of mistakes and inadequate knowledge. Ways grow up in professions to deal with these risks. Professionals see mistakes as inherent in judgment and believe that if one tries, then responsibility for the decision has been met. When problems are beyond knowledge, accommodations to the inadequacies are essential. Socialization in ways to deal with mistakes and inadequate knowledge protects the authority of the profession.

The knowledge base of professional authority may lead the public to expect more than the professional can deliver. Conversely, students may be socialized to expect greater use of knowledge and thereby greater authority than the profession is allowed. The careers they follow may encompass tasks that nonprofessionals could do equally well (Carlin, 1962). If the work of a profession does not include making decisions informed by specialized knowledge, its members' authority to impose sanctions and exert influence by recourse to professional knowledge is limited. This is especially true of semiprofessions whose work is in bureaucracies that specify the roles of their workers. When, on the other hand, workers can legitimately claim to possess important and specialized knowledge not possessed by others, they can escape compliance with bureaucratic rules by asserting a higher, professional authority, as in the case of physicians who can flout hospital rules (Smith, 1955).

Cell D refers to the autonomy claimed by the collegial group to be the sole judge of its performance, preferably in a way that defines proper conduct of others with respect to its function. Members of the occupation hold that only they can define what constitutes a good and a bad job of performing its service. Outsiders are not considered appropriate judges. Evaluations of performances are made from the perspective of the occupation. This kind of autonomy enables the occupational groups to claim that a practitioner has done a good job even though the patient has died or the client has lost the lawsuit. Orientations to autonomy lead an occupation to resist encroachments on its activities, to defy challenges to its word, and to protect the members from outside sanctions. Mistakes by professionals, which the public might regard as evidence of incompetence or negligence, are defined by members of the profession as inherent in professional judgment and unavoidable and are shielded from the public. This view of the mandate, granted by the license, helps to reduce if not eliminate external control over the profession (Hughes, 1958; Goode, 1957).

The colleague group's claim to autonomy to regulate its work maintains the profession's monopoly. Autonomy is too important to a profession for a school not to train students to appreciate the colleague group, which defends autonomy. The school emphasizes the colleague group in many ways. Students are taught from books and articles written by members of the profession. Reference to the profession occurs over and over again in the titles of books, journals, and course offerings. Students learn that professional associations are important through the associations' sponsorship of professional journals and professional meetings and the attention faculty give the associations.

Our classification of components of occupational license and mandate sets forth the ideal typical charge to a professional school from its parent profession for the training of students. The relationship of the license to the mandate can, however, be expected to vary with the nature of the service the occupation provides and even more with the extent of its authority.

Semiprofessions

Semiprofessions deal in valued services but lack a full mandate. Nursing, the occupation we study, is an example. Some semiprofessions may even lack a license. Social work is one. The work of semiprofessions is organized by bureaucracies, higher-ranking professions, and elaborate legal restrictions. It is externally controlled to a significant degree. The semiprofessions do not have an authority base to undergird their workers in all lines of their work. They are able to claim little autonomy. Their workers are subject to external constraints from clients as well as bureaucracies and sometimes other occupations. For the most part, the knowledge they use is developed by others. Their attempts to develop their own codified bodies of knowledge on which to base claims to collegial authority have met with little success (Strauss, 1966; Goode,

1969). Their work is done largely in organizations that define their work functions and set forth rules for carrying them out. Their roles have little scope for professional judgments informed by generalized knowledge.

Semiprofessions also differ from professions in the extent to which they are organized around collective interests and can promote them. Occupations may be differentiated horizontally or vertically (cf. Barnard, 1938). Different work settings, work functions, and working hours divide an occupation horizontally. Professions, when differentiated internally, get divided along such lines. Semiprofessions, in contrast, are differentiated vertically. Because their work is organized by bureaucracies and other external sources, their work roles are arranged vertically and differ in authority and prestige. These vertical differences are often reinforced by differences in educational requirements for work roles. Horizontal differentiation arranges the interests of an occupation around different loci, but vertical differentiation undermines collegialism through its invidious distinctions and power differences among occupational members. When workers in the same occupation differ sharply in what they do, grounds for collegiality and other common interests are reduced.

Professions and semiprofessions also differ in the sequence of power relations residing in the roles of student and practitioner. Students are subordinates even if they are being trained for roles as wielders of power. The student and practitioner roles are not always identical; they may be opposite from the standpoint of power. For this reason, it is not surprising that investigators focusing on power find little carry-over from school to professional practice. Yet their point can be overgeneralized. Although the roles of students are those of underlings regardless of what occupation they are being trained for, their subsequent occupational roles differ markedly from occupation to occupation: Doctors have authority, nurses have authority over some people but are themselves subject to physicians' authority, and so on. For this reason, conclusions affected by the difference in power between students and practitioners may not be generalizable from one occupation to another – for example, from medical school to nursing school – when the positions of practicing professionals in systems of power are not alike.

Leaders of semiprofessions have typically tried to increase occupational control by locating their schools in universities. This is typically the route professions have followed in securing a license over their work. Gaining a stronghold in universities increases control over selection of students and their education but does not ensure control over the occupation's work (Wilensky, 1964). License involves more than education and who enters the occupation; it also concerns the institutionalization of work in the marketplace and the kinds of services wanted from the occupation. Controlling the entry and education of practitioners enhances control over the occupation most when the education given is related directly to work in the occupation, with a curriculum focused on skills and knowledge used in later practice.

Hughes (1961) has noted that schools of semiprofessions, in their efforts to upgrade their standing, stretch out their periods of training. The rationale is that added time is necessary to teach the generalized knowledge one must draw upon in making professional judgments. But what is taught as additional generalized knowledge is often nothing more than a few survey-type liberal-arts courses during the early years of professional education; collegiate nursing education provides an example. Schools of semiprofessions may also try to enhance the caliber and image of their training by borrowing general concepts and methodology from other disciplines and watering them down to serve as "sensitizing ideas for students." Such education serves more as an admission card for the individual and a status badge for the occupation than as a knowledge base for the work of the occupation.

Such licensing by education has been shown by Oppenheimer (1970) to be a frequent characteristic of female occupations, including semiprofessions. All the qualifications for work can be obtained during education, and experience adds little to the market value of a practitioner. These training and work requirements adapt occupations to the transitory nature of the female labor force. A woman worker may switch back and forth from work to child rearing or move from one job to another without significant change in prestige or income.

In the semiprofessions, discontinuous careers do not impair claims to occupational membership. These occupations' lack of the kind of collegialism that comes from having a full mandate limits the influence of professional schools over the career routes of their graduates (Hall, 1949; Kendall and Selvin, 1957). Paradoxically, however, in such an occupation the educational program's influence in instilling a perspective toward service viewed as the performance of tasks through the application of special techniques may be enhanced. It is the knowledge of these techniques, all of which can be learned in school, that qualifies one for the occupation.

Nursing, the occupation we study, is a semiprofession. Its primary service is patient care, but physicians, not nurses, decide what the care will be. Since the time of data collection for this study, new specialties have developed within nursing that have increased its authority over patient care. Most notable is the family nurse practitioner, who works out of public-health departments. The family nurse practitioner has expanded the de facto influence of nursing over patient care but has not altered the de jure authority of physicians over nurses. The nurse practitioner makes routine checkups and reports findings to physicians. Physicians monitor the work of the nurse practitioner, but the nurse may initiate lines of patient care that were heretofore the work of physicians. This new specialty is an example of a dominant occupation passing on to a subordinate some of its routine tasks. Its development has paralleled the increased specialization and centralization of medicine in hospitals. From 1949 to 1973, general practitioners declined from 64 percent of all physicians to 24 percent (Rogers, 1977:85). Though some medical specialists give the primary care that is associated with the general practitioner, pediatricians for example, nurse practitioners fill a special part of the void created by the movement of medical practice to hospitals. They conduct clinics and follow up hospital discharges. But in this primary-care role, nurse practitioners report to physicians. The specialty has expanded the primary-care responsibilities of nursing but has not significantly increased its autonomy in the health field. The ceiling of nursing remains the floor of medicine.

Summary

The fit of a profession or semiprofession and its schools to the categories we constructed on the basis of Hughes's concepts of license and mandate may vary from occupation to occupation and, within an occupation, among work settings and schools. Nevertheless, we find the categories useful in specifying occupational concerns around which role orientations develop and in generating measurable variables corresponding to them. The prevailing expectation, inside and outside an occupation, is that new practitioners will go about their work in ways consistent with the occupational group's customs and preferences. Each cell of our classification specifies an orientation whose development in students we shall observe. These four orientations, however, provide only cognitive guides for occupational role behavior; they tell us nothing about the recruit's personal stake in the occupation. The personal stake is the essence of motivation to stay in the occupation. If this motivation is to be satisfactorily developed or maintained, the professional school must somehow build a relationship of the person to the occupation. The individual's stake in an occupational career is as important a dimension of occupational socialization as is cognitive development. It is included in our definition of professional socialization, which will be presented in the next chapter.

3. Dimensions of professional socialization

We regard professional socialization as a directional change or pattern of changes that persists across situations, including status changes. We see it as consisting of three analytically distinct dimensions or categories of variables: education or the imparting of occupational knowledge and skills, development of occupational orientations, and forming personal relatedness to the occupation. The first two of these are mainly cognitive; the third, motivational. The occupational orientations we specify pertain directly to the occupation's interests discussed in Chapter 2. The forming of personal relatedness joins the person to the occupation.

Education

Socialization includes developing technical abilities to perform expected duties of a role. Professional school programs are designed for that purpose. A school's program is the pivotal structure of the entire recruitment process (Hughes, 1955) in that it moves the novice from lay culture to the status of practitioner. The school admits annual cohorts. Passing from one academic year to the next signifies that students want to stay in the program and have acquired the qualifying knowledge and skills. This arrangement steadily moves students toward professional status while allowing them to drop out and the school to weed them out. Education is the master socialization process, the context for forming cognitive occupational orientations and relatedness to the occupation. The school's educational program corresponds to movement up through the academic years, so that our proxy measure of the acquisition of knowledge and skills is academic class status. This status will be the context within which we observe the development of cognitive occupational orientations and personal relatedness to the occupation.

Cognitive occupational orientations

The orientations we will observe pertain to the occupation's interests specified in the cross-classification of license and mandate in Chapter 2. Their development may be in the direction of the school's ideal charges or in some other direction consistent with other influences. Ideally, the school prepares its students to:

1. see service as the performance of tasks that apply specialized knowledge,
2. uphold the professional group as the definer of its service and the developer and/or specifier of appropriate knowledge,
3. uphold a conception of the professional role that gives the practitioner authority to make and execute decisions consistent with the occupation's knowledge, and
4. uphold the profession as the regulator and judge of professional conduct.

The first and third of these direct students' attention to the occupation's service and to how the recipients of service – and, sometimes, others involved in giving it – are expected to behave. Through having their attention directed to these concerns, students are supposed to learn how to approach and carry out work. We shall call these orientations to the functions of the occupation's work *cognitive orientations to the occupational role.*

The second and fourth charges orient students to the occupation as a collectivity. Students are expected to acquire an appreciation of the occupation as a collectivity and to aspire to positions that bring collegial recognition. The second of the four pertains to the internal organization of the occupational collectivity and the fourth to its position in the labor force and its career lines. *Cognitive orientations to a place in the occupation* express these interests.

Orientations to the occupational role

An orientation to an occupational role includes a conception of its work activities and of the boundaries of its authority. The role's activities and authority may be integrated as one configuration of behavior or be perceived separately. If they are seen separately, students may perceive activities not accompanied by commensurate authority; or they may perceive authority over activities and not know how to do them. Ambiguity in one's personal approach will increase with disparity between perception of the role's activities and authority.

The professional school defines the principal activities of the occupation and its spheres of authority, but its definitions do not always match those of other influence sources. For nursing, the occupation we are studying, there are four sources of definitions of appropriate nursing activities. These are the lay culture, the school ideology, the specific knowledge and skills being taught, and the work organization of the hospital where students obtain clinical experience. Authority to make decisions varies in response to differing role alters and activities. When sources of influence agree in their definitions of an occupational role, the development of orientations to the role should proceed smoothly; but when sources of influence disagree, as in the case we study, the development requires selection of relevant guides in varying contexts where the role is learned and enacted. An orientation may fluctuate in response to these different sources before settling down to a consistent pattern. Development has occurred when the view becomes consistent and persists or continues to grow in a given direction.

When students are subject to differing definitions of roles, in which of the possible directions will their orientations develop? Some research emphasizes that the orientations will develop in conformity with expectations of training agents who serve as role models in training situations (Merton, 1957). Training agents have expectations of students in their training roles. The agents impart expectations as instructions, or students emulate them in coping with problems encountered in their training. From the rewards received for conforming to expectations of training roles, students learn the expectations and incorporate them into orientations. The presumption is that expectations of training roles coincide with those of professional roles.

Other research holds that the values students bring to their education direct the development of their orientations (cf. Goldsen et al., 1960). What they learn and retain must fit the expectations they hope to realize from their education. If the program fails to provide opportunities for students to act on their long-range perspective, students may see no relevance of what they learn to their goals and defer further development of orientations until after they have graduated (Becker and Geer, 1958). The assumption is that value predispositions limit and direct the development of professional orientations.

Each explanation stresses only one influence. To look at only one influence on orientations oversimplifies the explanation of their development. Clearly, no amount of learning is likely to enter into students' orientations if it is incongruent with their values or with the expectations of their training roles. In our view, an educational program will develop orientations consistent with its objectives or with students' predisposing values if it can successfully link faculty values as expressed in program objectives with students' values (Wright, 1967) and provide training opportunities congruent with students' values (Becker and Geer, 1958) and with its own objectives.

Our explanation is a variant of the "learning" hypothesis. Students develop orientations that fit the technical knowledge and skills most heavily stressed in their education and the role relations associated with their application. They know they are expected to apply knowledge that will yield the performance expected by others; it is the use of technical knowledge in the context of an occupational role that will make them "professional." They develop orientations fitting the knowledge and skills they can use in meeting professional role expectations as they perceive these in the student role. The major influence on development of their orientations is professional knowledge and skills – the role's technology – as these converge with the demands they face in the student role. The orientations tell them what stance to take in enacting the role, and the enactment is the carrying out of duties using knowledge and skills they have been taught. Technical knowledge is carried over from the student role to the professional role. With it go orientations to its use in social settings that involve authority. In this way continuity of orientations across the transition from student to professional status occurs.

Orientations to a place in the occupation

Nursing is differentiated horizontally by work setting and function and vertically by type of educational certification, degree and scope of authority vested in work positions, routes of access to work positions, and prestige and other rewards of work. Cross classification of authority base by work setting (Table 3-1) shows the variety of major types of nursing positions. Most nurses work in hospitals. Their authority is bureaucratically based and primarily scalar. Nursing positions in public health and schools of nursing carry functional authority and are free from direct surveillance by bureaucratic superiors. But these employ

Table 3-1. *The authority base of nursing roles in different work settings*

Type of authority	Work setting		
	Hospital	Public health	Education
Scalar	+		
Functional		+	+

only a minority of nurses. Hospital bureaucracy, not nursing as an occupation, controls most nursing positions.

Collegialism in nursing is further weakened by differentially valued kinds of training programs. At the time of this study there were three types of nursing-education programs, which varied in length of training and type of certification. Their differences, however, were not institutionalized in the marketplace so that credentialism might regulate access to different nursing positions. Standards for staffing were formulated by nursing associations, but their ability to enforce them was limited because they lacked control over the hospital settings where most nurses worked.

Nursing's inability to control its labor force has limited the institutionalization of career lines reflecting collegial recognition and authority. Positions are ranked more by occupational title, hours of work, financial rewards, and other symbols based on workplace than by collegial concerns such as those that predominate in academic work and medicine. Access to positions is regulated largely by demand in the marketplace, not mediated by the occupational group. The lack of control by the occupation over much of its work means that positions are chosen and evaluated more on the basis of their extrinsic aspects than from a collegial frame of reference.

Yet, collegiate schools of nursing uphold a philosophy of occupational control over nursing. The school we studied was collegiate and conformed to the collegial philosophy in its teaching methods and in the kind of nurse it hoped to produce. But it also used a hospital nursing service to give its students practical experience. Students acquired experience in a bureaucratic work organization with nursing positions laid out in an explicit hierarchy of authority and rewards. The hospital practicum was a major influence source, at odds with the school's ideology and with some of its specific attempts to transmit technical knowledge of a kind that might develop collegial orientations.

During their professional schooling, then, the student nurses we studied were subject to disparate sets of criteria for viewing work: the collegial standards embedded in the school's program and the very different ones dominating the main nursing marketplace, the general hospital. In addition, they retained in some degree the lay culture's notions of the service function of nursing, which if employed in evaluating nursing positions might lead in still different directions. Moreover, the students were all women who, as we will show later, prized family over work. Desired family roles might restrict their opportunities to seek positions on the basis of occupational considerations.

As students near completion of the program, the impending status transition from student to worker looms large. During most of the professional school years, the press of academic demands keeps students focused on ways to get through school (Becker and Geer 1958). Toward the end of the program, however, students become increasingly concerned with what will happen once they have left. As student nurses near the transition, their interests turn toward the kinds of positions their education has prepared them to aspire to and the fit of these aspirations with nonwork roles, such as family ones. Students' interests might have turned away from collegial orientations insofar as these were not in tune with the realities of the main marketplace of nursing and the highly prized family roles.

Timing and origin of development of different orientations

Do orientations to the occupational role and to a place in the occupation develop simultaneously or in a predictable sequence? Do the same influences develop both sets of orientations, or do they arise from different influences?

Conceivably, the different kinds of orientations might develop cumulatively because they are inextricable parts of a global process that encompasses both. The reasoning behind this view is that different kinds of work organizations and positions involve different kinds of work; in orienting to a place in the occupation, one orients simultaneously to its mode of work. To put this possibility the other way around, the argument would be that a student who is oriented to a particular kind of work role knows its place in the occupation and simultaneously develops orientations to the occupational role and to a place in the occupation. Similar reasoning would lead us to expect the same influences to develop both sets of orientations: wanting a place in the occupation implies anticipating its characteristic work role along with its collegial patterns.

Our view is that the orientations are subject to different predominant influences, which are experienced at different points in the program. Orientations to the role develop first and orientations to a place in the occupation later. The school's educational program strongly influences both kinds of orientations, and its influence is felt early in students' training. The program remains the chief influence on orientations to the occupational role throughout professional education. Orientations to a place in the occupation are, however, subject to a second major kind of influence besides the program. As a student envisions the life that will follow graduation, extrinsic considerations concerning the relation of work to nonwork roles and the occupation's labor market come into play. In thinking about a career a student considers income, hours of work, and other criteria reflecting the lay culture because these things relate the person to roles outside the occupation, mainly family roles. These lay-culture considerations grow increasingly salient as the student nears graduation and can think realistically about moving from the status of student to worker. Because the program remains the main influence on orientations to the occupational role, even though extrinsic considerations come to exert strong influence on orientations to a place in the occupation, we should expect orientations to the role to stabilize first.

Relatedness to the professional role

Orientations students develop during their education provide cognitive standards that enable them to perceive an occupational role and a place in the occupation. Orientations do not, however, necessarily generate motivation to pursue the role or to be identified with the occupation. Nor does a lack of development of cognitive orientations indicate absence of occupational motivation. Developing a sustained interest in an occupation relates the self to the occupation. This relatedness is motivational and is not the same as cognitive orientations telling how to behave if one is in the occupation. Both are parts of socialization but neither can be derived from the other. The self is related to the occupation in three ways: status identification, commitment, and attraction.

Status identification

Status identification has been called by other names – occupational self-image (Huntington, 1957), public identity (Becker, 1963), and professional self-concept (Kadushin, 1969). We consider our term the most descriptive of the phenomenon. It refers to taking the occupational title as a label for the self to answer the question "who am I?"

Completion of professional education confers the right to call oneself by the professional title. Studies (Huntington, 1957; Kadushin, 1969) have found, however, that students come to use the professional title to think of themselves as professionals prior to their certification. These findings tell us that status identification is not a simple reflection of actual attainment of professional status. Instead, it evolves through transactional processes, the nature of which has been conceptualized in different ways. Huntington (1957) sees it emerging through a looking-glass process of enacting the professional role in conformance with others' expectations. As students perceive that others expect them to perform the role, they reciprocate by enacting it. Through repeated experiences of this kind, students adopt the label of the role as an identity. The critical phases of interaction that develop status identification are role alters' seeing the students as occupying the professional role and the students' enactment of the role in conformity to alters' perceptions of them. This repeated interactive process builds a professional self-view reflecting a feeling that one is competent to enact the professional role in a way that meets others' expectations.

Becker (1963:30-1) observes essentially the same transactions but conceptualizes them differently. His writings on deviant careers indicate that others' expectations that one perform in a role constitute a public identification of the individual with the role. Such identification objectively limits the availability of alternative roles for the person to relate to situations, thereby entrapping the person in the role. As others repeatedly identify a person with a role, "he is pushed in the direction of assuming the identity" (Becker and Carper, 1956:297). Alternative roles are closed out of one's perceptual field by the role label others have attached. In this formulation, others' expectations are seen not as guides to individuals for enacting the role but as enforcements of others' views of what their status should be (Hughes, 1945; Becker, 1963: 22–39). The process corresponds to the mechanisms of the self-fulfilling prophecy described by Merton (1949:179–95). What Huntington sees as a substantive development arising from a reciprocal process of role enactment and role alters' expectations, Becker sees as stemming from objective constraints on individuals that arise from their symbolic encasement in the role.

Whether status identification occurs in the way analyzed by Huntington or by Becker, mechanisms to develop it are potentially present when a school's program includes a practicum. To see whether role enactment or status labeling is the more critical influence requires disentangling role enactment from others' assignment of an identity and expectations. The measures and analyses in earlier studies have confounded these variables. Their findings are remarkably similar but might be interpreted to support either view. Official class – first year, second year, and so on – was found by Huntington (1957) and Kadushin (1969:401–2) to be closely related to status identification. A similar relationship of length of time in school to status identification was found by Holley (1971:2). These authors have largely ignored the theoretical implications of this finding because they have concentrated their analysis chiefly on within-class variations in status identification. Their data do not show a simple additive time effect in which each year of study contributes equally to status identification. Status identification may remain constant for long periods, then rise sharply as professional role enactment increases. For example, paid performances increased status identification among music students (Kadushin, 1969), serving as teaching fellows increased it among graduate students (Holley, 1971), and interactions with patients resembling doctor–patient relations increased it among medical students (Huntington, 1957).

Not only do the clinical years of professional education – or their equivalent such as paid performances by music students – allow the enactment of the professional role mentioned in these studies. The role is enacted in a social context of professional work where others identify students as at least partial professionals. Clinical-year students remain students in the formal structure of the school, but added to the student role are aspects of the professional role that associate the students in the eyes of others, including even the faculty, with a professional public identity. This shift toward professional status moves students from academic settings into settings more in keeping with the professional role. The shift may be symbolized in some highly visible way such as wearing a uniform. The student nurses we studied were expected to wear student-nurse uniforms on days when they had classes in the hospital. Status identification is not only a matter of accepting others' definitions. It also involves, perhaps more importantly, being in a situation where the actor's behavior is clearly linked to the professional status and the accompanying status arrangement that controls one's options.

This linkage of students to the professional status need not be simply a matter of others' imposing a label on them regardless of their wishes. Students enter a professional school for the explicit purpose of gaining the requisite training for careers in their chosen professions. They want to become identified as professionals. When an opportunity arises for them to achieve such an identification, they are likely to embrace it actively and approvingly. We should not be surprised that their status identification is not a continuous process of reacting passively to professional training situations but jumps substantially with any possibility for others to consent to a view of them as professionals.

Occupational commitment

Commitment is the pursuit by an individual of a consistent line of activity in diverse situations (Becker, 1960). It is inferred from consistency of present with past actions and from the intention to continue the pattern of activity. It includes activity and the intent to continue it in the future. Occupational commitment rests on objective investments in the occupational role. Such investments are made, intentionally or unintentionally, through linkage of other values and activities to the occupational role so that their realization is facilitated through its continued pursuit and would be impossible or difficult if one abandoned it.

The linkages, called side-bets by Becker (1960), are structurally embedded in the organizational and interpersonal arrangements of situations in which the individual participates. Some are specific to one's own network of personal relationships (cf. Alutto et al., 1973), whereas others arise from the rules, regulations, and program design of organizations. Kanter (1972:80-2) found that nineteenth-century communes that required the irrevocable signing over of property at admission and the contribution of all fruits of members' labor were more viable than communes without such requirements.

The investment potential of activities that make up a side-bet varies inversely with their ability to be detached from the occupational role. If benefits of these activities can also be realized from their attachment to alternative pursuits, the investment in the occupational role can be withdrawn. The less detachable a value is from the occupational role, the more it commits the student to the role. Commitment is built through structural arrangements that make it costly for students to abandon the occupational role.

Becker's analysis of commitment is consistent with his analysis of status identification as an entrapment of individuals in statuses through others' pinning labels on them. In commitment, individuals pursue lines of action that foreclose alternatives, whereas in status identification others label them in ways that propel them in a single direction. The conception of a sequence of labeling followed by unavoidable reactions to the label may inhibit the analyst's seeing a dialectic in which actors not only are acted upon but also act in a cumulative process, though one controlled through the arrangement of the educational program and the broader recruitment process.

In our research we shall look for structural contingencies (side-bets) in the recruitment process that commit students to the pursuit of nursing. Such contingencies may help to create commitment mechanisms. Once the student reaches a point in her education where pulling out would entail the loss of time and money, the dashing of hopes of parents, and other sacrifices, her commitment might be expected to grow.

Occupational attraction

Attraction refers to high evaluation of an occupation, of participation in it, and of being identified as a member of it. It differs from commitment in that attraction is wholly positive and cannot be accounted for by objective costs one would incur in abandoning the occupation. Occupations, like other social units, have no appeal from that which is attributed to them (cf. Mills, 1953:215). The process of attraction involves that attribution of value to the occupation as a collectivity and to its activities. The attributed qualities transform the occupation so that it embodies the values one has attached to it. Experiences in the occupation are then seen and felt from the perspective of these qualities. Participating in the occupation and identifying with it enhance the self.

Attraction to an occupation may arise from values or sentiments. We define values as conceptions of the desirable, and sentiments as values with persons, groups, or collectivities as their objects. Values originating in lay society as qualities imputed to occupations may guide occupational selection (Rosenberg, 1957; Davis, 1965) and be brought by a student to an occupation (Becker and Geer, 1958; Wright, 1967); or they may emerge from a student's experiences within a professional school (cf. Becker and Carper, 1956). The imputation of valued qualities to an occupation may help to justify or validate one's attraction to the occupation but is not enough to sustain the attraction or promote its growth. If a value is to sustain continuance in an occupation, it must effectively tie the person to the occupation as an object of sentiment. The growth of sentiments leads the person to feel an intrinsic connection between the occupation as a collectivity and its imputed values.

Sentiments are bred through interactions and common experiences with others (Homans, 1950). If enduring sentiments are to be directed toward an occupation, the interactions that give rise to them must be encompassed within and directly linked to the occupation. The occupation must be clearly delineated, commonly perceived, and considered salient by the individuals within the occupational context. Growth of attraction depends upon a clearly delineated, perceptibly distinctive, and salient occupational context to embrace the student's interactions and relate them to the occupation as a collectivity.

A social unit is delineated through insulation of members from interaction with members of other social units or through mechanisms to preserve the salience of the unit's identity when its members interact with outsiders. In some social units, membership imposes constraints on the frequency or nature of interaction with outsiders. The more a unit provides a setting and resources for activities meeting a variety of its members' needs, the more likely it is to be an inclusive locus of their interactions and to insulate them from outside contacts (Etzioni, 1961: 160-4). The social boundaries of a unit are most effectively maintained if it is geographically isolated from other units so that members are fully protected from contacts with outsiders, including negative evaluations of the membership unit itself. Lesser insulation and inclusiveness have similar though lesser effects. In other instances, cross-unit interaction is frequent but its nature is such as to emphasize the identities of the units as mutually exclusive categories. In these instances, a sense of membership in a unit may be maintained through structural and symbolic means to uphold its salience in contacts with outsiders. Members may participate in other social units as representatives of their own; they may maintain their social distinctiveness in symbolic ways such as dress, demeanor, and title; or occasions of contact may involve sufficiently large numbers of the unit's members to preserve its distinctiveness and salience in situations that include outsiders. All of these boundary maintenance mechanisms were present in the school we studied. Students' interactions were fairly tightly bounded within the context of the nursing school in the university community.

Group boundaries separate individuals from outsiders, but in themselves they do not ensure interactions of the kind that breed collective sentiments. Collective sentiments express a unit's solidarity; members must feel a sense of unity and common destiny. Common backgrounds and values foster interests common to all and lessen the likelihood of the unit's splintering into cliques and other internal divisions. Individuals with similar histories and earlier socialization feel a sense of camaraderie and can comfortably interact with one and all. A basis for collective sentiments is laid by the dispositions and outlooks that individuals bring to a social unit. But their development and persistence require unity of purpose, continually nurtured by members' involvement.

Student cultures are born of common experiences (Becker et al., 1961; Olesen and Whittaker, 1968). These are generated by a program that brings in students and educates them as cohorts. In going through the program together, they hold the same status, take the same courses, and face the same requirements. Their common experiences breed collective ways of doing things and encourage mutual aid. Common and collective experiences minimize individual competitiveness and the internal dissensions that might divide members into factions to divert loyalty from the collectivity to primary groups within it. If tightly bounded primary groups develop within the larger group, they may command the devotion of the members involved, who may lose sight of the interests that join them to the larger group (cf. Kanter, 1972). The arrangement of the nursing-education program we studied included devices that promoted common experiences and interests among students.

The program of a professional school may foster the development of a cohesive student group, but such a group may or may not generate attraction to the occupation. It may serve only to mediate the demands that students face as students. For the interactions of students within a collectivity to develop occupational sentiments, they must involve occupational concerns and cross-cut academic classes. Students must see their activities as contributions to the occupation and, through it, to a collective endeavor broader than that of the occupation. Mutual aid among students in their educational assignments, particularly those within a practicum, relates their interaction to the occupation. In a practicum, students are brought into work settings where the occupation is functionally related to other occupations. A practicum exposes students to others' evaluations of the worthwhileness of their own occupation and the work they do in its name.

On the other hand, if others' evaluations are unfavorable, students may acquire negative views of their occupation or of their performance of its role. Still another barrier to occupational attraction may inhere in a highly formalized, impersonal division of labor that inhibits interaction across occupations or the expression of others' appreciation of the occupation. It is a dilemma of the division of labor, seen long ago by Durkheim (1964; orig. 1902), that it is socially integrative only if each functional group is internally unified and at the same time bound to the others in a larger collective moral order.

For hospital experiences to generate sentiments for the occupation, the contribution of student nurses to nursing and to the work of the hospital must be communicated to the students. In particular, hospital nurses and physicians must let students know that their work is facilitated by what the student does in her training role. If the school faculty retains its authority over student nurses during their hospital practicum experiences, as it did in the program we studied, this may lead hospital nursing personnel to regard students as outsiders and not fully accept them. Lack of such acceptance seems likely to undermine students' identification with nursing and reduce their attraction to it.

Thus, practical experience might either promote or retard occupational attraction. It might promote attraction to the extent that students are able to engage in nursing activities and to be identified as nurses. It might impede it if students receive little indication that their occupation is considered worthwhile or that they are accepted into it.

Development of relatedness to the occupation

The processes that relate students to the occupation involve the narrowing of options to exclude nonoccupational alternatives. The arrangements supporting the three distinct components differ, as our discussion has shown. The school's program charts the roles of students and their access to experiences. In so doing, it controls their status and role options and their relations to role alters and other occupational groups, which are conditions underlying the three components of relatedness. Status identification arises from enacting the professional role or from others' identifying one with the role and thereby limiting one's access to alternatives. Commitment to the occupation is built from specialty study, whose payoff can be realized only through pursuit of the specialty. Attraction occurs through occupationally bounded experiences. All of these processes are relational. They arise from the school's control of role and status options.

The structure of socialization

If occupational socialization is multidimensional, an essential question concerns how its dimensions and the components of each dimension develop in relation to each other. Conceivably, the components of a dimension might develop so as to become separated from each other, or to cohere in a cluster that is distinct from other dimensions, or to merge with those of other dimensions.

If the conceptual categories are in fact empirical dimensions and not just figments arbitrarily defined, the components of each should come to cohere during students' education if they do not cohere from the beginning. The question then becomes whether the three dimensions develop independently of one another or in a definable pattern of interrelationship. If they develop independently, this does not mean their development reveals no pattern. The pattern is one of differentiation, with orientations to the occupational role distinct from those to a place in the occupation and each of these is unconnected to relatedness to the occupation.

Our study of the socialization of nurses found differentiation of the dimensions. This pattern may not occur in all occupations. How the dimensions develop in relation to each other may depend on occupations' recruitment processes. Recruitment processes vary with occupations' authority and collegialism because these affect occupations' control of their markets, the dispersal of their markets, and the diversity of career patterns. Recruitment processes vary also with students' exposure to competing occupational influences and definitions during their education. Our discussion will show how occupational and educational characteristics of nursing differentiate the dimensions of socialization and will present an explanation of the persistence of the differentiation across the status transition from student to professional.

In occupations with differentiated dimensions of socialization, the dimensions' development need not proceed from an undifferentiated state. Differentiation may involve resocialization in which relations among the components are realigned. The beginning state at entrance into a professional school and the subsequent pattern of development should vary with the extent and nature of anticipatory socialization and its congruence with influences from the occupation, from the school, and from other sources of control over the occupation, and also with the continued influence during education of lay agents important in the anticipatory socialization. At the extremes of anticipatory socialization – virtual ignorance of the field and few if any opinions about it at one extreme, and at the other extreme the internalization of cognitive views as moral prescriptions that attach the recruit to the occupational role – an undifferentiated initial state would seem likely to prevail. In the instance of ignorance, the components are insufficiently developed to aggregate or interrelate, and at the opposite extreme there is a Gemeinschaft condition with the components all interrelated. The latter seems to occur among religious novitiates and to have characterized the Kansas medical students (Becker et al., 1961; Becker and Geer, 1958).

Just as we do not see occupational socialization as necessarily following an evolutionary pattern from a simple to a complex state, neither do we see it developing mechanically through transmission of culture. The view that socialization proceeds in a simple cumulative manner with earlier learnings providing a foundation for later ones might be called a cultural view. The end product is assumed beforehand: a practicing member of the occupation with certain beliefs. The product is made through transmission of cultural content – knowledge, skills, and norms of the occupational role – and through a companion process of internalization of norms. Faculty and other role alters of students, knowingly and unknowingly, use a sanctioning system to regulate the cultural transmission. From the pleasures and pains of sanctions, and from the role models the faculty provide, students internalize the norms passed on to them. In this view the occupation exists within the persons of its workers. This interpretation is an example of what Wrong (1961) has called "the oversocialized conception of man."

The cultural view of professional socialization fails to take into account the fact that an occupation is centered in a marketplace and is subject to external influences. It also ignores other roles and interests of students. The cultural content transmitted to students may include norms respecting the interests of the occupation, including ways to control its relations with clients and competitors. These are important substantive lessons, which may correspond to the cognitive orientations the school we studied tried to impart in teaching the occupational role. But learning them well or even acting on them does not demonstrate motivation to enter the marketplace in pursuit of an occupational role, even one that embodies the norms that have been learned. An occupational role is attached to positions in an occupational marketplace. Persons will not enter the market to sell their labor unless they are motivated to do so. Cognitive elements of a work role are specifically occupational, and a school can teach them. Motivation to work is essentially an individual matter, even though investment in professional education reinforces it. One decides to work or not to work on the basis of personal concerns. These concerns are likely to be beyond the reach of a professional school. For these reasons, motivational dimensions of socialization are unlikely to develop in concert with cognitive elements to form a single cumulative pattern.

Differentiation of the dimensions of socialization means that a change in any one of them may or may not affect the others, depending on the conditions accompanying the change. Orientations to a work role may shift to fit the exigencies of a work situation without any effect on commitment, as the reaction model emphasizes. On the other hand, with marriage and the beginning of a family, commitment may decline precipitously if work is to be left for family roles, whereas cognitive orientations to the occupational role and even to a place in the occupation remain stable. Our view of socialization as a differentiation of dimensions overcomes, we feel, the oversocialized view of workers implicit in the induction approach. At the same time, we draw ideas from the induction model to overcome limitations of the reaction studies. The induction model's stress on cultural content acquired in conformity to expectations of work roles helps to explain the persistence of orientations in the transition from student to professional status.

4. Studying directional change: study design

Our definition of socialization consists of three main aspects; each is important in its measurement. It is social psychological; it is temporal; and it is multidimensional. To capture these aspects we have taken several considerations into account in designing our research. These considerations are all too often glossed over.

Socialization is individual change. Cross-sectional designs are inappropriate to study it. It can be conceived as process or as outcome, but its measurement necessarily entails looking at responses from the same individual at different points in time. Selection of responses from the life of an individual to determine a change unavoidably imposes an outcome perspective on the research. An outcome perspective need not be static, however. Ours is not. We regard socialization as the development of dispositions to actions that tell the person what to do in various types of situations. It is evidenced in the stability of or continued directional change of responses to questions about nursing. We say development has occurred when a response settles down to a persistent state or persistent direction that is continued, not erased or reversed by a status transition.

Directionality and persistence of responses across status transitions are the criteria we use to distinguish socialization from other kinds of individual change. As the training situations of students change, do their response patterns to earlier ones persist? This is the basic question we ask to determine whether or not the program has socialized students. The question requires that we take a long-range view and that the view incorporate the status transitions that move students from novices to licensed practicing nurses. Our research is longitudinal and it is designed around status transitions. The transitions are the steps in the recruitment process: entering the school, going through its program, and exiting as practitioners. Observations will be long-range, paralleling the recruitment process. They will enable us to extract patterns of directional change and distinguish them from temporary fluctuation in responses

46

to immediate situations. Short-lived responses tell how students experience a program, but these are not our interest. We want to see beyond temporary adaptations.

How are we to determine multidimensionality, the other main aspect of our definition? We argue that socialization is multidimensional, and that different conditions develop different dimensions, possibly at different times. Our observations must enable us to determine independence of the dimensions. Design problems pertain to when and how to observe students. In deciding when and how to observe, we have taken two additional considerations into account. We want to avoid conceiving socialization as having a specifiable end product laid down by official socializing agents. Persistent change may occur but in directions not advocated or wanted by the faculty. We do not want our design to hide unintentional socialization. The other consideration is to avoid seeing socialization as a simple change from a beginning state to an end state. The difference between the two states gives the amount of socialization that has occurred, but that is not our major interest. We want to see socialization instead as a complex process with its dimensions possibly developing at different times and under different conditions. We are not so interested in the gross or net change in responses as in the times of onset of their stabilization into coherent and persistent patterns.

Studies too often put aside these considerations by defining socialization as the learning of specific role behaviors. The definition is then taken as a standard for observing both the direction and the extent of change necessary for socialization to be said to have occurred. The model usually accepts official agents' definitions of appropriate behavior or attitudes. Measurements are made at the beginning and end of training to gauge increased conformity to the specified socialization criteria. A before-and-after design is useful for studying many problems of personal change, but it is not very useful to trace the course of a change or the continuance of a stable pattern. It cannot tell when or why a response stabilized. Moreover, in assuming a priori a specified end product (Olesen and Whittaker, 1968:5) and accepting one definition of socialization – usually an official one – it ignores unofficial socialization agents, whether their definitions be complementary, antithetical, or irrelevant to the official one. Through its focus on change in states, it slights continuity across situations.

Our research is designed to view socialization as a complex set of dimensions, to examine the extent of their directionality and persistence over time without specifying in advance what these must be, and to observe the varied conditions and influences underlying the development and differentiation of dimensions of socialization.

Research design

Data for this study come from research initiated in 1959. The framework of the research as initially planned followed closely the induction model of socialization (see McKinney and Ingles, 1959). It assumed that nursing could be conceived as a subculture and a nursing school as an agency for transmitting the subculture to students. Acquisition of the subculture was seen as preparing students for roles predefined by the profession as the end product of socialization. The objective of the research when it was begun was to ascertain the processes through which students learned nursing subculture – nursing values and expectations of their relations to patients, physicians, and others in the nurse's role-set – and the relation of these learnings to their ability to work successfully during their first year as registered nurses. The learning process was conceived as paralleling the succession of students' roles from those of entering freshmen to first-year graduates, and the research was designed to measure rigorously the acquisition of nursing subculture as students progressed through their education and into the world of work.

We have extended our view of socialization from that of the initial proposal, but the design of that research anticipated the issues we have raised about measuring socialization for our study to be reported here. The research design combined longitudinal and cross-sectional representations of students. This study views socialization as consisting of different dimensions that develop over time. To study them requires that we observe the same individuals over time to see whether a directional change occurs in their responses and if it persists at subsequent times. The longitudinal features of the design permit such observations.

We also need indicators of the program's influence on the individual changes in behavior, which we argue are produced by the program. Because we studied only one school and its program was essentially unchanged during the period of our observations, we must infer effects of the program from the timing of stabilization of responses as students moved through the program. Each academic year laid out an arrangement of role relations with different role alters for students. The options these arrangements allowed and the kinds of experiences they provided in each academic year are our indicators of the program's influence. The observations by academic class year enable us to indicate the changing role arrangements corresponding to different influences (independent variables). Matching the development of a dimension of socialization with a role arrangement in the program gives confidence that the influences contained within the role arrangement produced, or at least were associated with, the socialization result. Having the longitudinal observations classified by academic year enables us to relate individual changes to movement through different role arrangements within the program. In this way we hope to pinpoint the kinds of arrangements that initiate consistent directions of change in the different dimensions of socialization.

The longitudinal design overcomes limitations of a cross-sectional one in studying individual change, but it creates other difficulties not easily dealt with. Three are relevant for our study. One is attrition from the study population. Many students whom we observed during the early years of their education failed to complete the program, and our data for some of those who completed the program do not cover all academic statuses. The more worrisome loss is withdrawal from the program. It reduced the study population and thereby introduced unknown biases. We know school mortality was not random; students who completed the program differed from those who left, if in no other way than that they got the desired degree. To check for biases, we will compare panel responses with those for other aggregations of students.

A second difficulty associated with a longitudinal design involves the confounding of effects of aging and of school experiences on individual change. Aging and experience are not easily separated (cf. Glenn, 1977: 46–57). The aging of students cannot be separated from students' movement through the program to see their separate effects. All the students were virtually the same age at each academic status, so we cannot control age to see the effect of movement through the program separate from age. Socialization is by its nature temporal; to age is to experience and to learn and develop therefrom. But if aging is the dominant influence and not experiences within the school, socialization should occur continuously and cumulatively to parallel the aging process. We will show that socialization was not continuous or linear. Instead, it followed the shifts in the school program and fitted the experiences organized by the program. We conclude that aging alone did not produce our findings. We use timing of the stabilization of responses to infer the effect of program experiences on socialization.

A third difficulty arising from the longitudinal design pertains to repeated measures. The data gotten at the different times are not independent. In the interest of rigor, we asked the same individuals the same questions six times – at entry into the school, at the end of each academic year, and after one year of work. With the exception of the freshman year, a calendar year separated the observations. Conceivably, students may have remembered their earlier responses, but more likely they did not. A year between the data collections lessens the likelihood that our data are contaminated by repeated observations. This opinion is supported by the low intracorrelations of each dependent variable. The intracorrelations do not increase consistently from one academic year to the next as bias from repeated measurement would produce. (See Appendix A.) The absence of a consistent unilinear pattern of intracorrelations gives confidence that repeated measurement did not produce our findings.

Study population

The population included in the study consisted of three panel classes and five additional cohorts followed for varying periods of time. The panel classes were followed from the first week of their matriculation as freshmen, year by year through the four years of schooling, and through at least one year as graduates. Table 4-1 presents the study design, schematically showing the cohorts observed, the times when they were observed, and their academic status at each time. Each cohort is designated in the figure by year of its graduation and its academic class status. In all, eight cohorts of students were observed from the fall of 1959 through 1965. The three panel classes were observed from entry to at least one year after graduation as alumnae, and the additional cohorts for varying successive years, with the exception of the 1961 seniors, who were observed only at the time of their graduation. The panel cohorts are shown in the space between the broken lines in Table 4-1. Looking cross-sectionally at the design, we see that six cohorts were observed at entry and at the end of the freshman year; five of these were observed in each of the remaining academic years and three as alumnae. Two cohorts were observed for briefer periods to fill out the cross-sectional population.

Table 4-1. *Sample and research design*

	Academic year data collected															Academic class total
Status at time of administration	1959-60		1960-61		1961-62		1962-63		1963-64		1964-65		1965-66		
	Class of[a]	Cases[b]	Class of	Cases	Class of	Cases	Class of	Cases	Class of	Cases	Class of	Cases	Class of	Cases	
Entering freshmen	1965[c]	88	1964	88	1965	89	1966	87	1967	84	1968	81	d	d	517
End of freshman year	1963	80	1964	82	1965	82	1966	77	1967	78	1968	76	d	d	475
End of sophomore year			1963	67	1964	73	1965	68	1966	57	1967	69	d	d	334
End of junior year			1962	41	1963	59	1964	58	1965	48	1966	47	d	d	253
At graduation			1961	54	1962	39	1963	58	1964	48	1965	48	d	d	247
Alumnae[e]									1963	45	1964	42	1965	35	127

[a] Year of graduation.
[b] Number who completed questionnaires.
[c] Administered in fall; all others in the spring.
[d] Panel classes.
[e] Alumnae were sent questionnaires in the fall of the calendar year following their graduation: The 1963 class received theirs in the fall of 1964, the 1964 class in 1965, and the 1965 class in 1966.

Table 4-2. *Yearly attrition in enrollments*

Class of	Entering freshmen-freshmen	Freshmen-sophomore	Sophomore-junior	Junior-senior	Senior-graduate
1961					1.7
1962				7.1	13.3
1963	0.0	11.2	16.5	12.1	1.7
1964	2.3	8.1	20.0	5.4	0.0
1965	5.6	7.7	24.3	5.7	2.0
1966	0.0	11.5	31.2	7.5	0.0
1967	0.0	11.8	16.0	12.5	
1968	0.0	12.3	23.9		

Note: Dotted line denotes panel classes.

Table 4-1, under the heading Cases, gives the number in each cohort for each academic status who completed the questionnaires for each time period. The numbers of cases for all cohorts declined as they moved through the academic statuses. But the drop was sharpest between the sophomore and junior years and between graduation and the alumnae. The two points of loss represent two kinds of attrition from the sample. The attrition from the sophomore to the junior class arises principally from students' leaving the program; that between graduation and the alumnae is due to other reasons. We had difficulty in locating and getting alumnae to complete the questionnnaires; and some loss came from clerical problems in preparation and storage of alumnae data.

Table 4-2 gives the yearly attrition in school enrollments for each class as they moved from one academic status to another. The sharpest yearly drops consistently clustered between the sophomore and junior years. This was a major turning point in the program. Not only was the absolute yearly loss greatest at this point, but so was the percentage of the gross loss from time of entry to graduation. For the classes of 1963 through 1967, the percentage of the gross attrition occurring between the sophomore and junior years was respectively 71.8 percent, 91.4 percent, 73.2 percent, 82.9 percent, and 75.9 percent. The other main point of attrition in the sample occurred in the alumnae status. All students who graduated were by definition alumnae, so all the alumnae loss arose from incomplete information. Table 4-3 gives the percentage of enrollees in each academic status for whom we have usable data on most questions.

Table 4-3. *Percent of enrollees in usable sample*

Class of	Entering freshmen	Freshmen	Sopho- mores	Juniors	Seniors	Alumnae
1961					93.1	
1962				73.2	76.5	
1963	98.9	90.0	84.8	89.4	100.0	79.9
1964	100.0	95.3	92.4	98.3	90.6	79.2
1965	100.0	97.6	87.2	92.3	98.0	72.9
1966	100.0	87.5	74.0	88.7		
1967	98.8	91.8	92.0			
1968	100.0	93.8				

Aggregating respondents for analysis

The study design allows several ways of aggregating subjects. The panel classes give the individual histories of students undergoing the recruitment process. Idiosyncrasies of a panel are discernible from its comparison with other panels or from a norm based on all panels or classes. Data on academic classes are another population base; these are provided by the longitudinal data on different cohorts as they moved from one to another academic class. Agreement among the cohorts when all were in the same academic class at different times gives evidence that the influence of the structure of the program overshadowed temporal and cohort differences. Still another way in which subjects could be aggregrated is by the years when they were observed, were one interested in effects of notable events on all cohorts who were in school when they occurred. Because we do not have such an interest and the program's structure did not change during the period of our observations, we have not aggregated the students by the years when they were studied. Cohorts at the same points within the program differed little on measures of the dependent variables, and the three panel classes likewise showed high agreement on these measures (Miller, 1967). We have therefore grouped the three panel classes together for analysis, and we have grouped together the cohorts observed as members of each academic class for cross-sectional analysis.

For purposes of analysis the panel classes include only respondents who completed the program and on whom data are complete from entry to graduation. We also extend the period of observation of the panel to one year as alumnae. Panel classes are defined for analysis in two different ways because some data are missing on some alumnae. For some analyses the panel classes are defined as including only those respondents with complete data on all variables. For other analyses they are defined to include those who graduated from the program and on whom the data are complete through graduation on all variables, but some of whom are excluded from analysis of the alumnae population because of incomplete information for the year after graduation. The panels, defined by the criterion of completion of the program, are biased as samples of students through their exclusion of students who left the program. The year-by-year analysis of individual progression discussed below includes the dropouts, thereby avoiding the possible bias that is built into a panel design through its exclusion of dropouts. (On the other hand, it introduces another kind of bias. Each year's dropouts were absent from the data on the next year, and they may have been different from those who remained in the kinds of socialization processes they underwent. We were forced to risk one or the other of two types of bias.)

An additional way to aggregate respondents is to analyze the year-by-year progression of students through the academic classes of the program. The year-by-year progression aggregation includes the panel classes and also members of other cohorts who were observed through at least one status transition. This method gives a larger base than the panel classes. It is obtained by matching responses of each student from one class year to the next. We begin with entering freshmen; for all students who completed the freshman year we match responses at the beginning and end of the year; for all second-semester freshmen who completed the sophomore year we match responses at the ends of the freshman and sophomore years; and so on.

These different methods of aggregation enable us to consider different units of analysis simultaneously with the same data. Data on academic classes provide a view of the structure of the program to show between what points in the program the most pronounced aggregate differences occur. The year-by-year aggregation permits us to look at individual students to see continuity in their views as they moved from one academic class to another. The panels of those who completed the program enable us to look at year-by-year responses of graduates. To anticipate our findings, the results do not differ noticeably when different methods of aggregating the subjects are used. This fact suggests that those who were included in the study population during the earlier years of the program but subsequently left without graduating experienced the early parts of the program in essentially the same ways as those who graduated; missing data on early or late years did not bias the findings. Of these two inferences, the more significant is that differences in the processes of socialization up to the time of attrition were not the reasons for students' dropping out. Warnecke (1966) in a study of dropouts found that academic failure and marriage were the main reasons for withdrawing from the program.

Data collection

Several kinds of data were collected on students over the period when each cohort was observed. The main data are from questionnaires that gave repeated observations at entry into school, at the completion of each academic year, and approximately one year after graduation. The questionnaires were constructed with the help of two members of the nursing school faculty to ensure the asking of meaningful questions about nursing and nursing education as students were experiencing it. The questionnaires included open-ended questions that asked students about their experiences and reactions to them. As Table 4-1 has shown, questionnaires were administered each spring shortly before the end of the semester to all four academic classes. Entering freshmen within the first two weeks after matriculation completed questionnaires containing the items that were to be repeated at the end of each academic year and also containing questions about the hows and whys of their decisions to study nursing and their social backgrounds. The questionnaire data obtained from all students were supplemented with data from diaries kept by the first of our panel classes and with interviews with students from the same class, selected by nursing instructors as representatives of the best, the average, and the poorest students.

The school's program was assumed to be designed around a specific model of nursing that the school hoped to inculcate in its students. The ideals in the model are valued images, if not norms, that the faculty upheld for students and wished to pass on to them. Faculty questionnaires were constructed to ask about faculty views toward the curriculum, their teaching aims, the kinds of graduates they hoped to produce, and the problems they encountered in trying to develop their students into the kind of nurses they hoped they would become. During the six years of our observations there were thirty-three different faculty members including about twenty-four at any given time; all, including those who left their positions during the study, completed the questionnaire. These faculty data enable us to see the extent to which students acquired the orientations to nursing upheld as ideals of their program.

Still another kind of data comes from parents of students. Parents of all but the pilot class were sent questionnaires inquiring about their socioeconomic status, values, and lifestyles. Usable questionnaires were returned by 99.3 percent (452 of 455). These data give us information on the kinds of social settings and cultural climates from which students were recruited. We use these data to explore the relations of students' backgrounds to their orientations and personal relatedness to nursing and the extent of homogeneity of their backgrounds. Background data obtained from parents and entering freshmen also permit us to see the similarity of the population we studied to other collegiate and noncollegiate nursing students and nonnursing collegiate students described in other research. These comparisons enable us to relate our findings to a broader universe, though, of course, such comparisons cannot eliminate the intrinsic limits on the generalizability of our findings beyond the school and the time when it was studied. But we are less interested in the specific empirical findings on a school of nursing than in theoretical efforts to extend research on occupational socialization so as to integrate what have previously been treated as disparate aspects.

Organization of the book

Having developed our own conceptualization of socialization in Part I, we use it to investigate the socialization of student nurses in the remainder of the book. Empirical findings are reported in three main parts. Part II examines the development among students of orientations to the occupational role, orientations to a place in the occupation, and relatedness to the occupation, and the persistence of these dimensions of socialization among alumnae. Part III looks at individual differences among students to see if characteristics of individuals modified the pattern of development of the processes as shaped by the school. Part IV uses findings to discuss the utility of our model of socialization and implications of nursing education and socialization for the labor force of nursing.

PART II

The school's program and development of socialization processes

5. Social and cultural backgrounds of student nurses

This chapter shows that the cultural backgrounds of Duke School of Nursing students were relatively homogeneous in ways that fitted the values traditionally associated with nursing.

Demographic characteristics

The backgrounds of the student nurses reflected aspects of the traditional social origins of nurses and also of the student body of Duke University as a whole during the period of this study. All were white females. Like most nurses (Olesen and Whittaker, 1968:83) and most Duke undergraduates, they were predominantly Protestant, with high-status Protestant denominations overrepresented among them: 24.8 percent were Presbyterian, 23.8 percent Methodist, 14.9 percent Episcopalian, 6.1 percent Baptist, 6.1 percent Lutheran, 9.2 percent Catholic, 2.3 percent Jewish, and 12.8 percent from other Protestant denominations or religiously mixed families. (Percentages in this discussion of demographic backgrounds are based on all entering freshmen. N's range from 510 to 517.) Like most nurses at the time of the study (McPartland, 1957:31), they had grown up mainly in small communities or middle-sized cities: only 28.9 percent were from cities of 100,000 or more or their suburbs. Their regional origins resembled those of the Duke undergraduate student body: 45.5 percent were from the Northeast, 43.5 percent from the Southeast, 8.2 percent from the Midwest, and 2.8 percent from other regions.

Although their religious and community backgrounds typified the recruiting grounds of nursing, the social statuses of their families were higher than those of the average nurse. Most nurses come from working-class or lower-middle class families (Hughes et al., 1958:22; Martin and Simpson, 1956:14; Bressler and Kephart, 1955:116). Duke student nurses resembled most college students, especially those in expensive private colleges, in coming predominantly from the middle class. When

59

classified by their fathers' occupations using the Duncan (1961) Socioeconomic Index, student nurses came about equally from the upper-middle and lower-middle classes: 44.1 percent of their fathers' occupations scored 74 or above on the Duncan Index, 50.3 percent scored from 50 through 73, and 5.6 percent scored 49 or below. Occupations typical of those scoring below 74 included low-level adminstrators, school teachers, and clerical and sales workers. The yearly incomes of their families reflected the same predominantly upper- and lower-middle-class distribution: 42.7 percent of their families earned $15,000 or more (in the early 1960s), 28.6 percent earned from $10,000 to $14,999, and 28.6 percent earned less than $10,000. (During the early 1960s when these data were collected, family status was determined primarily by the father's work. If the mother worked, her work was not seen to affect significantly the family's status. Our measure of family status reflects this view. Income and occupational data are taken from questionnaires filled out by parents. All other demographic data are from questionnaires completed by student nurses at the time they entered Duke).

Thus the average parental social class of the Duke student nurses was higher than that of most nurses, though similar to that of collegiate student nurses as reported by Olesen and Whittaker (1968:86). But slightly more were from the lower-middle class than from the upper-middle class, and the lower-middle class has been one of the strata from which nurses have traditionally been recruited. Duke was an expensive school to attend, but a number of the student nurses were receiving scholarship aid, so that quite a few in modest financial circumstances were able to attend.

Recruitment to nursing and the Nightingale pattern

The pattern of student nurses' background characteristics suggests that they were not a random cross-section of undergraduate college students but a selected group, relatively homogeneous in significant ways. Selectivity of social and cultural characteristics of recruits tends to occur in any occupation. The principal selectivity of student nurses' characteristics was self-regulated through their decisions to apply for admission to the school. Unlike most women students, student nurses in applying for admission are at least tentatively committing themselves to an occupational choice. Can the students' backgrounds help to explain their initial interest in nursing? We cannot answer this question definitely, but the fact that the Duke student nurses shared background characteristics with other nurses despite their higher socioeconomic origins suggests that the kinds of community and religious backgrounds from which they came may generate a special affinity to nursing.

Why is it that small communities produce more than their share of nurses? A convergence of facts suggests that the association of nursing with small-community backgrounds is not fortuitous. The stereotype of the ideal nurse, which took root in reality, was conceived during the later part of the nineteenth century (Strauss, 1966; Olesen and Whittaker, 1968:62–4). This was a time of the rapid growth of cities, occasioned by migration from farms and small towns and by massive immigration of poor Catholics and Jews, successively from Ireland, Italy, and Eastern Europe. The nation as a whole was Protestant, rural, and small town in population and in ethos. The conditions that reformers of nursing sought to change were attributed to the foreign immigrants to the growing cities (Strauss, 1966). In identifying cities and their immigrant populations as the cause of the low state of nursing and in looking to small towns and farms as sources of recruits to upgrade nursing, the reform strategy invidiously evaluated the different types of communities and populations and cast nursing's lot with the small Protestant community and its way of life.

Delineation of a desired population from which to recruit does not guarantee that the preferred population will want to enter the occupation. At the time of the nursing reform movement, however, conditions were especially ripe for the recruitment of nurses from rural Protestant communities. Hospitals and medical and nursing care were undergoing phenomenal growth (Strauss, 1966:75–7). The rapid growth of hospitals and nursing jobs was not confined to the big cities but was also taking place in small cities and towns. The availability of nursing work in small communities provided job opportunities for women from farms and small towns, who had begun to enter the labor market in substantial numbers by the turn of the century (Smuts, 1959:20, 49–50). The desired pattern of selective recruitment of nurses came about automatically as a result of broad social changes. The range of suitable occupations for rural women was quite limited. Within this narrow range, nursing was highly visible, obviously feminine, and morally acceptable. The individualized service orientation personified by the nurse has historically pervaded the idealized ethos of the small town (Hilfer, 1969:3–

24). More than any other orientation, it describes the attraction of nursing for its recruits to the present day.

Another characteristic of the small-town population and its prevailing imagery that seems to have been linked to nursing is the middle-class concern with self-betterment and purposefulness. Utilitarian concerns of this kind are evident in the emphasis nursing leaders have placed on housekeeping efficiency and order (Strauss, 1966:87). On the personal value level of the recruit, the utilitarian values might be expressed in a concern with improving oneself. Because women were taught to orient themselves to maternal and familistic concerns, their desires for self-improvement were largely confined to outlets that would have social utility. What better way for a respectable young woman to exemplify the complex of small-town values than to be a nurse? Nursing enabled her to improve herself in a socially useful way. Daughters of working-class or lower-middle-class families who went into nursing did not have to choose between the values of self-improvement and nurturance. The two values were conjoined in nursing.

The overrepresentation of small-community backgrounds among the Duke student nurses suggests that nursing is still perceived in small towns more than in big cities as a highly appropriate occupation for women. Small communities remain less occupationally diversified than larger ones and present young women with fewer visible occupations identified as suitable for middle-class or upward mobile women. The convergence of the traditions of nursing with the way of life of the small town apparently continues to enhance the attractiveness of nursing to small-town women. Nursing is respected, and the esteem in which nurses are held adds to the occupation's intrinsic attractiveness.

The slight predominance of lower-middle-class familial backgrounds among Duke student nurses also fits the historical pattern of nursing recruitment. This stratum is noted for a concern for self-improvement. (For a summary of research findings on values of this class see Broom and Selznick, 1973:183-5.) Parents work and plan for a college education for their children. A collegiate nursing program would seem especially attractive to the lower-middle class; it provides a college degree and it gives training in an occupation having job opportunities widely dispersed throughout the country.

The sizable proportion of upper-middle-class backgrounds among the Duke student nurses departs, however, from the traditional recruitment pattern of nursing. Values commonly attributed to this stratum are more diverse than those identified with the lower-middle class. A concern for self-improvement and community betterment coexists with an emphasis on expressing one's personality (Banfield, 1970:48–51). The latter value is sometimes seen as antithetical to a concern with helping others, the core value around which the image of nursing has been formed (cf. Rosenberg, 1957). Self-expression may, however, take the form of working to improve one's community. This kind of self-expression is quite consistent with a service orientation: One expresses oneself through activities aimed at community betterment. Emphasis on community service over more individualized modes of self-expression would seem more possible for the average upper-middle-class resident of a small community than of a large one. The upper-middle class is relatively much smaller in small cities and towns. Members of this stratum not only initiate service, but are expected by others to do such work. Such an expectation should lead to a deemphasis of interest in purely private self-expressive activities.

If interest in community betterment is more prevalent in the upper-middle class of small than of large communities, the high proportion of Duke student nurses from upper-middle-class backgrounds may not have been a departure from the pattern of values traditionally associated with the recruitment of nurses. If the student nurses from the higher social strata were overrepresented among those from the smaller communities, then the traditional recruitment pattern had not been sidetracked but expanded in a way that was consistent with the pattern of values underlying the traditional recruitment pattern. These students would have come from social settings whose value climates coincided with most aspects of the value climates prevalent in most recruits' backgrounds. This appears to have been at least somewhat the case. In descending order of parental status, 20.0 percent, 21.1 percent, 32.0 percent, and 31.7 percent came from cities of 100,000 or more population or their suburbs. (The categories of parental status are Duncan Socioeconomic Index scores of 85 and above, 73–84, 57–72, 56 and below.) Students from the highest-status families were more likely than others to be from smaller communities. The special characteristics of the upper-middle-class role in small communities may have helped to instill in them the service values commonly associated with attraction to nursing.

In general, the backgrounds of Duke student nurses seem to have resembled in significant ways the backgrounds of most nurses. Their

Table 5-1. *Percentage of parents of student nurses who said that they participate more, the same, or less than other families in their communities in various activities*

| Activities | Comparison of own participation with that of other families | | |
	More	Same	Less
Community civic affairs (PTA, Community Chest, etc.)	50.0	42.5	7.5
Political affairs	18.1	45.0	36.9
Fraternal and women's clubs	25.3	33.6	41.0
Church affairs	55.3	34.0	10.7
Informal social life	27.6	58.9	13.5

Note: The number of parents responding ranged from 446 to 450.

community and family backgrounds were fairly homogeneous in terms of the conditions most conducive to the perpetuation of the nurturant service orientations of what has been called the Florence Nightingale or ministering angel pattern of nursing. The Duke student nurses tended to have some structural attachment – community or social class – associated with parochialism. And these parochial values, inferred from an emphasis on local community, appear to give strong impetus to the selection of nursing as a career by many young women.

Parental value climates

On the basis of previous findings on the backgrounds of nurses and of our findings on the Duke student nurses, we have argued that social attachments and values associated with localism support recruitment to nursing. Students were attached to local community and social class structures through their families. The value climates of their families constituted intimate settings for inculcating values and orientations that might support attraction to nursing. Their family backgrounds were congenial to traditional nursing values.

As one way of measuring family values, we asked the parents about the families' involvement in various kinds of community participation and about the kinds of concerns emphasized within their homes. Table 5-1 shows the percentages of parents who rated the family's participa-

Table 5-2. *Rank order of concerns parents say are emphasized within their families* more *than within most families*

Activities ranked	Percent
Children's education	84.1
Children's opportunities	70.6
Close family life	70.2
Literature, art, music	61.1
Current affairs	57.2
Religion	56.1
Home and garden	51.4
Science	34.2
Father's occupation	33.5
Proper standing in the community	30.7
Fashion	23.5

Note: Parents responding numbered from 430 to 452.

tion in different kinds of community activities as being more than, the same as, or less than that of "other families" in their communities. (One parent answered for each student's family.) Using a standard of at least 50.0 percent of the families saying they participated more than other families as an indication of heavy participation, we see that only church and civic affairs (PTA, Community Chest, etc.) were widely supported by the student nurses' families. The families tended to consider themselves typical of their communities ("same") in informal social life and tended to describe themselves as less active than most families in fraternal and women's clubs and political life. The relatively low involvement in these activities, which might link a family to events outside the local community – fraternal and women's clubs and political affairs – coupled with their high participation in church and local civic affairs suggests that the families were highly localistic in orientation.

The parochial orientations of student nurses' families are even more evident in the kinds of concerns that parents said were emphasized in their homes. Table 5-2 ranks different concerns by the percentages of families in which they were said to be more emphasized than in other families. Three clusters of endorsed concerns appear. The families overwhelmingly stressed familistic concerns, especially the children's education. Evidently the parents had strongly supported and planned for the college education of their daughters. Another type of concern, emphasized by slightly more than half the parents, pertained to leisure pursuits: literature, arts, music, current affairs, religious matters, and home and garden. These leisure activities are primarily of the self-improvement type. Although they may be enjoyed for the pleasure they give, they are also "educative" and would fit the interest of parents concerned with education and other opportunities for their children. About a third of the parents said that science was strongly emphasized in their families. A concern with science might also fit the value placed on self-improvement and children's opportunities.

The self-improvement value evident in the stress on "cultural" pursuits stands in sharp contrast to the low amount of expressed concern with father's occupation, social standing in the community, and fashions, which are endorsed by only about a fourth to a third of the families. These last concerns, like the "cultural" ones, are consumptive in nature, but they symbolize a desire for status recognition in the community, whereas the more strongly endorsed cultural pursuits symbolize "higher" moral objectives. Moreover, social status concerns direct a family's attention outward to invidious comparison of itself with other families, so that activities of individual members of the family may be only tenuously linked to an activity pattern of the family as a group. Cultural pursuits need not have this effect of orienting the family or its individual members outward. Because the purpose of cultural pursuits can be fulfilled within the family circle, they might tend to integrate family activities and foster familism.

We have argued that concerns with culture and current affairs might fit the self-improvement aspect of traditional familistic orientations. An argument might be made that they are, instead, highly cosmopolitan. Evidence that suggests they were not a part of a cosmopolitan outlook among student nurses' families comes from responses to a question that presented forced-choice value alternatives and asked parents to choose the preferred value from each pair for a son and a daughter. The alternatives pitted cosmopolitan against parochial values (cf. Merton, 1957: 387–99): work autonomy versus secure income, creative versus helpful, successful versus happy home life, well-off financially versus helpful, advanced education versus faithful to religious beliefs. The first value of each pair reflects cosmopolitanism; the second, parochialism.

Table 5-3 gives the value preferences for sons and daughters, sex differentiations of the values, and the rank order of the sex differentiations. Value preferences shown in the third column were obtained by

Table 5-3. Sex differentiation of values by parents of student nurses[a]

Value choices a choice, b choice[b]	Percent choosing value	Value preference[c]		Sex differentiation of value[d]
		Son	Daughter	
Work autonomy vs. secure income (N = 379)		+12.4	−49.2	+30.8
1. a both	23.0			
2. a son, b daughter	33.2			
3. b son, a daughter	2.4			
4. b both	41.4			
Creative vs. helpful (N = 387)		−12.1	−65.9	+26.9
1. a both	14.0			
2. a son, b daughter	30.0			
3. b son, a daugher	3.1			
4. b both	53.0			
Successful in work vs. happy home life (N = 318)		−56.9	−95.3	+19.2
1. a both	2.4			
2. a son, b daughter	19.2			
3. b son, a daugher	0.0			
4. b both	78.5			
Well off financially vs. helpful (N = 387)		−60.8	−80.4	+10.3
1. a both	8.5			
2. a son, b daughter	11.1			
3. b son, a daughter	0.8			
4. b both	79.6			

Table 5.3 (cont.)

Value choices a choice, b choice[b]	Percent choosing value	Value preference[c]		Sex differ- entiation of value[d]
		Son	Daughter	
Advanced education vs. faithful to religious beliefs (N = 369)		−20.4	−38.8	+9.2
1. a both	30.6			
2. a son, b daughter	9.2			
3. b son, a daughter	0.0			
4. b both	60.2			

[a] Only parents who chose for sons *and* daughters were included.

[b] *a* choice refers to first mentioned value; *b* refers to second value. E.g., *a* signifies creative; *b* helpful.

[c] Value preference is obtained by subtracting total preferences of *b* value from total preferences for *a* value. *a* value is assigned a plus (+) and *b* values a minus (−). Thus, a sum designated by a minus sign indicates that parental preference is for the *b* value.

[d] Sex differentiation is obtained by the following: (*a* son, *b* daughter) − (*b* son, *a* daughter). It shows the linkage of a value with either sex.

subtracting the number of parents preferring the parochial *b* value (the second in the pair) from the number preferring the cosmopolitan *a* value (the first in the pair). A negative (−) figure indicates overall parental preference for a parochial *b* value and a positive (+) figure indicates overall parental preference for a cosmopolitan *a* value.

These data show that parents preferred parochial to cosmopolitan values for both daughters and sons, with the exception of the value pair "work autonomy vs. secure income." By 10.4 percent they chose work autonomy over secure income for sons (55.2 percent vs. 44.8 percent). However, they heavily preferred secure income for daughters. The values they wanted least for their children relative to the alternatives were financial well-being and success in work. They heavily chose helpfulness over both creativity and financial success for both sons and daughters. They preferred faithfulness to religious beliefs over advanced education, an especially strong indication of the strength of religion in these homes in view of the fact that 84.1 percent of them said that they stressed their children's education more than most families, as was reported in Table 5-2.

The values that nurses expect to realize from nursing are ones associated with the traditional role of the woman. They are part of a generally traditional orientation. We have seen that parents tended to endorse traditional values for both sons and daughters; the endorsement, however, was greater for daughters than for sons, as is shown in the fourth column of Table 5-3. The measure of sex differentiation of a value is obtained by subtracting the third from the second figure shown for the value in the first column: (*a* son, *b* daughter) minus (*b* son, *a* daughter). It shows the link of a value to either sex, with a positive figure (+) indicating greater cosmopolitanism of preferences for sons than for daughters and a negative figure (−) indicating greater cosmopolitanism of preferences for daughters than for sons. The sex differentiations of all values were positive in sign, indicating that parents were more parochial in their aspirations for their daughters than for their sons. The value pairs are listed in order of sex differentiations, from most to least differentiated. Although some of the value preferences were substantially different in the aggregate for children of the two sexes, the most common pattern for every value was to choose the parochial alternative for both daughters and sons.

Because cosmopolitanism and parochialism tend to be associated with social class, and because the statuses of parents were widely distributed, the variation in value preferences and in the sex differentiation of the values might simply have corresponded to the parents' statuses. Table 5-4 shows that this was not the case. The table cross-classifies parents' status and their value preferences and sex differentiations of values. As before, the four parental status categories are Duncan SEI scores of 85 and above, 73–84, 57–72, and 56 and below. Controlling parents' status does not alter the overall pattern of wide support for localistic and familistic values or of the sex differentiation of the values. The only deviation appears in value preference between work autonomy and secure income for sons; parents of status groups I (the highest-status group) and III were about evenly divided between preferring one and the other, whereas in the total sample work autonomy was mildly preferred for sons. In all status groups parochial values were preferred for daughters, and although the extent of sex differentiation varied somewhat by status, the overall direction of sex differentiation of the values was the same in all social classes.

The data strongly suggest that the parents of the student nurses tended to uphold strong moral codes for their daughters. The daughters were expected to be helpful, to favor security, to value the home, to behave in such a way as to beget respect, and to maintain religious faith. These are the kinds of expectations that promote nurturant orientations toward others. Parents placed relatively little emphasis, even for sons, on values identified with individualism or achievement. Because the communities in which the students grew up were relatively small, the climate of the home could be meaningfully extended to organizations serving the community as a whole, to judge from parents' concern with church and civic affairs. The lifestyle of these students' families was organized around collective moral ends but limited to the local community.

The many background characteristics show that Duke students did not bring new blood into nursing but came from the backgrounds that have traditionally produced nurses. The early socialization of nurses is typically in small communities, and our students fitted the pattern. Their parents stressed tradition, family, helpfulness, and religious faith; and students incorporated these values into service goals. They wanted to help others and to do so directly. Small communities seem to produce in girls the kinds of values that make nursing an attractive occupation. The students in the Duke School of Nursing reflected these traditional patterns, as we shall see more directly in Chapter 6, which exam-

Table 5-4. *Social status of parents and value preferences for sons and daughters and sex differentiation of values*

Value pair	Value preference *sons*				Value preference *daughters*				Sex differentiation of value			
	Status groups				Status groups				Status groups			
	I	II	III	IV	I	II	III	IV	I	II	III	IV
Work autonomy vs. secure income	0.9	27.0	−1.5	21.6	−53.1	−54.0	−46.5	−38.8	27.0	40.5	27.5	30.4
Creative vs. helpful	−11.4	−9.0	−15.5	−12.7	−62.8	−66.2	−85.9	−57.1	25.7	28.6	35.2	22.2
Success in work vs. happy home life	−52.2	−57.4	−71.4	−52.8	−98.4	−92.0	−97.2	−93.4	23.0	17.3	12.9	20.3
Financial well-being vs. helpful	−60.8	−54.4	−57.1	−66.7	−84.0	−74.6	−77.1	−85.7	11.6	10.1	10.0	9.5
Advanced education vs. faithful to religious beliefs	−20.4	−4.2	−30.4	−23.3	−52.8	−15.4	−51.6	−41.7	10.7	5.6	10.6	9.2

ines the values of entering freshmen. Data in Chapter 7 will show that orientations to individualized patient care and holistic views of patients were emphasized in the school's ideology and program, which were thus congruent with these traditional values of students.

6. Orientations of entering freshman students toward nursing and nursing education

The initial views and orientations the Duke student nurses brought with them as entering freshmen included values they sought to express through nursing and conceptions of nursing work and nursing education. If entering students hold values congruent with those of practicing nurses and their faculty – which, we will later show, was the case among the Duke students – this prior inculcation of values congruent with those prevalent in the occupation should foster a sense of commonality with the school among its students and allow the faculty to focus mainly on the teaching of skills and knowledge on the assumption that what they teach fits students' expectations. The lack of such congruence may lead to student disenchantment, as was found by Wright (1967) among sociology graduate students; he found immense differences in the first-year dropout rates between students whose values concerning the nature of sociology were and were not represented in the program of study.

We have seen in Chapter 5 that Duke nursing students came predominantly from communities and families whose value climates resembled the cultural settings and values of typical recruits to nursing over the years. From this we would expect student nurses to have entered Duke anticipatorily socialized in the service values of nursing. Recruitment on the basis of normative considerations increases the likelihood of heavy emotional involvement in an occupation, thus enabling educators to feel a sense of control over their products (Etzioni, 1961:152). Chapter 8 will show that the values the Duke student nurses invoked to explain their choice of nursing were in fact the same as the criteria the faculty used to evaluate students for admission.

Personal values and choice of nursing

Our data on values of entering student nurses support our contention in Chapter 5 that student nurses were self-selectively recruited and that

73

Table 6-1. *Values entering freshmen associated with nursing*

Values associated with nursing	Percent
A. *Most important consideration in decision to enter nursing*	
Extrinsic rewards	18.4
Desire to help people	79.6
Self-expression values	1.9
B. *What is liked best about the work of a nurse*	
Being able to help people	68.4
Working with people	22.2
Extrinsic rewards	8.8
Self-expression	.6
C. *The best description of nursing*	
Descriptions of people in nursing	8.1
Descriptions of service to others	88.9
Descriptions of work tasks	3.0

Note: Respondents numbered 407 for question A, 510 for B, and 514 for C. The pilot class was not asked question A.

the selectivity was value-based, resulting in a congruence of students' values with the traditions of nursing. Students were motivated to help others and saw nursing as an occupation that rendered service. Section A of Table 6-1 is based on a question that asked students to select from a list of five considerations the main one in their decisions to enter nursing or to write in the main consideration if it did not appear in the list. "The desire to help people" was selected by 79.6 percent of the students as their main consideration in deciding on nursing. Extrinsic rewards, which included job security and good pay, were designated by 18.4 percent as their main consideration. Only 1.9 percent based their choices on values concerned with self-expression.

Part B of Table 6-1 shows that when asked to select from a list of eleven job characteristics the one they liked best about the work of a nurse, 68.4 percent of the entering students chose "being able to help people" over ten other characteristics grouped under the categories working with people (working with people directly, having interesting people as colleagues, being a part of a health team, and developing warm personal relations with patients), extrinsic rewards (five job features), and self-expression (one job feature).

Their images of nursing were based largely on the values they hoped to realize. They were presented eleven descriptions of work and were asked to select the one that best described nursing. Two of the descriptions pertained to personal service, and these were selected over the other nine descriptions by 88.9 percent of the students as the best descriptions of nursing. (See Table 6-1, Section C.) They saw nursing as a helping occupation and that is why they had chosen it.

The students saw the same kinds of service-oriented values as being expressed in the characteristics highly important for an ideal job (Table 6-2). These correspond closely to a value profile of the traditional image of a nurse. Using a standard of at least 50 percent of the students endorsing a value as highly important, we observe from the rank order of endorsed values that they wanted a chance to help people, to learn continually, to work with people, to use judgment and assume responsibility, to feel able to use their own special abilities and aptitudes in their work, to feel that their work was effective, and to combine career and family. These endorsed values add up to a picture of students' wanting to give dedicated and effective service to others, using their special abilities in giving it.

Their heavy endorsement of service values contrasts sharply with the pattern of value endorsement by female college students in the early 1950s in Rosenberg's (1957:49) sample, also shown in Table 6-2. The contrast is especially evident when we look at the one value from the list selected by the students as *the* most important one in making a job ideal. Rosenberg's college women were about four times as likely as the Duke student nurses to choose self-expression values (37.0 percent vs. 9.2 percent) and little more than half as likely to choose people-oriented values (36.0 percent vs. 67.8 percent) as the most important ones. Looking at these same figures differently, the Rosenberg students were about equally likely to choose self-expression or people-oriented values, whereas the Duke students were about seven times as likely to choose people-oriented as self-expression values. Even between the students in the two samples who chose people-oriented values as the most important, there were differences in which people-oriented values were preferred: Student nurses selected a chance to help people by a more than 4 to 1 margin, whereas the Rosenberg students selected working with people by almost 2 to 1. These comparisons agree with

Table 6-2. *Occupational values rated the most important and highly important in an ideal job by entering freshmen and by female students in the Rosenberg sample (in percent)*

Occupational value	Most important value		Highly important values	
	Student nurses (N = 444)	Rosenberg sample (N = 750)	Student nurses (N = 444)	Rosenberg sample (N = 750)
Self-expressive values	9.2	37		
Special abilities and aptitudes	9.2	27	77.5	80
Creative and original	0.0	10	28.8	54
Extrinsic reward values	.7	19		
Social status and prestige	.2	1	11.5	15
Stable, secure future	.5	15	41.6	51
Earn a great deal of money	0.0	3	4.9	19
People-oriented values	67.8	36		
Work with people	11.7	23	79.4	54
Chance to help people	56.1	13	92.4	53
Others	22.3	1		
Exercise leadership	0.0	1	39.6	29
Use judgment and responsibility	4.7	NA	78.1	NA
Combine work and family	7.3	NA	67.4	NA
Work is effective	3.5	NA	71.8	NA
Learn continually	5.6	NA	81.1	NA
Adventure	.7	2	5.2	17

Note: NA signifies "not asked."

those of Davis (1964:172–180), who found that senior students who planned to go into nursing led all students in the choice of people-oriented values, were next to the bottom in endorsement of creativity and originality and interest in making money, and led in conventionality. Freshman medical students resembled freshman nursing students in their emphasis on service (Bloom, 1973:104). Duke students in 1958–64 did not appear to be any more traditional than nursing students in other parts of the country.

The heavy emphasis on service rather than on self-expression suggests

Table 6-3. *Goals incoming freshman students wanted much to have achieved within twenty years*

Goals	Percent
Full-time housewife	54.7
Part-time work	48.3
Contributions to nursing	65.5
Nursing supervisor	44.6
Served fellow man	98.1
Member of the faculty of a school of nursing	11.1
Active in professional nursing associations	38.7
Gratitude of many patients	45.2
An important place in my community	50.2

Note: Respondents ranged from 504 to 514.

a deemphasis of individuation, competitive achievement, and recognition. As Chapter 5 has shown, this deemphasis was in accord with the expectations of student nurses' parents. Students' aspirations were little inclined toward self-oriented achievement. Table 6-3 shows the percentages of students who wanted "much" to attain various roles and objectives within twenty years. Nursing supervisor and faculty member of a school of nursing are positions of achievement in nursing careers, but these positions lacked attractiveness to most students, especially the faculty position, which is the more prestigious of the two. In contrast, virtually all students wanted much to have served their fellow man, though fewer than half wanted gratitude from patients. About two-thirds wanted to have contributed to nursing; but because they viewed nursing as a series of helpful acts rather than as a professional entity, the contribution they hoped to make lay mainly in helping patients. Table 6-6 will give data on the attractiveness of nursing activities directed toward the profession of nursing, and these data will further support the evidence in Table 6-3 that students' attraction to nursing lay in helping patients, not in the expectation of success in the career sense.

The relative lack of interest in occupational careers is further evident in the entering students' answers to a question about their plans for work and family roles. (These figures are not shown in a table.) Only 8.8 percent expressed hopes for continuous full- or part-time work with

Table 6-4. *Freshman student nurses' preferred values for life and work*

Value	Percent choosing first-named value
Happy marriage vs. successful and rewarding career	83.3
Close relations with patients vs.	
judgment and responsibility	75.9
new problems	74.5
dependable income	81.3
Judgment and responsibility vs.	
new problems	54.2
dependable income	60.8
New problems vs.	
dependable income	57.2

Note: Respondents ranged from 468 to 482.

minimal interruptions. The percentages giving other responses were 20.6 percent not wanting to work at all or only until marriage or the birth of the first child, 46.5 percent wanting to work until the first child was born and not return to work until after the youngest child was at least eight years old, and 24.1 percent wanting to work until the birth of the first child and return before the youngest child was eight. The familistic aspirations of the students were consistent with their lack of interest in careers aimed at attaining recognized places in the profession. The role of a housewife, whether she is employed full time, part time, or not at all, involves identifying the self with the welfare of the family, an orientation similar to the service motives of nurses.

The service-oriented values of the student nurses were part of a general nurturant orientation. They were interested in helping flesh-and-blood people directly, not humanity in the abstract. Their desire for traditional female roles reflected their nurturant view of interpersonal relations. The values they sought in work were concerned with nurturance. Table 6-4 shows the greater appeal of nurturance than of self-oriented values to these students. The data are based on a question that gave seven pairs of alternatives and asked students to indicate, by checking a four-point scale, toward which alternative in each pair they leaned. The seven pairs of values where happy marriage versus a successful and rewarding nursing career, having close relations with patients versus using judgment and having responsibility, close relations with patients versus dependable income, judgment and responsibility versus new problems, judgment and responsibility versus dependable income, and new problems versus dependable income. Examples of the alternatives and format of the question are:

Having close relations with patients and having an irregular, nondependable income	____: ____: ____: ____	Having little or no relationship with patients and being able to count on a dependable income
Having a happy marriage and never working as a nurse	____: ____: ____: ____	Not getting married and having a successful and rewarding nursing career

The seven pairs of alternatives involve six values. Table 6-4 shows the percentage of respondents who chose each alternative in each pair and the preferential ordering of values. The most preferred value was a happy marriage. Next came close relations with patients, preferred over three alternatives by large margins. Third was judgment and responsibility, preferred slightly over new problems and substantially over dependable income.

The importance placed by the students on close relations with patients and on judgment and responsibility corresponded closely to the values the faculty hoped to develop in the students. As Chapter 8 will describe, the primary objective of the faculty was the development of orientations concerned with individualized patient care, in which the ability to relate to the patient – an ability requiring judgment and responsibility – was a critical component. Because students entered with orientations similar to those the faculty wanted graduates to have, no redirection of these student orientations was necessary and the faculty could concentrate on teaching the skills that would enable students to translate the values into performance. Moreover, the accommodative attitudes of students suggested by their low evaluation of self-expressive values, coupled with their concern for being responsible, should have fostered easy compliance with the expectations of the educational program. As we shall see, the program was highly structured, with little opportunity for students to choose even their liberal arts courses and no freedom to evolve individualized programs of nursing study. These students, who had little desire for autonomy or novelty, should have liked a highly structured program and readily accepted faculty authority. These data show a consistent value profile among entering students. They placed high value on giving nurturant service, an orientation consistent with the values of their parents and faculty. A main desire in life was to help others. They lacked strong interest in self-expression and had little conception of the occupation apart from service to patients. They were favorably inclined toward exercising judgment and responsibility and dealing with new problems but much more attracted to having close relations with patients. Their desires mirrored the public image of nursing as an occupation that gives unselfish service. Their invoking of values consistent with society's expectations lent public sanction to their choice of occupation. The values that students brought to their education from lay society endorsed and reflected nursing's service mandate. Collegial and other occupational interests were relatively undeveloped in students' conceptions and values. This is not surprising, because an occupation's work interests tend to be insulated from public visibility within occupational associations and work organizations, and when brought before the public they are clothed in the occupation's service ideology.

Although societal validation of their occupational decisions presumably enhanced their commitment to nursing, their actual choice of nursing over other helping occupations was furthered more through the favorable recommendation of nursing by advisers and confidants with whom they discussed their educational and occupational plans. We turn now to an examination of this and related aspects of the decision to enter nursing school.

Occupational advice and deciding on nursing

The first step in committing oneself to a role is thinking about it. The Duke student nurses had long played the role of nurse in imagination: 53.4 percent of entering students had thought of becoming nurses while in grammar school and all but 16.5 percent had considered becoming nurses before they had begun high school. The actual choice of nursing was made, on the average, about four years after the occupation was first considered. The time at which the decision was made varied: 30.7 percent had definitely decided on nursing before they entered the tenth grade, an additional 50.7 percent by the end of the eleventh grade, and the remaining 18.6 percent during the year before they entered the

Duke School of Nursing. Although the decision to study nursing brought girlhood fantasies to fruition for many of the students, 72.2 percent of them had also considered other occupations and 47.8 percent said that their decisions to enter nursing had not been easy.

Because the alternative occupations considered by student nurses were almost entirely other helping occupations, the choice of nursing did not involve competition of basic occupational values. The competition among different occupational choices pertained to training requirements, the work situation, and the precise nature of the work. Medicine was the only other occupation considered by more than half (69.3 percent) of the entering student nurses. Those who had considered medicine said they had decided against it because the training was too prolonged (74.8 percent) or too expensive (29.9 percent) and/or that the occupation was incompatible with marriage and family life (51.8 percent). (Most students who had considered medicine mentioned more than one reason for having chosen nursing instead.) Social work had been considered by 46.7 percent of the students and teaching by 42.6 percent. Students had rejected teaching mainly because they did not feel that the work would be interesting. Of those who had considered social work, 70.5 percent still gave some thought to combining it with nursing for a career in medical social work. Others had rejected social work because of its prolonged training and/or because they thought the work would be less interesting than nursing.

The high identification of these student nurses with health occupations – not only nursing, but in many instances medicine or medical social work – is noteworthy. A high proportion of the students had close relatives in health occupations: 55.2 percent were closely related to a registered or practical nurse or a nurse's aide, and 29.4 percent to a physician. A specific example of a nurse was said by 48.7 percent of the students to have provided some inspiration in their decisions to become nurses.

The rejection of other occupations, especially medicine, by these students because of the prolonged training requirements and perceived incompatibility with female domestic roles indicates that in making decisions they had considered expectations and demands of occupational roles as well as the general nature of the work and the values they might express in it. Such consideration involves bringing relevant information about the work expectations to bear on the alternatives being chosen among. Students had actively sought advice on their career plans and information about the expectations of different occupations. They had gotten advice from a wide range of people of diverse occupations with whom they had social relations of various kinds. The median number of advisers was 6.3 and included ministers, parents, teachers, counselors, doctors, nurses, nursing students, friends, and relatives. Parents and representatives of health occupations had been the most frequently used kinds of advisers. All but 10.8 percent of the students had been advised by a doctor, a nurse, a nursing student, or a specialist in some other health field. Most had been advised by more than one health representative.

With few exceptions the advisers of the students had supported their decisions to go into nursing. Representatives of health professions had been the most favorable. Advised to go into nursing were 97.1 percent, 96.0 percent, 95.8 percent, and 89.8 percent of the students who talked respectively with student nurses, nurses, doctors, and specialists in other health fields. Parents were also highly supportive of their daughters' decisions. Only 10.2 percent of the mothers and 10.1 percent of the fathers whose advice was sought advised against nursing.

Although students received advice from a variety of sources, their main reliance was on their parents and on specialists in health fields: 57.4 percent ranked advice given by a family member as the most influential in their decisions and 30.1 percent ranked advice from someone in a health occupation as most influential. The wide use of occupational advisers, especially of advisers representing health occupations, and the favorable support of nursing by the vast majority of the advisers constituted pressures on the students to select nursing. The advice probably furthered students' anticipatory socialization into the role of nurse. Not only did students learn about nursing from these advisers; the advisers' endorsement of nursing deepened their attraction to nursing.

Students' expectations of nursing

We have seen that student nurses chose nursing in order to help people and that what they wanted most in work was close relations with patients. We would therefore anticipate that their expectations of nursing and their attitudes toward nursing would be patient-centered rather than collegially oriented and would mirror their nurturant orientations. This proved to be the case. Evidence that the opportunity for close relations with patients guided their attitudes toward patient care is given in Table

Table 6-5. *Freshman students' attitudes toward the care of different kinds of patients*

Kinds of patients	Percent who would like to give the care
Critically ill	95.5
Terminally ill	76.1
Mentally disturbed	70.1
Mutilated	63.6
Patients in respirators	62.9
Unconscious patients	45.7
Care of corpse	10.8

Note: Respondents ranged from 511 to 515.

6-5, which ranks different kinds of patients by the percentages of students who said they would like to care for them. The most favored kind of patient care was for the critically ill. Next, close together though with slightly declining attractiveness, came care of the terminally ill, the mutilated, the mentally disturbed, and patients in respirators. There was then a sharp drop in favorable evaluation, to care for the unconscious. Care of a corpse ranked a distant last, with nearly nine-tenths of the students saying they would not like this kind of nursing care. This preferential rank of types of patient care shows that as the likelihood of a close nurse-patient relationship decreases, the attractiveness of a particular type of patient care also decreases.

Further evidence that the expectations of students toward nursing were built around nurturant relations with patients is indicated in Table 6-6. It gives data on the attitudes of students toward engaging in various nursing activities, classed as person-centered activities, physical-care activities, clerical and administrative activities, professional activities, and activities relating nurse to doctor. Among the most favorably perceived of the nursing activities were the first eight in the person-centered category. All of these involve the nurse in an interpersonal relationship with the patient. Favorableness toward activities declined with perceived interpersonal separation of the nurse from the patient. An exception to this pattern was making phone calls for patients. Offhand, this activity seems as nurturant as bringing water to a patient, but the students perceived it differently. Possibly they interpreted making a

Table 6-6. *Attitudes of entering freshman students toward nursing activities (in percent)*

Nursing activities	Like	Have no opinion	Dislike
Person-centered activities			
Bedside care	95.3	2.7	1.9
Reassuring patient before operation	95.3	3.9	.8
Reassuring patient's family	92.6	5.6	1.7
Counseling newly admitted patient	90.9	5.6	3.5
Assisting patient to walk	89.3	8.9	1.8
Convincing difficult patient to follow doctor's orders	81.7	12.1	6.2
Bringing water to patient	81.5	16.5	1.9
Teaching health habits to patients	78.8	11.9	9.3
Tidying patient's room	65.7	23.1	11.2
Making phone call for patient	38.1	41.8	20.0
Custodial care	33.3	19.9	46.8
Physical care activities			
Taking blood pressures	90.1	9.1	.8
Preparing dressing for sterilization	72.1	24.1	3.7
Charting food intake	59.6	29.1	11.3
Giving narcotics	44.4	45.6	9.9
Giving enemas	20.0	50.4	29.6
Clerical and administrative activities			
Coordinating and planning	69.9	15.7	14.4
Formulating and revising nursing techniques	38.5	39.6	21.9
Simplifying record keeping	34.9	32.5	32.5
Supervising	27.5	33.3	39.1
Keeping records	27.0	22.6	50.4
Professional activities			
Keeping up with current research	82.5	5.3	12.2
Contributing to professional meetings	66.5	21.0	12.4
Training auxiliary personnel	43.6	23.9	32.5

Table 6-6 (*cont.*)

Nursing activities	Like	Have no opinion	Dislike
Doing research on nurses	39.1	30.7	30.2
Teaching colleagues	35.7	17.7	46.6
Writing professional articles	26.8	23.5	49.6
Activities relating nurse to doctor			
Making rounds with doctors	95.5	3.7	.8
Reporting to doctor	89.9	9.7	.4
Taking patient's orders from doctor	79.1	18.5	2.3
Assisting doctor in physical examination	75.3	21.8	2.9

Note: Respondents ranged from 512 to 516.

phone call for a patient as performing an activity in the name of the patient, which would relate the patient to another person rather than to the nurse and would involve the nurse as an instrument of the patient and not as a significant role alter.

That students looked for close relations with patients is further indicated by the data in Table 6-6 showing attitudes toward nursing activities concerned with physical care, administration, and the nursing profession. Whereas nine of eleven person-centered activities appealed to more than half the students and all of the nurturant ones were endorsed by more than three-fourths, half or more of the students said they would like only three of five physical-care activities, one of five administrative activities, and two of six professional nursing activities. The nursing activities concerned with physical care received higher endorsement than those concerned with administration or the profession. There was little negative opinion about physical-care activities other than the giving of enemas; in general, students either liked the physical-care activities or had not formed an opinion of them. Although these activities may have been seen as less nurturant than the patient-as-person activities, they are obviously a part of patient care. In contrast, the administrative and professional activities are removed from patients and are parts of occupationally oriented career lines. The students' relatively low interest in these activities reinforces the impression that their primary orientation was to direct-patient care and nurturance.

Clerical, administrative, and professional activities involve symbol manipulation rather than personal nurturance. The students' attitudes reflect the differences between the objects involved in these activities. Not only do the percentages of students who said they would like to engage in activities drop as the activities' distance from personal care increases, the percentages who said they would *dislike* the activities rises sharply. Students tended either to like the person-centered activities or to have no opinion about them. The average percentages of dislikes for administrative and clerical and professional activities exceeded the average percentages of "no opinions," 31.7 percent versus 28.8 percent and 30.6 percent versus 20.3 percent. Clerical and administrative activities received the lowest favorable endorsement by entering freshmen of any of the kinds of nursing activities, 39.6 percent. Supervising and keeping records were more disliked than liked.

That coordinating-and-planning was an exception to the unattractiveness of clerical and administrative duties may have reflected the connotation of the term to the student more than it reflected the work activities ordinarily denoted by the term. In high-school extracurricular organizations, students plan and coordinate group activities such as dances, picnics, and other social affairs. Planning and coordinating these activities bring together the peer group, an intimate experience in which the planners have close cooperative relations with those they plan for. If such a personal interpretation underlay students' favorable view of planning and coordinating, their positive evaluation of this activity fitted the person-centered perspective evident in their other attitudes rather than an administrative or careerist perspective.

The professional activities, though less attractive than person-centered ones, had greater appeal than clerical and administrative activities (49.0 percent versus 39.6 percent liked). Most of this favorableness is attributable to the high evaluation of keeping up with current nursing research, and, to a lesser extent, of contributing to professional meetings and conferences. These favorably endorsed professional activities may have connoted getting together in a sociable way with other nurses to talk about nursing experiences, a very different kind of thing from the solitary intellectual effort or task and authority orientations involved in the other professional activities: research, writing, professional articles, training auxiliary personnel, and teaching colleagues. Scales that we will use to observe changes in students' orientations toward nursing during their education, in Chapter 9, show the same kinds of orientations indicated in the preceding discussion.

The incoming students' relatively unfavorable feelings about administrative and professional activities provide additional evidence that they had gone into nursing to help people and had built images and expectations of nursing around their desires for nurturant relations with patients. As entering freshmen they lacked appreciation of a collective view of the occupation and their own participation within it as workers and as guardians of its interests. If they were to develop orientations favorable to nursing as an occupational collectivity, their thinking concerning patient care would have to become distinct from collective occupational interests so that the two would not collide but might be simultaneously served.

Another set of nursing activities involves duties that relate the nurse to a physician. Unlike professional and administrative activities, the doctor–nurse relationship is publicly stereotyped as a handmaiden relationship with the nurse a helper of the doctor and subordinate to him. Activities that relate the nurse to the doctor tended to appeal to incoming students, as is seen in the last section of Table 6-6. These activities had the highest average appeal of any of the nursing activities, including even those in the person-centered category. The attractiveness of this subordinate relationship contrasts sharply to the unattractiveness of superordination implied in the low appeal of administrative duties.

These data show that entering students held markedly differing attitudes toward different role relations within nursing. Their image of nursing work mirrored the traditional conception of the nurse as personal helper of the patient and handmaiden of the physician. Their views of professional achievement and of administrative and clerical work – which constitutes much of the actual work of hospital nurses, especially of those from collegiate nursing programs – were strikingly negative or unformed. Most students aspired to heavy involvement in the feminine family role rather than to continuous nursing careers. Their relative lack of commitment to careers did not mean they did not expect to work, but that the great majority expected to stop working for long periods while they had young children.

Students' expectations of education

The well-defined values of students, focusing on personal service and deemphasizing solitary intellectual effort, fixed their expectations of

college primarily on training in nursing with only secondary consideration given to general academic learning. Many would have forgone a college education if forced to choose between it and nursing. They were
asked, "If you had not been admitted to a collegiate school of nursing
would you have entered a hospital school of nursing?" Only slightly
more than a third (35.5 percent) said they definitely or probably would
not have enrolled in a hospital school or associate degree program; virtually all of this minority (97.4 percent) would have gone to college. Incoming students did not, however, expect to have to forgo a college
education. They were confident of admission to a collegiate school of
nursing. Only 2.1 percent applied to hospital schools, whereas 57.5 percent applied to four or more collegiate schools. Students thus expected
a college education but wanted it in nursing. Only 7.9 percent applied
for study in fields other than nursing.

Their interest in nursing coupled with their expectation of a college
education was reflected in the kinds of considerations they had pon-
dered in deciding to matriculate at Duke. When they were asked to rate
the influence of different factors in their decisions to come to Duke, factors rated very influential by 50 percent or more of the students included interest in nursing and in a broad education (80.5 percent), the reputation of Duke Hospital (76.9 percent), and the liberal arts emphasis at
Duke (76.9 percent). Although the students were attentive to the larger
university, the nursing program exercised a stronger influence on their
decisions to enroll at Duke. When asked the main reason for coming to
Duke, 65.7 percent cited the Duke School of Nursing, its program, or
the Duke medical complex of which the nursing school is a part (in the
order of frequency in which they are listed); only 30.7 percent cited
features of the university as a whole, such as its academic reputation;
and 3.6 percent named family concerns such as financial considerations
and family ties to Duke.

Students' interest in college education centered largely on the most
direct kind of preparation for nursing. The Duke School of Nursing cat-
alogs sent to prospective students emphasized broad liberal arts education as an essential part of the educational program. Despite this, entering students relegated academic learning to a secondary position in their
evaluation of components of a nursing education. Table 6-7, which
shows the percentages of students who rated different aspects of nursing education as very important, indicates that the students perceived
caring for patients and nursing courses as the core activities of a nursing

Table 6-7. *Experiences considered by entering freshmen to be very important in the education of a nurse*

Experiences	Percent saying very important
Caring for patients	97.9
Nursing courses	94.2
Contact with ward nurses	64.8
Reading nursing literature	58.5
Contact with doctors	58.3
Academic courses	57.6
Informal discussions with classmates	54.8
Reading medical literature	43.1

Note: Respondents ranged from 513 to 515 for all but the next to the last, which was not included in the questionnaire of the pilot class of 1963 and had only 427 respondents.

education. Personal relationships involved in clinical-nursing experience were assigned slightly more importance than classroom nursing courses and much more importance than nonnursing academic courses. These findings suggest that the students may have valued college more for the bachelor's degree it conferred than for the actual education other than nurses' training. They came from the kinds of middle-class homes where a college degree is sought as a badge of self-improvement or is taken for granted. But their basic values, supported by the value climates in their homes, restricted their interests principally to the nurses' training part of the actual education received.

Their greater interest in nursing than in academic courses did not stem from an expectation that nursing education would be easy. They were asked to compare the difficulty of education for nursing and for other female occupations. Nurses' education was perceived as more difficult than that of a librarian by 66.5 percent, a dietitian by 56.5 percent, a dental hygienist by 54.3 percent, a grade-school teacher by 51.2 percent, and a social worker (who requires a master's degree) by 38.2 percent.

Not only did students regard direct nursing experience as the essence of their education; they wanted their social contacts to be within the nursing context. Incoming students knew that during the first year they would have little contact with patients or others in the hospital and that most freshman work would be in academic courses. Yet only 28.1 percent desired much contact with the academic faculty. The contacts they hoped to have as freshmen were mainly with people in nursing: other student nurses (76.7 percent), the nursing faculty (74.7 percent), practicing nurses (44.2 percent), and patients (36.1 percent). The opportunity to be a part of general campus life was relatively unappealing. Almost half hoped for a great deal of contact with male students, but only slightly more than a fourth hoped for such contact with nonnursing female students. They had less desire to form relationships with nonnursing female Duke students (26.8 percent) than to maintain friendships formed earlier (32.8 percent). Thus they sought not only an education but also a social life anchored in nursing.

The limited focus of their social and educational expectations of college life, coupled with their strong desire for involvement with other people, forecast a cohesive in-group. Entering students expected close personal ties with their peers in nursing school. In response to a question asking, "To what extent do you think the first-year nursing students will try to help each other?" 60.1 percent felt that they would help each other a great deal.

Summary

The student nurses went into nursing in order to help others. They were strikingly unconcerned with self-expression, competitive achievement, or other values that would individuate them. Their expectations of nursing work were built around nurturant values. They looked forward eagerly to nursing activities focused on the patient as a person, but not nearly so much to activities involving superordination, manipulation of symbols, or separation from close relations with patients. The interest in nursing was of long standing, having been nurtured by contacts with relatives and specialists in health work. Medicine was the main occupation they had considered as an alternative to nursing, and although most had considered alternative occupations, only a few had considered occupations not involving personal service.

Their highly developed interest in nursing narrowed their educational interest to the part of their education directly pertinent to nursing; they wanted college degrees but as incoming freshmen they were relatively unattracted to academic courses or to experiences such as contact with nonnursing women students, which would deemphasize their status as student nurses. Their interest in nursing was intense but was largely a matter of training for work that would complement family life and take second place to it during the child-rearing years, not an interest in continuous achievement-oriented professional careers. Most of them hoped for contacts with male Duke students, presumably seeing college as providing an opportunity for marriage as well as for degrees in nursing.

The students thus began their nursing education not with open minds but with preconceived ideas of what a nurse is, of the relevance of different experiences for the development of an ideal nurse, and of how much of the self was to be committed to nursing. All of these preconceptions are variables that can promote, retard, or complicate the course of socialization, depending at least partly on the extent of their congruence with faculty expectations of nursing and student roles, which we will examine in Chaper 8.

7. The collegiate movement and nursing service

The initial values of entering students were congruent with the idealized objectives of the Duke School of Nursing program, but both of these diverged at some points from the actual expectations imposed on students by the program. This incongruence, which will be discussed in detail in Chapter 8, was not unique to the school we studied. It is characteristic of collegiate nursing education as a whole, reflecting a separation between collegiate nursing education and the realities of nursing service (Hughes et al., 1958). The separation has resulted from developments within both nursing education and the organization of nursing service, especially in hospitals (cf. Mauksch, 1972). This chapter will look briefly at this separation to indicate its sources in the culture and organization of nursing.

Both the ideal patterns of nursing upheld by collegiate nursing schools and the patterns of hospital nursing service are focal parts of nursing as an occupation, but the structures that carry the patterns differ. Collegiate nursing education represents a relatively new movement to professionalize nursing by giving it status as an intellectual discipline; it has been successfully sponsored by nursing educators, who have dominated nursing as an organized occupation (Strauss, 1966:65-96). As a collegiate school, the Duke School of Nursing is attached to the collegiate nursing ideology. The ideology's influence on the school is furthered by the faculty's participation in the activities of nursing associations and through the school's compliance with requirements established by educator-dominated accreditation agencies. At the same time, the program of the school is influenced by the hospital nursing service pattern by virtue of its use of Duke Hospital as a training facility, despite the school's administrative autonomy and the lack of authority of the hospital over its program.

92

Collegiate nursing education

Following World War II the collegiate education movement within nursing developed rapidly, first at the undergraduate level and later at the graduate level. The movement was aimed at gaining full academic status for nursing within the structure of the university so as to give nursing the freedom to develop its own programs apart from hospital administration. Leaders of the movement felt that in this way nursing education could be upgraded to prepare "professional" nurses. Schools carrying the title of university programs had been created earlier in university settings in conjunction with the establishment of medical schools, but these early programs were patterned after the three-year hospital diploma programs. The Duke School of Nursing, founded in 1931, had this origin. Even when these programs began to award college degrees, as Duke's did soon after its establishment, most of them remained attached to medical-school hospitals; they retained the three-year nurses' training programs operated by the hospitals and added two additional years of liberal arts academic study to run concurrently with or following the nursing training to earn the college degree (Strauss, 1966:80).

The collegiate movement as it developed after World War II broke with the earlier pattern of hospital control over administration of the nursing program and set the objective of giving a fundamentally different kind of nursing education. Collegiate degree-awarding schools grew rapidly, from 61 (in addition to 45 offering a choice of degree or diploma programs) in 1949 (National Committee for the Improvement of Nursing Service, 1950:1) to 152 degree-only programs in 1959 (American Nurses Association, 1966:95), the year our study began, to 198 in 1965, the year our data collection ended (U.S Bureau of Health Resources Development, Division of Nursing, 1974:95). During the ten years after that they continued to grow annually, reaching 329 in 1975 (American Nurses' Association, 1977:98).

The growth of baccalaureate programs is only one of the major changes occurring in nursing education. (See Table 7-1.) Nonbaccalaureate programs have grown even more dramatically. The associate degree program was started in the 1950s as one of the vocational programs offered by the community colleges. Its purpose was to prepare technical nurses, and its autonomy led nursing leaders to endorse it over the hospital diploma program. Nursing educators hoped the associate degree programs would in time replace hospital diploma programs.

Table 7-1. Nursing programs, enrollments, and graduates by type of education

Year[b]	State approved programs[a]			Enrollments			Graduates		
	Diploma	Associate	Bacca-laureate	Diploma	Associate	Bacca-laureate	Diploma	Associate	Bacca-laureate
1946	NA	NA	NA	94.4	0.0	5.6	NA	NA	NA
1950	85.1	0.0[c]	14.8	91.3	0.0	8.7	NA	NA	NA
1952	84.3	0.0	15.7	89.3	0.0	10.7	92.1	1.0	6.9
1955	84.5	2.9	12.6	84.7	1.4	13.9	89.9	.7	9.4
1959	80.7	4.2	15.0	80.7	2.0	17.2	85.5	1.5	13.0
1965	68.8	14.6	16.6	69.1	8.5	22.4	77.2	7.2	15.5
1970	47.3	32.8	19.9	43.2	27.1	29.7	52.4	26.8	20.9
1975	32.6	44.0	23.4	24.0	35.7	40.2	29.1	43.8	27.1

Note: NA signifies "not asked."

[a] Some schools had more than one type of program; this tendency declined as the percentage of baccalaureate programs increased.

[b] The reporting date for 1946 and 1950 was January 1; thereafter it was October 15.

[c] In 1950 there was one associate degree program; in 1952 there were four.

Sources: Data for 1946–70 are from U.S. Bureau of Health Resource Development, Division of Nursing, Source Book: Nursing Personnel, DHEW publication (HRA) 75–43, December 1974, p. 95. Data for 1975 are from American Nurses' Association, Facts about Nurses, 1977, p. 94.

Their hope seems near realization. These programs now outnumber hospital diploma programs. In 1975 they produced 1.5 times as many graduates. Though not as spectacular as the growth in associate degree programs, that of baccalaureate programs has added significant numbers of college-educated nurses. Baccalaureate programs prepared slightly more than a quarter of all registered nurses who graduated in 1975; their percentage of all graduates more than doubled in the twenty years from 1955 to 1975. But their graduates remain a minority of all nursing students graduated yearly. The changes within the education of registered nurses give no indication that baccalaureate programs will replace nondegree programs or compete with them. Instead, these programs have added an elite education in nursing. Their graduates have the inside track to elite nursing jobs. The composition of the nursing labor force is beginning to reflect the changes in nursing education (Table 7-2). Though diploma programs have declined, diploma nurses will still predominate for some time because of the age distribution of nurses.

Simultaneous with the differentiation of registered nurses by type of education has been the development of lower grades of nursing personnel. One is the licensed practical nurse, trained to rank just below the registered nurse. State-approved practical nurse training programs grew from 296 in 1953–4 to 1,306 in 1972–3, and their annual number of graduates increased from 7,109 to 46,456 (U.S. Bureau of Health Resources Development, Division of Nursing, 1974:100). There were al-

Table 7-2. *Type of nursing education of registered nurses working in the United States, 1952–74*

	Master's or doctorate	Baccalaureate	Diploma	Associate degree
1952	1.0	7.2	91.8	
1956	1.5	7.0	91.5	
1960	1.7	7.4	90.9	
1964	2.3	9.0	88.7	
1968	2.5	10.8	84.9	1.8
1972	3.1	13.7	78.7	4.5
1974	3.3	15.2	75.5	6.0

Source: U.S. Bureau of Health Resources Development, Division of Nursing, *Source Book: Nursing Personnel,* DHEW Publication No. (HRA) 75-43, December 1974, p. 69.

most fourteen times as many licensed practical nurses employed in hospitals in 1972 as in 1941, an increase from 17,332 to 237,346. They are rapidly swelling the lower ranks of nursing. In 1953–4, nursing programs graduated 4.0 registered nurses for every practical nurse; this ratio had dropped to 1:3 by 1972–3. Almost one-third as many practical as registered nurses were employed in 1970. But practical nurses are not the bottom stratum of nursing; aides, orderlies, and attendants rank below them and do less skilled work. This bottom stratum has grown, but less sharply than practical nurses. Aides, orderlies, and attendants in hospitals increased from 119,829 in 1941 to 543,871 in 1972 (U.S. Bureau of Health Resources Development, Division of Nursing, 1974:143). The total number employed in 1970 was about six-sevenths of the number of employed registered nurses (U.S. Bureau of Health Resources Development, Division of Nursing, 1974:16).

A four-way differentiation internally stratifying nursing service has been occurring. Aides, orderlies, and attendants are at the bottom. Practical nurses are over them and immediately under registered nurses. Baccalaureate education is adding a layer of degree-holding nurses above nondegree registered nurses. The direction of development of the baccalaureate movement has been to upgrade nursing education while holding on to the ideology and traditions of nursing, thereby ensuring an elite corps of nurses for the top positions in nursing service.

There were baccalaureate programs before World War II, but the organization of the postwar baccalaureate programs differed in significant ways from the earlier ones. They required four years instead of five and combined academic and nursing study. Control of schools of nursing was shifted from the hospitals to the universities. Schools of nursing were physically as well as administratively housed outside the hospitals. Nursing schools were given authority to establish their own curricula under the guidance of their own university-appointed governing boards. This is the organization of the Duke School of Nursing, which changed to a four-year program in 1953 and gained national accreditation of its undergraduate program during the time of our study.

This new plan of organization gave nursing educators the authority to plan their programs without regard to the staffing needs of hospital nursing services. The subordination of educational objectives to hospital staffing needs had been a major complaint against the previous type of collegiate program (Strauss, 1966:68; Olesen and Whittaker, 1968:67–8). Nursing educators had felt that the training given by hospital schools, whether in university or other hospitals, was compromised by the poor teaching qualifications of the instructional staffs, which were drawn from the regular hospital nursing services supplemented by lectures by physicians, and by the hours students had to spend assisting on the wards in what the nursing educators considered educationally unprofitable ways. Freed from the requirement of educationally unproductive ward duty, students' time could be devoted fully to preparation for nursing and to the academic course work leading to the bachelor's degree. Although moving physically and administratively away from the hospitals, schools of nursing retained the right to use the university hospitals, or other hospitals, for clinical-training experiences geared to the schools' curricula; but the faculty held positions only within the schools of nursing, not in the hospital nursing services.

The new collegiate movement involved changes in the philosophy of nursing education along with its separation from the hospital. In building nursing curricula, educators turned to an emphasis on the psychological-moral side of nursing, rejecting the narrow emphasis on physical care that had characterized the hospital diploma programs (Strauss, 1966:88–93). The general focus on psychological-moral considerations was not new, but a legacy of the traditions of nursing established by the Nightingale reform movement around the turn of the century, which we have discussed in Chapter 5. The way in which it was now conceived as a core aspect of nursing care was, however, new.

The Nightingale reforms and the traditions built around them had conceived the psychological-moral dimension of nursing in terms of the values and personal characteristics of the nurse, manifested in a dedication of the self to nursing as a *calling*. These personal qualities were to be built into nursing through selective recruitment of women who measured up to the desired moral and personal standards and through inculcating in student nurses an exacting code of conduct emphasizing decorous behavior and unstinting service. The psychological-moral characteristics took hold and were generalized to form occupational values. The values stressed nurturance and subordination of self-interest to the care of others.

The values and behavior singled out as personal standards for nurses expressed essentially the values that were associated with motherhood, thereby linking the occupational values of nursing to the idealized complex of values surrounding the role of the self-sacrificing nurturant woman (Strauss, 1966:84–90). These ideals as they applied to the role of the nurse were expressed in the normative form of "tender loving care" at the bedside of the patient. Tender loving care was nursing's charisma; a nurse had it if she was able to instill confidence in patients and their loved ones that the patient was being cared for and watched over. The institutionalization of psychological-moral values in the norm of tender loving care conceived nursing as an art resting on motherly nurturance and devotion to service. Training could develop and channel these qualities but could not implant their natural base, which was seen as inhering in the personal characteristics of the nurse.

The collegiate nursing movement set out to transform nursing from an art to a profession. A profession requires an articulated body of knowledge from which occupational skills and procedures are derived. The Nightingale ideal had not involved an abstract knowledge base; leaders of the collegiate movement sought to create one. The direction in which they moved kept the essential core of the Nightingale pattern – the meeting of patients' socioemotional needs through the nurse-patient relationship – but conceptualized the relationship in a way that enabled it to be taught as a body of abstract and systematic intellectual principles.

The principal sources of inspiration for the development of an abstract knowledge base for professional nursing were the disciplines concerned with individual needs and interpersonal relations, such as psychiatry, psychology, and sociology (Strauss, 1966:92-4). Medical aspects of nursing were retained in the new curricula but with relatively diminished emphasis. Nursing care at the time of our study was conceptualized from the perspective of the "total patient" who had physical needs but also psychological needs, social needs, religious needs, and other needs to which the nurse should attend. To care for the total patient called for an individualized approach to the patient because each patient would have a different constellation of needs. The nurse was to use her judgment, based on the knowledge she had acquired in nursing education, as a resource for dealing with each patient as an individual. The approach thus involved an understanding of the patient's needs and of the dynamics of patient-nurse relationships. The nurse was expected to control the relationship according to her professional judgment of what was therapeutic for the patient.

Thus the collegiate movement did not abandon the traditional focus on the psychological-moral aspects of nursing. The only basic change from the old to the new ideal of nursing has been a change from the motherly nurturance of tender loving care to an intellectually based structuring of the nurse's relations with patients. The conception of the nurse's role as one of relating individually to patients and of structuring the relationship on the basis of patients' individual needs has not changed. The personal-service values of nursing recruits fit the traditional Nightingale ideology and the new professional ideology equally well.

Nursing roles in hospitals

Although the essential ideals of nursing have not changed, the locus of most nursing work has changed. The traditional conception of nurturant individualized care fitted the patterns of nursing that prevailed at the time when the old traditions took root. Until the 1930s most nurses were in private practice (Brown, 1966:278). The private-duty nurse was employed by a patient or a patient's family and was responsible to the employer. Her overall program of care may have been guided by a doctor's orders, but her care was personalized and was expected to include the extras that communicated nurturance combined with attentive observation and control of the illness. These expectations fitted best the work situation of private-duty nurses but were not at marked variance with the work patterns of nurses employed by the hospitals of the time (Brown, 1966:179–180). The daily censuses of most hospitals were small and so were their staffs, both in numbers and categories of personnel. Nursing services were expected to keep hospitals operating smoothly and efficiently, but nurses were also expected to watch closely over the needs of individual patients. Nursing roles were diffuse in focus, allowing nurses to act on the holistic person-centered orientations of the traditional ideal, and the informal patterns of small hospitals carried interpersonal sanctions to reinforce the traditional expectations.

In the decades since the 1930s, the diffuse, personalized nursing roles around which the traditional ideals were shaped have been largely displaced as the structural locus of nursing has shifted from private-duty nursing in the home or work in small hospitals with informal atmospheres to large bureaucratic hospitals where individualized care would be difficult if not impossible. The functional units in the organization of the modern hospital are not patients but wards, and the focus of nursing roles has accordingly shifted from patients to wards. Nurses still care for patients, but the pattern of care is defined within the context of ward responsibilities. These responsibilities are structurally segmented and allocated to varying categories of nursing and nonnursing personnel according to the kinds of duties the responsibilities involve and the level or type of training required to carry out the duties or associated with their performance. The roles of nurses and other personnel are specified by their official positions in order to facilitate the control and coordination of the myriad activities that go on. Nursing procedures are standardized to ensure accountability of performance; routines and schedules are established to maximize efficiency in running the ward. This bureaucratization of nursing work has been reinforced by technological innovations in medical care, which have necessitated the systematic observation of patients and the monitoring of equipment. The standardization of procedures has deindividualized patient care, narrowed the conception of the nurse's role, and focused the nurse's responsibility on precise execution of doctors' orders and adherence to hospital procedures and ward routines.

This functional pattern of the organization of nursing roles in the modern bureaucratic hospital is extended vertically into administration. Nurses occupy a large proportion of hospital administrative positions, and the career lines of nursing have come to be oriented to the administrative hierarchy. The hierarchical pattern begins on the level of the ward, with the team nurse, who leads the nursing team composed of less experienced or less highly trained nurses, practical nurses, and aides. From the ward the hierarchy extends upward through the assistant head nurse, who assists in the management and supervision of personnel and activities; to the head nurse; to the assistant supervisor; and so on. As one proceeds up the line, patients are increasingly perceived in categorical terms to facilitate the planning of nursing activities; and as one proceeds down the line to the lowest level, patients are increasingly perceived in terms of delimited tasks to be performed in accordance with hospital rules and routines.

The bureaucratization of nursing work within narrowly defined roles limits not only the relations that nurses can establish with patients, but also the relation they can establish with physicians. The patient's chart is the medium of communication between nursing and medicine. The formality and social distance created by the chart does not reduce the subordination of nursing to medicine, but increases it. What a nurse may do for a patient must be specified by a physician or by the established routine of hospital procedures. "The system [of nursing] is task oriented rather than patient oriented; getting the work done is the primary focus of attention" (Brown, 1966:190).

The nursing-care approach of individualized patient care adopted by the collegiate nursing schools was in large part motivated to counteract the task-oriented patterns of nursing that had evolved in the modern hospital. But the intellectualization of the traditional ideal has failed to come to terms with the most basic change in nursing work: its movement into a setting where it is not feasible to maintain individualized nursing care, whether it be defined as tender loving care or intellectually conceived, as the essential task and orientation of the nurse, or to maintain the autonomy of the nurse in deciding what to do and how to do it. The contradiction between the professional ideal of collegiate nursing education and the bureaucratic realities of hospital nursing creates problems regarding the employment of collegiate nursing graduates, for most nurses now work in hospitals. Although opportunities for nursing jobs outside the hospital have increased in absolute numbers (Davis et al., 1966:162–5), the hospital is the main employer. The percentage of employed nurses practicing in hospitals steadily increased from 48.6 percent in 1951 to 59.3 percent in 1957 to 65.2 percent in 1966 (Bureau of Health Professions Education and Manpower Training, 1969:26–9) and remained at that level in 1972, when the last survey of nursing employment was done (Roth and Walden, 1974:7). The 1972 percentage is not completely comparable to earlier ones. Earlier surveys were not careful to separate nursing and convalescent homes from hospitals as distinct employment fields (Roth and Walden, 1974:8). Nursing homes are second to hospitals in the employment of nurses (Table 7-3); together they employ almost three-fourths of all nurses.

Cognizance of the problems of the place of collegiate nurses in nursing practice was implicit in the recommendations on staffing by the Surgeon General's Consultant Group on Nursing (1963). Its recommendations were later adopted in a report by the American Nurses' Association (1965). The recommendations drew a distinction between baccalaureate and diploma nurses on the basis of the level of patient responsibility their education prepared them to assume. Baccalaureate education programs were seen as preparing "professional" nurses and the diploma or associate degree programs as preparing "technical" nurses. According to these reports, technical nursing is organized around the

Table 7-3. *Fields of employment of registered nurses, 1972*

Field	Percent
Hospital	65.2
Nursing home	7.1
Office nurse	6.9
Public health	5.1
Private duty	5.0
School nurse	3.9
School of nursing	3.8
Industrial	2.5
Other	0.5

Source: Aleda V. Roth and Alice R. Walden, *The Nation's Nurses: 1972 Inventory of Registered Nurses.* American Nurses' Association, 1974, p. 7.

performance of tasks specified by the employing hospital, whereas professional nursing is oriented mainly to individualized patient care in which the nurse assumes direct responsibility for decision making about the needs of patients and the nursing activities best suited to meet them.

Specifically, the American Nurses' Association report stated that graduates of diploma and associate degree programs were prepared for staff duty nursing in hospitals, clinics, and nursing homes and that baccalaureate graduates were prepared for supervisory and administrative positions in hospitals from the level of team leader through head nurse and for settings where they would not be subject to hospital authority systems, such as public-health nursing and directorships of nursing in nursing homes. In all of these recommended settings the baccalaureate nurse can make decisions about nursing care, though only in public-health nursing is her role organized around giving direct individual care to patients. The classification of nursing jobs by level of educational preparation was backed up by the terminological distinction of baccalaureate versus other nurses as professional versus technical nurses respectively.

The actual employment distribution of baccalaureate degree program graduates departs substantially from the recommendations of the American Nurses' Association. Excluding those engaged in teaching, who constituted about a seventh of the total, and those with master's and doctoral degrees, more than half of whom were engaged in teaching, data compiled by the Bureau of Health Professions Education and Manpower Training (1969:44) indicated that in 1966 there were about 55,000 employed baccalaureate nurses. Of these, 29 percent were staff nurses in hospitals; 35 percent held positions as head nurses or higher administrators in hospitals; fewer than 2 percent worked in nursing homes; 27 percent were in public health, school nursing, or industrial or occupational nursing; and the remaining 7 percent were divided among private duty, office nursing, and other work settings. The fact that only 29 percent of these collegiate nursing graduates, some of whom had been trained in early collegiate programs in which the training was essentially the same as in diploma programs, were hospital staff nurses conforms rather well to the American Nurses' Association recommendations; but it does not seem likely that as many as half the remaining 71 percent were practicing the professional ideal of individualized patient care. A reasonable estimate might be that fewer than a third of the nonteaching graduates of collegiate programs were in situations where they could function in accord with the ideology of collegiate nursing education; these would be found mainly in the public-health, school, industrial, and private-duty categories. (A hospital head nurse is thoroughly embedded in the bureaucratic structure of the hospital and does not usually spend time in giving individualized patient care.)

The employment of baccalaureate nurses has not changed much since 1966, when the last Duke graduates in this study entered the labor force. In 1972 most baccalaureate nurses worked in hospitals and most were general-duty nurses. The fields and positions of baccalaureate nurses (Table 7-4) suggest that the American Nurses' Association recommendations for the employment of baccalaureate nurses are still for the future.

Perspectives implicit in the pronouncement of appropriate jobs for differently trained nurses failed to claim autonomy for all nurses. Positions providing authority and decision making were hierarchialized and confined to specified administrative positions or types of employing organizations. Scalar, not functional, authority was emphasized. Thus, in an effort to enhance the authority of nursing in health organization, the employment guides set forth by nursing associations unwittingly lessened the collegialism that a functional claim to authority gives. In effect, nursing sought to move in directions that would further the gap between collegiate nursing education and the market for nursing services.

Table 7-4. Employment of baccalaureate-educated registered nurses by field and position, 1972.

	Total	Administrator or assistant	Consultant	Superior or assistant	Instructor	Head nurse or assistant	Staff nurse	Other	Not reported
Total	100.0	5.5	1.7	10.6	11.9	11.7	51.8	4.2	2.6
Hospital	56.3	3.0	.5	6.5	2.5	9.1	32.3	1.1	1.3
Nursing home	4.2	.7	.1	1.0	.1	.9	1.3	a	.1
School of nursing	9.9	.5	.1	.2	8.7	a	.2	a	.2
Private duty	2.5	—	—	—	—	—	—	2.5	—
Public health	10.8	.7	.6	2.0	.3	.4	6.2	.1	.6
School nurse	8.8	.2	.3	.4	—	.4	7.4	.1	—
Industrial	1.2	.1	.1	.1	a	.2	.7	a	—
Office nurse	4.1	.1	a	.2	a	.5	3.2	.1	a
Other	.7	.1	a	.1	.1	a	.1	.2	a
Not reported	1.5	.1	.1	.1	.2	.1	.4	a	.5

(a): Less than 0.1 percent.
Source: Aleda V. Roth and Alice R. Walden, *The Nation's Nurses: 1972 Inventory of Registered Nurses.* American Nurses' Association, 1974, p. 43.

The discrepancy between the individualized approach to nursing care upheld by collegiate education and the realities of nursing work would seem likely to create problems for the baccalaureate student whose clinical experiences are in a hospital, and it has led to some questioning of the relevance of collegiate nursing education to the main markets for nurses (Davis et al., 1966:167-9). As we will show in the next chapter in examining the roles of Duke student nurses as they were structured by the curriculum, students in collegiate programs are not sheltered from the bureaucratic realities during their education; their clinical experience is obtained in hospitals where the nursing services are bureaucratically organized. Moreover, educational requirements for accreditation of nursing schools and for licensing of their graduates call for knowledge of the very procedures that are used in bureaucratically operated hospitals. As students learn the procedures of physical care of patients and gain proficiency in carrying them out in hospital settings, problems inevitably arise concerning the integration of these learnings with the ideal of individualized patient care, which is taught by the nursing faculty and which agrees with the students' initial orientations toward nursing.

Summary

The collegiate nursing education movement formulated a conception of nursing care that embodies traditional individualized nurturance ideals of nursing in an intellectualized form but which deviates in its orientation from the roles of nurses institutionalized in what is now the main work setting of nursing, the large bureaucratic hospital. Collegiate nursing educators have used the terms professional versus technical nursing to distinguish the individualized care pattern emphasized in collegiate education from the more narrowly conceived task-oriented pattern of hospital nursing. They have recommended certain work settings as offering scope for professional nursing and therefore as appropriate for graduates of collegiate programs; they consider hospital staff positions as offering scope for technical nursing only and as inappropriate for baccalaureate nurses. But most graduates of collegiate programs are employed in positions not providing opportunities for individualized patient care, and the clinical training of collegiate student nurses occurs in bureaucratic hospital settings, so that neither the education nor the employment opportunities of collegiate nurses are wholly consistent with the ideology of the collegiate nursing movement.

8. Professional ideology versus bureaucratic training roles

The program of the school encompassed a dilemma faced by the profession of nursing as a whole. Its objective was to produce professional nurses, but its use of the hospital as a teaching resource led to an unintended emphasis on orientations very different from those of the professional nursing movement. This chapter will describe the idealized objectives of the program, indicate their congruence with the predisposing orientations of students, and then examine students' hospital training roles to show how the curriculum unwittingly incorporated the very expectations of technical nursing roles and bureaucratic places in the occupation that the faculty saw as antithetical to its model of professional nursing. This chapter's discussion of the disparity between objectives and training roles is preliminary to an analysis in the next chapter of the development of students' orientations toward nursing.

Insulation of student nurses from other university students

The program was organized to minimize outside influences on students that might be incompatible with the professional nursing orientation. Besides moving its own authority structure into the clinical-training situation, the faculty exerted further control by organizing the curriculum around cohorts of students, moving each cohort in lockstep fashion through the four academic years. Requirements for each year were rather rigorously prescribed, so that the curriculum dictated what courses the students took and when they took them. Not more than 9 of the 135 semester hours' work required for graduation could be elective, and the catalog specified "preferred" courses for these electives. From the viewpoint of our research, the resulting absence of diversity in students' curricula virtually eliminates such diversity as a variable that might have influenced their orientations.

Student nurses were officially students in the university, but the organization of their roles within the school severely limited their ability to behave as typical female students or to mingle with other students. They were an identifiable and insulated group. They lived in student-nurse dormitories about a mile away from the women's college campus where other female students lived. They had their own student government, which included the rules governing other women students but was adapted to deal with their study of nursing as well as their social and personal conduct. They took many of the same academic courses as other Duke students, but the fact that all student nurses in a given academic year had the same courses led to the enrollment of sizable numbers of student nurses in the academic courses they took, thereby increasing their cohesion and reducing their mingling with other students. In the junior year there were special student-nurse sections of academic courses.

The structural separation that arose from this organization of student-nurse roles was manifested in a perception by student nurses that they were seen as different from other female students. When asked how they thought their liberal arts faculty saw them, 79.6 percent of student-nurse freshmen, 77.3 percent of sophomores, 73.9 percent of juniors, and 69.9 percent of seniors felt that the liberal arts faculty saw them as student nurses, not simply as students or as coeds. (Women students were called coeds at the time of this study.) It is significant that the slight but consistent decrease from year to year in the perception that liberal arts faculty saw them as a special category paralleled the decrease in academic study and the corresponding increase in concentration in nursing study. The reader will recall that freshmen and sophomores took academic courses with sizable enrollments of nursing classmates in courses that were not taught exclusively for nursing students. The steady decline in perception of being seen as student nurses reflects the tendency of tightly bonded groups to think of themselves as different when participating in situations with outsiders. Student nurses apparently did not object to being seen as a special group, for only 9.5 percent of freshmen, 11.7 percent of sophomores, 15.5 percent of juniors, and 11.4 percent of seniors preferred to be seen only as students or coeds.

Student nurses' contact with women's campus students was infrequent despite their sharing academic courses. It was limited largely to double dating, and even this form of contact was infrequent: 16.9 percent of student-nurse freshmen double-dated frequently with women's campus students, as did only 11.7 percent of sophomores, 7.3 percent of juniors, and 4.7 percent of seniors. "A great deal" of contact with other women students was desired by only 33.3 percent of freshmen, 24.6 percent of sophomores, 17.1 percent of juniors, and 20.9 percent of seniors. In view of the limited actual and desired contact between student nurses and other women students, it is not surprising that student nurses thought women's campus students saw them as different: only 10.7 percent of freshmen, 15.6 percent of sophomores, 17.7 percent of juniors, and 17.3 percent of seniors felt that women's campus students saw them as "fellow students." They had more contact with undergraduate men than with other women students, primarily in dating relations, which probably had little direct effect on their academic or professional outlook.

Thus, despite their official status as students in the university as a whole, their patterns of participation were organized around the special status of student nurse. They believed that others saw them as a special group, and this insulation from other students was entirely satisfactory to most of them. They liked being student nurses. In Part III we will consider the influence of identification with the status of student nurse on the different processes of occupational socialization. For Part II, however, the importance of student nurses' insulation from the rest of the university community is that it enables us to assume that the school of nursing and the hospital were the chief social contexts for their learning of nursing orientations.

The ideal objective of the program: patient-centered nursing

The school's philosophy emphasized professional nursing. School bulletins and course descriptions gave evidence of the main orientations by which the school defined professional nursing. These sources made clear that the professional nurse should ascertain the needs of patients and establish relationships with them to deal therapeutically with their needs. All patients should be viewed holistically in terms of their "total" needs, and the nurse should individualize her care so the therapeutic relationship would meet each patient's emotional as well as physical needs. Thus the professional nurse idealized in the program's stated objectives had a holistic view of patients, a feeling of direct responsibility to them, and an individualized therapeutic relationship with each patient. These themes in official pronouncements were equally evident in faculty responses to an open-ended question asking them to describe the kind of nurse they hoped to develop. Their teaching was aimed at developing a nurse who was patient oriented, able to make informed decisions about patient care, and able to relate to patients. The faculty gave about equal weight to decision making about patient needs and to interpersonal relations. Typical descriptions of their ideal product are:

A nurse who is able to identify and deal with the overt and covert nursing needs of her patients.

One who is able to problem-solve and to relate with empathy toward others.

A creative, logical thinking person who is able to do problem solving effectively, who is patient oriented, and sympathetic to the needs of others.

One who can relate to the needs of patients – is knowledgeable, creative, flexible, and organized, and able to work with others.

Only two of the twenty-three faculty members who described the kind of nurse they hoped to develop included technical competence among the qualities they mentioned in their descriptions.

The faculty's view of nursing corresponded much more closely to the traditional image of the nurse as a nurturant giver of care than to the technical conception. They assumed that their students would become proficient in carrying out technical nursing procedures but placed more emphasis on ability to relate to the patient. They saw the nurse–patient relationship as the essence of nursing and the ability of students "to relate to the patient" as essential. As a course syllabus stated, "The most effective nurse is the one who can give to the most patients the deepest feelings of being sympathetically understood as a person and lovingly and thoroughly cared for as a patient."

Professional nursing as espoused by the faculty has pinned a new label on the nurse, but for most of the faculty the nurse remains the traditional nurturant female who can communicate feelings of support to patients while proficiently carrying out standard nursing duties. The faculty view of the ideal nurse seems to presuppose a nurturantly oriented person. Most faculty members favored explicit use of personal qualities as criteria for recruitment of students. They were given a list of twenty-five attributes pertaining to academic ability, personal characteristics, and career orientations, and were asked to select the single one they felt was most valuable in evaluating candidates for admission. Personality characteristics were considered far more important than other attributes in selecting students for the program: 67.7 percent of the faculty designated as most important such personality characteristics as concern for others, practical efficiency, ability to get along with others, and social maturity; 29.0 percent saw characteristics related to academic ability as most important, and 3.2 percent selected characteristics pertaining to commitment to nursing.

Given the values underlying the self-selection and evaluation of applicants for admission, it is not surprising that entering students' conceptions of nursing largely coincided with those of the faculty. Students were patient oriented, wanted to serve patients directly, and were not averse to accepting responsibility. Because the anticipatory views of students corresponded closely with faculty expectations of entering students and with the qualities the faculty hoped to develop further in them, the educational program would seem to have required no significant resocialization of views, but mainly cognitive development of the initial patient-centered views if the critical condition in the development of orientations was sheer congruence of faculty and student perspectives. (We shall see later that this was not the critical condition.)

The curriculum

We have seen that the school had its own physical, instructional, and administrative facilities, housed separately on the campus and including dormitories for its students. It also had access to Duke Hospital and to academic classes and other university facilities for training purposes. In planning its curriculum it used all of these, but the one resource that all thirty-four faculty agreed was most important to the entire nursing curriculum was clinical experience in the hospital. Also considered important were nursing theory courses and academic courses, in that order.

In using the hospital for training, faculty members were aware that the kind of professionalism they sought to produce had not been developed within hospital nursing. To guard against influence by the hospital nursing pattern while students were receiving training in the hospital, the school moved its own authority system intact into the hospital to retain control over clinical experience. Students were directly responsible to school faculty members rather than to the hospital's nurses. The faculty selected patients for assignment to students, supervised students on the wards, and were accountable for student care of patients to the hospital administration rather than to the nursing service, though they had to work with the nursing service in coordinating students' and staff nurses' work. In this way the school hoped to keep control over both the classroom and clinical parts of the nursing curriculum.

The curriculum was supposedly structured to develop progressively the students' knowledge and skills and to integrate these with the professional nursing orientation of holistic individualized patient care. On paper the progression of study appeared well calculated to support these goals, but the actual roles of students as they underwent their education seem to have diverged from the intended objectives. We shall suggest how the divergence occurred after looking at the idealized plan.

The freshman curriculum consisted mainly of scientific courses aimed at teaching the basic knowledge needed to understand "total" patient needs and of general liberal arts courses necessitated by university degree requirements. Only one course in nursing, which was continued over the fall and spring semesters, was given in the freshman year. This course was entitled "Interpersonal Relations in Nursing" and was "designed to assist the student in . . . developing concepts and skills that are basic to competence in interpersonal relations and nursing therapy." The course introduced students to a professional conception of the role of the nurse, stressing concepts and principles that should be followed to "establish a therapeutic relationship with a patient." Role playing in the classroom assisted students in applying the principles and concepts presented in lectures and readings.

The sophomore year saw an increase in the proportion of time spent in strictly nursing courses, with thirteen semester hours of "Fundamentals in Nursing" – a two-semester course – and three hours of diet therapy. The course description of Fundamentals in Nursing suggests that the second-year curriculum was aimed at reinforcing and further developing the perspectives introduced in the freshman year and simultaneously teaching the core skills and procedures of technical nursing. The course in fundamentals taught, according to the catalog, basic technical skills and procedures for the physical care of patients within a context of patient-centered nursing roles. The course included two weekly laboratory experiences of two hours each in which students practiced performing nursing procedures and one weekly four-hour clinical experience in the hospital in which students were assigned patients for whom they administered the procedures discussed in class and practiced in the laboratory. Sophomore students received their uniforms and were required to wear them in the hospital during their clinical experiences. With the fundamentals course, according to the catalog, the curriculum began the systematic incorporation of limited aspects of actual patient care in the hospital as a main part of the student role. Skills and procedures increased in complexity during the year to enable the student to move from simple nursing tasks requiring slight technical knowledge, such as making a bed, to making a bed with a patient in it, to fairly complicated procedures such as the catheterization of patients. On the basis of the stated objectives of the fundamentals course, the development of students by the end of the sophomore year should have reached the point of their applying technical skills and integrating the physical with the sociopsychological care of patients.

The junior and senior years were devoted almost exclusively to nursing courses. Specialty nursing began in the junior year and included pediatric, obstetrical, medical, and surgical nursing. It continued in the senior year, adding psychiatric and public-health nursing along with advanced medical and surgical nursing. The senior year also included a course called "Social Foundations of Nursing," which looked at nursing as a profession. Except for this course, the student role as formally defined in the curriculum of the junior and senior years centered almost wholly on enacting the role of the nurse in clinical settings. Students were expected, according to course descriptions, to apply and integrate core nursing skills learned during the sophomore year to the practice of clinical specialities within a context of individualized patient care and also to learn additional skills related to the specialties they were studying. The individualized patient care context would, the faculty thought, integrate the clinical experiences with the philosophy of professional nursing: Instead of learning discrete skills and procedures as they had done in the sophomore year, students were now expected to develop patient care plans, adapting skills, procedures, and principles to particular specialties, and to carry through the plans in individualized patient care.

This description of the program shows that it gave little attention to matters related to the profession as a collectivity that would define and guard its service domain, or as a definer of quality nursing, or to students' future place in the occupation. Heavy attention was devoted to teaching students a conception of the role of the nurse – its principal duties of relating to patients in therapeutic ways, making decisions consistent with the role definition, and applying technical skills in carrying out nursing activities. Although only one course, and that in the senior year, pertained directly to nursing as an occupational group, the faculty in teaching the role of the nurse and especially the need for decision making imparted what was considered a view of the "professional" nurse.

Emphases of student training roles

In its structuring of the curriculum, as distinct from its statements of nursing education philosophy, the faculty did not confine its attention to orientations to professional nursing. It also emphasized, perhaps even more, the teaching of specific techniques and skills and an associated knowledge base, partly in classroom work but especially in the clinical experience. Much of the curriculum consisted of what Etzioni (1961: 148–9) calls instrumental socialization, although the goals embodied value orientations. The program was called professional nursing, but the organization of courses and much of their substance corresponded to the bureaucratic pattern of nursing that the faculty considered the antithesis of professional nursing. The technical skills and the organization of clinical training around specialties corresponded to the scalar and functional division of nursing labor in hospitals.

The nursing activities performed by students in their clinical roles were the activities needed by the hospital and were indistinguishable from the activities of hospital staff nurses, despite the philosophical emphasis of the school on a different approach to nursing from that of the hospital. Student clinical roles were enacted within the authority structure of the school of nursing, with supervision by school clinical instructors; but the nature of the learning experiences in which students assumed rather full nursing care of patients for extended periods of the day constituted, from the hospital's point of view, standard nursing work. The hospital counted student assignments as part of its daily nursing care service. Moreover, the students were in contact with nurses and other hospital personnel. Much of this contact was unofficial or subject to scrutiny by the nursing faculty, but it was nonetheless essential to students' carrying out the nursing activities assigned to them.

The faculty in no way disavowed the overlap between their program and the nursing activities of the hospital. The school was, in fact, required to instruct students in skills, techniques, and nursing specialties to meet accreditation standards and to prepare students for licensing examinations. But the technical training did not include specifically professional elements to match the orientations of the professional ideal. This failure to translate ideals into role assignments led the faculty to emphasize technical expertise more than professional orientations. Professional nursing, as we have seen, differs from technical nursing not so much in what the nurse does as in her approach to patients. Learning techniques and becoming proficient in applying them are concrete tasks whose performance can be measured. Even when more was said about the goals, as in the freshman interpersonal relations course, the implicit attention necessarily given to nursing activities called attention to what nurses *do* – that is, to technical procedures. The fact that students practiced the nursing activities by giving actual patient care in the hospital seems likely to have intensified the concern of both students and faculty with technical competence. The acquisition of specialized knowledge and skills is what makes one a nurse, and students trying to carry out nursing activities on real patients could hardly avoid perceiving a technical emphasis in their curriculum. Only by mastering technical skills and standard procedures could they carry out their assigned activities.

The faculty themselves felt that clinical experiences were highly important in their curriculum, and many faculty members felt that the proportion of students' time spent in clinical experiences should be increased. The faculty were asked if there were areas of the curriculum that did not receive enough attention. Of the thirteen who responded affirmatively, eight would have increased the time spent in the hospital. The others would not have changed the number of courses taken but would in two cases have ironed out duplications in nursing theory courses and in three instances would have improved the "quality of academic courses" either for background knowledge useful in nursing or for citizenship training. Those who favored increasing clinical time expressed such views as, " . . . our students need more . . . exposure to the realistic hospital and nursing situation"; they need "time necessary for assuming the feeling and responsibility of actually being a nurse"; " . . . the laboratory and service time now allotted is too short to really allow students to consolidate the skills they will use and to give realistic practice in applying nursing concepts and principles."

We do not have systematic data on what the students thought their teachers expected them to learn as they moved through the curriculum. Therefore, our observations are largely inferences drawn from the emphases placed on skills, techniques, and nursing activities in the course descriptions. These inferences about the emphasis on the technical and hospital pattern of organization of nursing are supported, however, by evaluations made by the faculty of what they considered important for students to learn and by faculty perceptions of what students thought it important to learn. Table 8-1 shows that the faculty said that they considered relations with patients the most important aspect of the education of students, but that they perceived students as considering technical proficiency almost as important as relations with patients. Emphases that pertained to nursing as a profession and toward claims to authority were intermediate in emphasis by the faculty. Faculty perceived students, however, as attributing the least importance to such emphases. Thus, in contrast to technical performance, faculty stressed them more than they perceived students as considering them important.

This discrepancy between the faculty's own evaluations and what they perceived as student evaluations of the relative importance of relations with patients and creative ability to plan nursing care on the one hand and technical skills and procedures on the other hand further suggests that the faculty were unable to integrate their goals of professional nursing fully into their teaching. This inference is supported by data from interviews with three sophomores selected by their fundamentals class instructor as being topflight, average, and poor students near the end of the first semester. The students all agreed that much emphasis was placed on trying to understand the needs of patients. To illustrate this emphasis, the average student reported that students had not known until they went onto the wards that they would be able to sit down and talk with patients, but that their instructors encouraged them to do so *after* they had finished their *assigned procedures.* The interviewees said that they talked about whatever interested the patients, and one added that "you certainly learn a lot talking with them." These students also reported that their faculty graded them on efficient use of time and that while on the wards they were expected to stay busy and not stand around talking with each other. It thus appears that individualized nursing activities in which students "related to patients" were not integral parts of the nurse–patient training experience but a crutch the student could lean upon to demonstrate efficient use of her time. During the same interview, the students said that they could not leave the ward until the assigned time of departure, though few would have

Table 8-1. *Faculty evaluations and faculty perceptions of students' evaluations of qualities' importance in nursing education (in percent)*

Qualities	Faculty considered very important	Faculty perceived students to consider very important	Faculty minus student
Relations with patients			
Ability to relate to patients	91.2	66.7	24.5
Help suffering humanity	27.3	50.0	−22.7
Abilities related to assuming authority for nursing care			
Creative ability	48.5	13.3	35.2
Ability to organize one's work	42.4	26.7	15.7
Orientations toward nursing as a profession			
Desire to advance nursing knowledge	36.4	13.3	23.1
Desire to be part of a professional group	42.4	20.0	22.4
Technical skills and procedures			
Mastery of highly developed nursing procedures	15.2	63.3	−48.1
Proficiency in meeting phsycial needs of patients	33.3	56.7	−23.4
To work effectively in the hospital	15.2	56.7	−41.5
Desire to do difficult things well	15.2	50.0	−34.8

Note: Faculty respondents numbered 33.

wanted to leave if they could. "We are *also* learning to understand patients, and the things we do 'special' *after* our assignments are a part of our grade." (Emphasis supplied.)

Program objectives and the marketplace of nursing

With the development of the collegiate nursing education movement, as described in Chapter 7, an elite type of practitioner was added to nursing, the baccalaureate graduate. Baccalaureate graduates have the inside track to elite nursing jobs, which tend to be in administration or nursing education. In each case the work activities are far removed from the direct patient care emphasized in the philosophy of the collegiate movement. Administrative positions are concerned with planning organizational practices and overseeing their execution in hospitals, public-health agencies, or other health-care agencies. Even though the objectives of the collegiate nursing movement and the organization and administration of baccalaureate schools separate the programs from hospital service, it is expected within schools of nursing and within nursing practice that the baccalaureate graduate should have the inside track to administrative nursing positions. This expectation is supported by standards for staffing proposed by the American Nurses' Association (1965) and by employment statistics. As we have discussed in Chapter 7, the hospital is the main employer of baccalaureate nurses; and of those employed by hospitals, more hold administrative positions, including that of head nurse, than hold positions as staff nurses.

The faculty of the school, even though they held an idealized view of nursing education, which pictured the nurse as giving direct care to patients, nevertheless recommended a pattern of employment in administration for baccalaureate graduates. When asked what the first and second positions held by a baccalaureate graduate should be thirty-three of thirty-four faculty members who answered the question recommended a staff position for the first position; but twenty-seven of the thirty-three felt that the graduate should move from an initial staff position after a period ranging from three months to two years into administration as a head nurse or assistant head nurse, two recommended that she return to school for graduate study, three felt that the graduate's own goals should dictate her second position, and only one felt that the baccalaureate graduate should remain at the bedside of the patient. (The one faculty member who did not recommend staff nursing as the first position selected instead a position with supervisory responsibilities as the most appropriate initial position.) Thus, although the idealized goals of the school focused on the direct care of patients, which within the existing structure of nursing practice is carried out in staff positions, the faculty saw their graduates moving rapidly into hospital administration.

An abiding concern of nursing educators, according to Strauss (1966), has been the desire to instill within students a consciousness of the occupation and its interests. The particular routes seen by nursing leaders as furthering the interests of the occupation have changed through the years (Strauss, 1966). The current emphasis, which developed concurrently with the collegiate nursing movement, is to professionalize the occupation, following strategies such as the development of nursing through research and the communication of this knowledge and the awareness of other collective interests through publications, professional conferences, and other media. Orientations toward such collective professional activities would provide the "leadership potential" that Davis, Olesen, and Whittaker (1966:157–62) hold is expected by nursing leaders from the graduates of collegiate programs, though these authors conclude from their research that the University of California School of Nursing they studied failed to instill the orientations needed for leadership potential.

Although orientations toward nursing as an organized professional community, which we will hereafter call collegialism, were not as dominant a theme of the school we studied as was patient-centered nursing, the faculty did give some support to collegialism – considerably more emphasis than they perceived students to place on it (see Table 8-1). The Student Government Association, in which membership by students was mandatory, gave students experience in participating within the collectivity of nursing and contributed to the development of orientations favorable to collegialism. Students highly involved in the association during the junior and senior years were more likely than those less involved to score high on our scale of collegialism, to be discussed in Chapter 9 (59.3 percent versus 39.0 percent among juniors and 70.8 percent versus 60.0 percent among seniors).

Thus, although efforts to develop orientations toward administration and professional activities were not centrally visible foci of the school's program, the entire organization of nursing and its work opportunities directed students toward administration, and faculty expectations coupled with Student Government Association participation gave attention to collegialism. Conditions thus existed within the program for the development of favorable orientations toward activities associated with administration and professionalism.

Summary

Thus a disparity between the idealized individual patient-care goals of the program and its bureaucratic, technical training roles characterized the educational situation of students in the school of nursing. That such a divergence of the actual emphasis from the idealized objectives occurred enables us to separate analytically the relations of ideal values and goals and of expectations structured by student roles to the development of students' orientations. Entering students' values were congruent with the ideal goals of the faculty, though less in the case of collegial than of role activity concerns, and would seemingly have needed only substantive elaboration through training experience for the goals of the school to be achieved. Students' hospital training was, however, incongruent with both. In Chapter 9 we shall examine the outcome of this situation, showing the relations of the influences discussed in Chapter 3 to the process of development of professional orientations.

9. Acquisition of occupational orientations in a bureaucratic context

In Chapter 3 we gave two general explanations from the literature, and one of our own, of the development of occupational orientations. The two from the literature stress congruence of entering students' values and orientations with the program's goals (Wright, 1967) and training experiences (Becker and Geer, 1958), respectively. In these explanations, orientations mature from predispositions. Maturation is aided when a program provides experiences and a value climate expressive of students' entering values and goals. Divergence of a program's goals and training experiences from students' entering values slows down the maturation of occupational orientations, but it is unlikely to redirect students' initial values or orientations.

Our explanation is a variant of the learning hypothesis. We hold that orientations are acquired; they do not simply mature. If students' initial values coincide with expectations stressed in their training assignments, the acquisition proceeds smoothly with no redirection. But when convergence does not occur, resocialization is needed. Students faced with a marked disparity between their initial expectations and the reality of the program may well drop out as Wright showed (1967). We do not see acquisition occurring through the imitation of role models, but through the application of the knowledge and skills that enable one to perform roles in compliance with training agents' expectations. Training agents' expectations specify tasks of the role, and knowledge and skills provide the means to perform the tasks. If the knowledge is so general that it cannot be consistently and routinely translated into techniques and skills to perform tasks, the transmission of the knowledge will not impart consistent orientations toward its use. Similarly, if training agents uphold one set of ideal tasks but stress another set in what they teach, students will learn what is stressed, not what is idealized. Students acquire their orientations from the expectations imparted toward the use of the knowledge and skills that enable them to meet their assignments. From continued use of the knowledge and skills to perform tasks, they develop personal stances toward them that they generalize to the occupational role. These personal stances are what we call orientations.

Regardless of which explanation one may favor, the influences that develop orientations are all organized and carried by the school's program and in the person of its students. Because we studied only one school and its program was unchanged and its students homogeneous in background and values over the period of our study, we have no comparison groups. We must infer influences from the fit and timing of the development of students' orientations with the ideology of the program, the provision of training experiences, and the skills and knowledge used to perform training roles. The program was so arranged that we can separate in time these three aspects. They differ in the manner and time of the influence each may have had, so we can confidently make inferences based on the timing and consistency of responses. Our analytic design must enable us to pinpoint when changes stabilize into consistent directions that persist across status transitions. The turnover table meets these requirements (Zeisel, 1957:219–38; Levenson, 1968: 372–8); it will be our main analytic technique to show the development of orientations. We will look first at the net change that occurs in students' responses as they move from one academic status to another; but net change cannot tell us whether the changes show consistent directionality and persist over time. To determine directionality and persistence, we will look to see whether or not responses in a given academic class status are retained the following year. Our academic classes will be paired thus: entering freshmen-freshmen, freshmen-sophomores, sophomores-juniors, juniors-seniors, seniors-alumnae. The responses for the earlier academic year in each pair will be the base for observing the subsequent year. To rule out the possibility of lagged effects, we computed correlations of each dependent variable with itself for all pairs of academic class years. This correlation matrix is in Appendix A. It shows no evidence of lagged effects.

For our analysis of development of orientations, we will use panel data. We have both a graduation and an alumnae panel. Most of our analysis will use the graduation panel, which consists of 128 students. To see the persistence of responses from graduation to a year following, we will use the alumnae panel. It has 89 cases (39 of the graduation panel were lost because of inability to locate them, their failure to complete questionnaires, and clerical problems in storage and retrieval of the alumnae data). As we discussed in Chapter 4, panel data are subject to unknown biases related to subjects' survival in a sample. To check for unknown biases, we have compared results of our panel analyses with those of other aggregations; the results are given in Appendix B. They are consistent for all aggregations.

Orientations to the role of the nurse

Professional nursing as expressed in the ideology of the school emphasized two main orientations, a holistic view of patients and individualized patient care; these defined the role of the nurse from the view of the school's ideology. We developed a Guttman-type scale pertaining to each of these orientations using a sample of students from each cohort at different academic statuses. Our measure of the holistic view of patients was counterposed against the bureaucratic pattern of nursing with its emphasis on the physical care of patients guided by hospital rules and doctor's orders. It was a six-item agree-disagree Guttman-type scale with a coefficient of reproducibility of .90, composed of items such as these: "It is all right to talk about total patient care, but when you come right down to it, all a nurse can do is see that the instructions on the chart are carried out." "Acting friendly and understanding is all right, but the important thing is to follow the prescribed routine." To make analyses in the turnover table manageable, scale scores were dichotomized around the median of all respondents in all academic classes. Scores 4–6 indicate a nonbureaucratic conception of the role of the nurse emphasizing a holistic view of patients, and scores 0–3 indicate a bureaucratic conception.

Our measure of orientation to individualized nursing inquired about the attraction of students to simple, nontechnical nursing activities emphasized in curriculum objectives as ways of "relating to the patient," observing patients' reactions, and individualizing care. This scale included five patient-centered simple nursing activities and had a coefficient of reproducibility of .95. Students were asked how much they would like or dislike performing activities such as "assisting the patient to get out of bed and walk" and "bringing the patient a drink of water." Scale scores were dichotomized around the median of respondents in all classes included in the sample with scores 4–5 classed as indicating high endorsement of individualized patient care.

Dichotomizing the scale scores unavoidably lost information on the distribution of responses and could possibly have distorted our findings

Table 9-1. *Orientations toward the holistic view of the role of the nurse and toward individualized patient care*

	Percent high	
	Holistic view	Individualized patient care
Faculty (N = 33)	60.6	NA
Entering freshmen	80.5	75.8
Freshmen	50.0	66.4
Sophomores	27.3	65.6
Juniors	21.9	46.1
Seniors	23.4	37.5

Note: NA signifies "not asked."

on the pattern of socialization. Scores clustered above and below the median are more proximate than scores one and two standard deviations above the mean that have been grouped together to form the high group. To see if the procedure distorted our findings, we computed means and standard deviations of all scales for each academic class. They are reported in Appendix C and show the same pattern yielded by dividing the scores into high and low groups. We use the dichotomy for our analysis here rather than the means and standard deviations in order to simplify construction of turnover tables, which we use to observe directionality and stability of students' socialization.

Table 9-1 presents data on orientations of students to holistic views of patients and to individualized, patient-centered nursing when they entered the school and at the end of each academic year. It shows that reinforcement or further development of student orientations emphasized in the goals of the school as central to professional nursing and already present in the anticipatory views of students did not occur. The orientations of students corresponded less to the ideal goals of the school when they graduated than when they entered. Instead of developing in the direction indicated in the students' initial values and those desired by the school, student orientations shifted toward conformity with the bureaucratic pattern of nursing, a pattern the school ideally opposed and sought to deemphasize. (The pattern is the same for all four ways of aggregating students; see Appendix B, Table 13-1.)

Table 9-1 also shows that the establishment of a majority point of view favorable to these bureaucratic orientations was not a gradual, cumulative development. The largest net changes took place mainly during the freshman and junior years. The times of onset of the changes were not the same for the two orientations, however. Orientations toward a holistic view of the role of the nurse changed most during the freshman year. Of the entering freshmen, 80.5 percent favored a holistic orientation, but by the end of the first year this figure had dropped to 50.0 percent. Net decline in holistic orientations continued in the sophomore year, stabilizing by the end of that year with about a fourth of the junior and senior classes favoring a holistic role orientation. The pattern of predominance of bureaucratically oriented views was well established by the end of the sophomore year and for the junior and senior classes without much further net change in extent of endorsement of bureaucratic views.

Academic class changes in the other variable shown in Table 9-1 – orientations toward individualized, nonroutine nursing care – followed a different course. The class patterns of these attitudes remained relatively stable from the time of entry through the sophomore year, during the time when holistic orientations showed a net decline. About three-fifths to two-thirds of each academic class were highly attracted to individualized care through the sophomore year. A fairly rapid net decline in this attraction began in the junior year, with the proportion favorable dropping to less than half by the end of the junior year and to slightly above a third by the end of the senior year.

The shift of student orientations away from their initial values and the goals of the school is indicated even more sharply in the year-to-year changes in attitudes of individual students. Tables 9-2 and 9-3 report these changes in the graduation panel. They show a decided shift toward a bureaucratic conception of the role of the nurse during the freshman year, which subsequent years reinforced with no reversals. Although only a small minority of entering freshmen favored a bureaucratic role conception (19.5 percent, as can be inferred from Table 9-1), that view was considerably more likely to persist than was the predominant view, which was in agreement with the faculty goals. For every student the program succeeded in converting to its values during the freshman year, it lost nearly six students to the bureaucratic view; and for every student it was able to hold to an initial view consistent with its ideal, three students remained unmoved from initially contrary views. The rate of movement away from faculty goals increased even

Table 9-2. *Yearly change in students' orientations toward holistic view of the role of the nurse (in percent)*

Year-to-year orientations	Entering freshmen-freshmen	Freshmen-sophomores	Sophomores-juniors	Juniors-seniors
Stable holistic	54.4	40.6	42.9	53.6
Holistic to bureaucratic	45.6	59.4	57.1	46.4
(Total holistic)	(103)	(64)	(35)	(28)
Stable bureaucratic	68.0	85.9	86.0	83.0
Bureaucratic to holistic	32.0	14.1	14.0	17.0
(Total bureaucratic)	(25)	(64)	(93)	(100)

Note: The base N's for percentages, in this table and in others, are the numbers who were low at the first of the two times.

Table 9-3. *Yearly change in students' orientations toward individualized patient care (in percent)*

Year-to-year orientations	Entering freshmen-freshmen	Freshmen-sophomores	Sophomores-juniors	Juniors-seniors
Stable low	67.7	41.9	68.2	84.1
Low to high	32.3	58.1	31.8	15.9
(Total low)	(31)	(43)	(44)	(69)
Stable high	77.3	69.4	46.4	62.7
High to low	22.7	30.6	53.6	37.3
(Total high)	(97)	(85)	(84)	(59)

more in the sophomore year and continued with little change throughout the remainder of students' education.

In contrast, there was no consistent drift away from individualized patient care until the junior year. Not only was the program able to retain beginning students' interest in individualized patient care; it was able to shift orientations toward individualized care during the first two years. In the junior year, however, the pattern shifted. No longer was the program able to change orientations to favor individualized patient care. The drift away from faculty goals accelerated in the senior year, with the result we have seen in Table 9-1 that only about a third of the graduates had the views the faculty had hoped to instill.

Thus the orientations of students toward nursing moved away from both the goals of the school and the students' own initial orientations. Inasmuch as the students' beginning views were highly consistent with the goals of the school and the curriculum included training situations valued by students from the sophomore year onward, the school's ideology and students' opportunities to act on their values cannot have been the determining factors in the development of student orientations. If the adherence to values had been the main shaper of orientations, the orientations would have remained fairly constant throughout student' education, even when the training situation was not consistent with the initial values. Becker and Geer (1958; see also Becker et al., 1961) argue that medical students retain their idealistic values despite the medical school's academic emphasis in the preclinical year and its emphasis on specialty practice in the clinical years. The pattern was strikingly different from this in the school of nursing we studied.

At the very point in the educational process when student values and the ideology reflected in course content converged the most – the freshman year with its interpersonal relations course – a sharp shift of orientations away from students' initial values and the goals of the school took place. Moreover, the introduction of clinical training congruent with students' evaluations of their learning experiences in the sophomore year failed to stop this shift. Students wanted to help patients, and almost unanimously and continuously throughout their education they rated contact with patients as highly important for their nursing education. At no time did the percentage considering it important drop below 98 percent. Students' entry into the hospital with its nurse-patient relationships during the sophomore year should have brought, according to the value congruence thesis, movement toward the initial anticipatory orientations of students, but, instead, the sophomore year continued the shift away from the holistic view with no letup in the rate of change away from the views sophomores had held as entering freshmen. Clearly, the individual subjective perspectives of students and their evaluations of educational situations on the basis of these perspectives were not the critical factors in developing their orientations.

One might see our findings as consistent with, not in disagreement with, the conclusions of *Boys in White,* which held that students evolved perspectives to meet the demands of their education but returned to their idealistic views upon graduation. Our evidence suggests, however, that the student nurses' evolving perspectives were genuine occupational orientations and not merely short-run views that fitted the student role of compliance with faculty demands. Once they developed, the pattern persisted. The perspectives were accepted most by graduating seniors, who within a few days after completing the questionnaires would be full-fledged nurses. No reversion to the idealistic orientations occurred among the graduates of the nursing school.

Having found that students' values did not develop in accordance with their own or the faculty's values, we now turn to the question, did the orientations develop in accordance with students' perceptions of what the faculty expected of them? We cannot answer it with as much certainty as was possible in answering the previous question, because we have only inferential data on the influence of students' role assignments on their perceptions of faculty expectations. However, our findings on the development of attitudes toward the holistic nursing role and individualized patient care parallel what appears to have been the major shift in the patterning of the expectations of student roles structured by the curriculum.

The student-nurse role in the hospital included two component social relationships, the student–teacher relationship and the nurse–patient relationship. The student–teacher relationship included expectations on the part of teachers that enabled the student to enter into the nurse–patient relationship and was therefore both a condition limiting access to the nurse–patient relationship and a provider of instrumentalities for carrying it out. Orientations to the nurse–patient relationship were thus built into the student roles structured by faculty expectations. Evidence supporting this interpretation is seen in the finding that change in the training situation of students to include the nurse–patient relationship in the sophomore year did not result in much modification of the pattern of development of orientations toward patient care observed in the freshman year. If the nurse–patient relationship had been a major determinant of orientations, its incorporation into the curriculum would have been marked by change in direction of the developing pattern; but we have seen that orientations toward individualized patient care remained stable during that year and the shift away from the holistic view of patients, begun in the freshman year, continued.

Another explanation of the development of orientations is that they are learned from occupational expectations of student roles. The faculty, in this view, regulate access to the professional role, structuring the student role to include elements of the professional role. What students think is expected of them is determined by the assignment and supervision of their role performances by the faculty. In the case of the school of nursing, an instrumental orientation toward patients as objects on whom faculty-assigned tasks were to be performed was implicitly built into the student role. The biggest shifts of student orientations away from the ideal occurred in the freshman and junior years, when the expectations implicitly built into the assignments of student roles diverged from the students' initial views of patient care.

The formal description of the curriculum indicated shifts in expectations of student roles in the junior year. In that year the students began specialty practice and were expected for the first time to perform the role of the nurse rather fully. We have seen that in the junior year, attitudes toward individualized nonroutine care of patients declined in favorableness and the bureaucratic conception of the role of the nurse was well established as the predominant orientation, though individuals continued to change to that orientation during the senior year. The division of labor in a hospital is organized around types of tasks, and the activities we have classified as individualized nonroutine ones are assigned as the main work of aides and practical nurses, though registered nurses may perform these tasks if they have time. The beginning of specialty nursing in which students were expected to integrate core skills and techniques learned earlier into an overall pattern of patient care expanded their access to the professional role. Their assignments stressed activities that *nurses,* not lower-ranking personnel, performed in the specialties; and time limitations alone would have fostered a deemphasis of individualized nonroutine nursing care.

Before the junior year, individualized nonroutine activities such as bringing water to a patient were things that students could do while being taught core skills in piecemeal fashion. The importance of these activities for sophomores was enhanced by the fact that students could do them on their own, meeting a faculty expectation that they should keep busy doing "useful" things while with the patient. But as our interviews with three sophomores selected by their fundamentals class instructors as outstanding, average, and poor near the end of the first sophomore semester suggested, individualized nonroutine nursing activities were not really an integral part of the nurse–patient training experience, but a crutch the student could lean upon to demonstrate her efficient use of time. Thus individualized nonroutine activities were tacked on to sophomore assignments but not made an essential part of students' education.

Changes in what was explicitly expected of students during the freshman year, of a kind that might have supported changes in their orientations to patient care, are not apparent in official descriptions of the curriculum. The freshman interpersonal relations in nursing course sought to teach a holistic conception of patient care, but most students came out of the course with a task perspective instead. Not only did 68.0 percent of those who began the course with a bureaucratic view (19.5 percent of the entering freshmen) fail to learn what the course had meant to teach them; 45.6 percent of those with initially holistic orientations consistent with the objectives of the course unlearned them. Evidently more went on in the course than meets the eye in the curriculum statement. If the view of socialization as role learning is correct, so that students learn what the faculty set forth as expectations of student roles, the bureaucratic perspective with which students ended the freshman year must somehow have entered unitentionally into the interpersonal relations course. The faculty members who taught this course were specialists in psychiatric nursing and strongly endorsed holistic views. The course, according to its catalog description, was intended to teach an approach to patient care: the importance of individualizing patient care through perception of patients' needs and the use of one's self to relate to patients on the basis of their needs. However, from the perspective of student roles, the course focused attention on a general approach as to how a nurse should be in charge of the nurse–patient relationship. This question of *how* the nurse should give care was not directly coordinated with the question of *what*, specifically, she should do in giving care in a way that would have met the intended objectives of the course.

An approach to a problem assumes a set of skills and procedures for carrying out the approach. If the base of knowledge and skills is stated in so general a manner that specific behaviors cannot be directly derived from it, the approach has little utility as a set of behavioral guides for role performance. Wilensky (1964) and Goode (1969) observe that occupational groups that expand their knowledge bases by borrowing abstractly defined concepts and theories from occupations or disciplines whose work functions are unrelated to theirs in their quest for professional autonomy, as nursing has done (Strauss, 1966), meet with little success because the public is unable to see any technical relation of the abstract knowledge to the occupations' core work functions. The lack of perceived technical relatedness of the interpersonal relations course to the work of a nurse, which the students pictured as helping patients by doing things for them, seems to have hampered their learning to see their own relationships with patients as an aspect of the nursing role. Untrained in *what* a nurse does, they lacked a frame of reference for integrating the lessons on how a nurse should give care.

The failure of students to learn what the course was meant to teach them does not, however, explain why many of them unlearned their initial orientations. What seems to have happened is that the holistic view purveyed in the course *focused on the approach of the nurse to patients;* the anticipatory views of students were also holistic, but they focused on the *patient as the alter of the nurse,* with the patient seen as the active partner in the interaction, in contrast to the course's view of the nurse as the active member of the pair. Students were anticipatorily oriented to nurturant care, but the course told them that the mere doing of what the patient wanted done was not nursing; it might be indicated for one patient but contraindicated for another. The course taught the students that the patient was the recipient of nursing care, not the determiner of it. Students lacked the preparation to ascertain what patients needed, and their teachers told them that patients' wishes and requests were not appropriate indicators of patient needs. The high generality of the holistic approach purveyed in the course, coupled with the faculty's discounting of students' initial nurturant orientations as appropriate guides to behavior, seems to have created a vacuum; students had no way to decide what they should do with or for patients. The vacuum was filled by a task perspective, which required only that they carry out activities called for by doctors' orders and hospital nursing procedures.

Orientations to a place in the occupation

Occupations are organized in varying degrees around positions within career lines and around collective interests of the occupational group, and practitioners are accordingly placed within an occupation on the basis of the positions they hold and seek and of their participation in the occupational collectivity. Socialization of students may include orienting them to careers and positions and to the occupation as a community. To examine this aspect of professional socialization, we constructed two Guttman-scaled sets of questionnaire items measuring orientations to a place in the occupation. One scale refers to orientations to administration and supervision and the other to collegialism. The administration and supervision scale, with a coefficient of reproducibility of .92, was made up of five activities; students were asked how much they would like to do each of the five. The activities in this scale, arranged from the low end to the high, included supervising all kinds of auxiliary personnel, coordinating and planning nursing activities on a ward, training auxiliary personnel, formulating and revising techniques and procedures used by colleagues, and finding ways to simplify record keeping. Authority for performance of these activities is given by the hospital. Thus, we consider the endorsement of items to be contrary to a view of nursing as a regulator of nursing activities. Scale scores were dichotomized as near as possible to the median response of all students, with scores 3–5 grouped as highly favorable toward administrative and supervisory activities and scores 0–2 grouped as not favorable.

The collegialism scale was similarly constructed, consisting of students' responses indicating how much they would like to do each of five things pertaining to participation in nursing as a collectivity; it had a coefficient of reproducibility of .94. The activities, arranged from the low to the high end of the scale, were keeping up with current research in nursing, teaching principles and techniques in a school of nursing, writing professional articles, doing research on nurses, and contributing to professional meetings and conferences. Scale scores were dichotomized at the median, with scores 3–5 classed as favorable to collegialism and scores 0–2 classed as unfavorable.

Students' orientations toward collegialism and toward administration and supervision as they progressed through the program of the school are shown in Table 9-4. The table shows a net decline in favorableness toward administration and supervision and toward collegialism during the freshman year; the losses were regained in the sophomore year; the aggregate levels of favorableness remained relatively constant through the junior year, the senior year saw a sharp increase in the levels of endorsement of both orientations. This pattern is even more evident in the year-to-year changes of individual students' views, shown in Tables 9-5 and 9-6. Examining the percentages of students in each year of the program who were highly favorable after having been less favorable the

Table 9-4. *Orientations toward collegialism and toward administration and supervision*

	Percent high	
Academic class year	Collegialism	Administration and supervision
Entering freshmen	52.3	64.8
Freshmen	36.7	50.0
Sophomores	50.0	58.6
Juniors	46.9	51.6
Seniors	64.8	71.1

Table 9-5. *Yearly change in orientations toward collegialism (in percent)*

Year-to-year orientations	Entering freshmen-freshmen	Freshmen-sophomores	Sophomores-juniors	Juniors-seniors
Stable low	85.2	66.7	79.7	57.4
Low to high	14.8	33.3	20.3	42.6
(Total low)	(61)	(81)	(64)	(68)
Stable high	56.7	78.7	73.4	90.0
High to low	43.3	21.3	26.6	10.0
(Total high)	(67)	(47)	(64)	(60)

previous year, we see the sharpest shift toward favorable orientation occurring in the senior year. The percentage of students who were unfavorable to collegialism as juniors and shifted to being favorable as seniors was about four times the percentage that shifted in the other direction. The same pattern occurred during the senior year with respect to orientations toward administration and supervision. Thus, at the point of graduation from the school, students appeard to have begun to look with favor toward administrative work and toward participation in a professional community of nursing.

Our findings on the development of favorable orientations toward professionalism differ from the findings of Davis, Olesen, and Whittaker (1966:160) on University of California student nurses whom they

Table 9-6. *Yearly change in orientations to administration and supervision (in percent)*

Year-to-year orientations	Entering freshmen-freshmen	Freshmen-sophomores	Sophomores-juniors	Juniors-seniors
Stable low	75.6	60.9	68.5	43.5
Low to high	24.4	39.1	31.5	56.5
(Total low)	(45)	(64)	(54)	(62)
Stable high	63.9	76.6	66.2	84.8
High to low	36.1	23.4	33.8	15.2
(Total high)	(83)	(64)	(74)	(66)

studied at about the same time that our data were collected. Although their measure of professional values was a forced choice, counterposed against vocational values, they found that the level of endorsement of professional values declined slightly from entry to graduation. Had we counterposed the items in the administrative and supervisory scale against those in the collegialism scale, it is possible that we would also have found a decline in collegialism; but, having observed orientations toward the two sets of activities separately, we found very favorable orientations toward both emerging. The sharp shift toward endorsement of administration and collegialism in the senior year among the students we studied cannot, of course, be taken as evidence of the development of the kind of professional nurse upheld by the faculty as its ideal; that kind of nurse was one who also was oriented toward patient-centered nursing activities, whereas the favorable views of administration and professionalism as we defined them only oriented students to positions within structures of the occupation. Had the students developed the kind of professionalism the school desired, their orientations toward administration and supervision and, especially, toward collegialism should have been positively related to the values of professional nursing activities emphasized by the faculty. We will see in Table 11-1, a correlation matrix, that orientations toward administration and supervision and toward collegialism were unrelated to holistic views of nursing, and that orientations to individualized patient care were not related to collegialism at any time and were related to administrative and supervisory orientations only among entering freshmen and only slight-

Table 9-7. *Persistence of cognitive orientations after graduation, alumnae panel*

Orientations	Percent
Individualized patient care	
Stable low	81.8
Low to high	18.2
(N = seniors low = 55)	
Stable high	38.2
High to low	61.8
(N = seniors high = 34)	
Percent of alumnae high = 25.8	
Administration and supervision	
Stable low	28.6
Low to high	71.4
(N = seniors low = 28)	
Stable high	90.2
High to low	9.8
(N = seniors high = 61)	
Percent of alumnae high = 84.3	
Collegialism	
Stable low	51.6
Low to high	48.4
(N = seniors low = 31)	
Stable high	69.0
High to low	31.0
(N = seniors high = 58)	
Percent of alumnae high = 61.8	

ly among them (r = .20). One would expect students who were oriented to administration and supervision to be relatively unfavorable to the activities included in the scale on individualized patient care, but the two were unrelated, not negatively related. This lack of relationship suggests that these orientations have no bearing on each other, a conclusion that would not be inconsistent with the interpretation of Davis et al. (1966). Table 11-1 will also show that commitment was not correlated at any time with orientations toward administration or collegialism. Students who oriented to elite positions in nursing were neither more nor less committed than those who did not.

Persistence of orientations among alumnae

Data given in the tables above on the orientations for which we have alumnae data show that the patterns of development of these orientations started during the educational program were maintained among alumnae a year after graduation. Orientations favoring administrative activities increased, whereas collegialism remained relatively stable. Orientations favoring individualized patient care dropped from slightly over a third to about a quarter of the responses. These data show that orientations developed during education tended to persist among alumnae and that changes tended to be in the direction of the pattern already established, not contrary to it (see Table 9-7).

Conceivably, the persistence of the patterns may have been supported by work in nursing settings similar to the bureaucratically organized

Table 9-8. *Work setting and stability of orientations from senior to alumnae status (in percent)*

	Nursing work setting	
Orientations	Autonomous (N = 19)	Bureaucratic (N = 87)
Individualized patient care		
Stable low	63.2	47.1
Low to high	10.5	13.8
High to low	10.5	26.4
Stable high	15.8	12.6
Percent of alumnae high	26.3	26.4
Collegialism		
Stable low	10.5	20.7
Low to high	31.6	12.6
High to low	26.3	16.1
Stable high	31.6	50.6
Percent of alumnae high	63.2	63.2
Administration and supervision		
Stable low	5.3	10.3
Low to high	10.5	20.7
High to low	10.5	6.9
Stable high	73.7	62.1
Percent of alumnae high	84.2	82.8

hospital used for clinical experience. Most of the alumnae – 82.1 percent – worked in such settings, with the remaining minority in jobs organized by the nursing profession such as those in nursing education, psychiatric nursing, and public health. But orientations did not differ by work setting, nor did one work setting promote stability more than the other (see Table 9-8).

Summary

Freshmen began their education endorsing views that fitted very well the conception of the ideal nurse the school wanted to prepare. Rather than develop and reinforce the ideal, their education shifted their views away from the goals of the school toward a bureaucratic conception of nursing, ideally opposed by the faculty. Their curriculum and student assignments on wards in the hospital emphasized technical, task-oriented nursing, and orientations consistent with this emphasis are what students developed. The pattern of development of the different orientations coincided with training experiences, with each set of orientations developed by distinctive experiences. Once developed, the orientations persisted without change in direction. Work as alumnae reinforced them.

10. Development of personal relatedness to the occupation

Chapter 9 has described the patterns of development of orientations to nursing. In this chapter we shall examine the development of personal relatedness to nursing and its roles. The learning of role definitions and skills enables students to perform a role, but these cognitive learnings alone are not sufficient to socialize students so that they identify with the occupation and are attracted and committed to it. Full socialization includes relating the self to the occupation so that it endures in the person. Chapter 3 has specified ways in which we expect the program of the school of nursing to relate students to nursing and its role through control of role and status options. A nursing-education program, through its regulation of the acquisition of knowledge and the opportunity to enact nursing roles, influences the extent and pattern of development of personal relatedness to nursing.

We will use the same analysis plan in this chapter as in the preceding one. The turnover table will show the academic year in which each component of relatedness to the role of the nurse developed and its direction. Our analysis will be done on panel data, but results of analysis using other aggregations of students to compare with the results from the panel data are given in Appendix B.

Status identification

Identification with the status of an occupation refers to acceptance of the occupational title as a self-description, a naming of one's social identity. Two main explanations of the process of status identification have been advanced. One is that identification develops through enacting the occupational role or aspects of it in response to expectations of role alters. In this view, factors affecting enactment of the occupational role in accordance with alters' expectations indirectly affect the growth of identification with the occupational status. For example, the acquisition of skills needed to perform activities expected by role alters affects

137

students' ability to reciprocate alters' expectations and thus affects their ability to identify with the status (Huntington, 1957:184–6). The other explanation sees identification occurring through persistent public identification of the person with the status. On the basis of Becker's labeling theory, the labeling of a student as a nurse by others, not her behavior in the role of the nurse, should develop her identification with the status of nurse. Were the student to become publicly identified with other statuses that overshadowed her public identification as a nurse, her identification with the status should decline.

The educational activities of the school were so arranged as to enable us to separate analytically the first year when students were identified with the status of nurse by others from the first year when they were expected to enact the nursing role. The principal movement toward identification of students as nurses by others occurred in the sophomore year, when weekly four-hour clinical experiences in the hospital began; but it was a year later, when students began specialty nursing as juniors, that they were expected to carry out rather fully the activities of the nursing role, combining and enacting the discrete basic skills they had learned as sophomores. In the junior year, the weekly four-hour clinical experience was increased to daily hospital assignments ranging from three hours to a full day. We will use the sophomore year as a gross indicator of the introduction of public identification of students with the status of nurse and the junior year as a gross indicator of their first enactment of the nursing role.

With the beginning of clinical experiences in the hospital in the sophomore year, students were expected to wear student-nurse uniforms in the hospital and were assigned patients on whom they performed the discrete core nursing skills they were being taught. Although these new experiences did not change objectively their essential status as students, they did introduce identification of students as nurses by patients and other hospital occupational groups. Patients undoubtedly saw distinctions between student nurses and nurses, but they were distinctions of seniority more than of function. Student nurses' visible activities and uniforms identified them with the functional status of nurses. Thus a sophomore experienced, week after week at firsthand, others' views of her as a nurse, even though a student nurse. She was identified in the hospital as a student nurse, not simply as a student. This labeling moved her own reference group orientation away from students and toward nurses. An academic year of such identification with the status of nurse should be expected on the basis of labeling theory to produce a sharp increase over the freshman year in the tendency of students to identify themselves with that status.

Not until the junior year, when specialty nursing was begun, were students expected to enact rather fully the role of the nurse. Sophomores were in the hospital only once a week for four hours, and the activities they performed there were geared to their learning specific skills and procedures in piecemeal fashion. The junior curriculum was devoted largely to nursing and included daily experiences in the hospital. Junior students were expected to integrate the separate skills and procedures they had learned as sophomores along with learning new skills in carrying out the nursing needs of patients. Thus if enactment of the role is the critical influence on status identification, one would expect the addition of specialty nursing in the junior year, with students assigned nursing roles including responsibility for planning and executing patient care, to bring the first sharp increase in the tendency of students to identify with the status of nurse.

Our measure of status identification is a modification of the measure used by Huntington (1957:180). Huntington's question asked, "In your most recent dealings with patients, have you tended to think of yourself primarily as a doctor rather than a student, or primarily as a student rather than a doctor?" Our question asked, "Do you think of yourself as a nurse?" We deleted the situational context from the question in order to inquire about a more generalized perception of the self in the status of the occupation.

Table 10-1 presents data on status identification by academic year. Status identification developed rapidly from the beginning of the freshman year through the sophomore year. Shortly after students had en-

Table 10-1. *Students' identification with the status of nurse by academic class*

Academic class year	Percent highly identified
Entering freshmen	20.3
Freshmen	55.5
Sophomores	89.8
Juniors	93.8
Seniors	93.8

Table 10-2. *Yearly change in identification with the status of nurse (in percent)*

Year-to-year status identification	Entering freshmen- freshmen	Freshmen- sophomores	Sophomores- juniors	Juniors- seniors
Stable low	51.0	17.5	30.8	50.0
Low to high	49.0	82.5	69.2	50.0
(Total low)	(102)	(57)	(13)	(8)
Stable high	80.8	95.8	96.5	96.7
High to low	19.2	4.2	3.5	3.3
(Total high)	(26)	(71)	(115)	(120)

tered the school as freshmen, one-fifth of them thought of themselves as nurses. This figure increased to slightly more than half at the end of the freshman year and 89.8 percent at the end of the sophomore year. The junior year, when students began specialty nursing training and were expected to assume rather fully the role of the nurse, produced little increase beyond the high identification already evident before specialty training had begun. Thus one year of classroom study as student nurses and a second year consisting mainly of further classroom study supplemented by hospital training in discrete nursing skills sufficed to produce status identification. These findings are in accord with a status labeling explanation. They suggest that when one is placed in a social setting that supports identification with a status, alternative statuses with which one might identify are closed out as options and actual role enactment is not necessary for status identification to occur.

The findings just discussed pertain to net development of status identification as students went through the program. Table 10-2 shows the influence of the program in molding the process as indicated in annual shifts by individuals. The table shows the freshman program more supportive than unsupportive of status identification, as one would expect from the aggregate pattern. Of students low in status identification when they entered the program, 49.0 percent shifted to high identification during the freshman year, whereas only 19.2 percent of those who were high in status identification at the beginning of the freshman year shifted to low by the end of that year. The program's influence on status identification was more strongly positive during the sophomore year.

The sophomore year program retained the high status identification of 95.8 percent of its already high identifiers; the corresponding figure for the freshman year was 80.8 percent. Of sophomores who had been low in status identifications at the end of the freshman year, 82.5 percent changed to high identification by the end of the sophomore year in contrast to only 49.0 percent who underwent a similar shift during the freshman year. These findings, coupled with the very high percentage of students highly identified as nurses by the end of the sophomore year (Table 10-1), suggest that the sophomore year was the critical part of the program for producing status identification. Further examination of the data shows that once status identification had occurred in the sophomore year, the program was generally successful in maintaining and even increasing it during the junior and senior years.

These individual patterns of change in status identification correspond closely to a status labeling explanation in which an individual identified with a status by others is likely to identify with it. Especially noteworthy is the large percentage of entering freshmen who were high in status identification; they had never performed any element of the nursing role but were in a situation where others identified them as student nurses and hence, to some degree, as nurses.

Occupational commitment

Occupational commitment refers to the process through which the student becomes motivationally attached to the occupation. It grows with the cost of changing to another line of activity. When the perceived costs of changing to another line of activity exceed the perceived rewards of change, the individual is committed (cf. Thibaut and Kelley, 1959). Costs arise from the institutional arrangements that entrap the individual (Goffman, 1961:88–91) by making alternatives too costly to be realistically considered. This does not mean that commitment is necessarily involuntary; one may be objectively entrapped even though one has no desire to escape and no feeling of entrapment [cf. Durkheim, 1951 (orig. 1897):152–216].

From this reasoning we would expect students' commitment to nursing to increase sharply at the point in the school's program when change to another program would entail severe losses of investments in nursing, with further increments of commitment added with each additional year of study that could not be transferred to another program

Table 10-3. *Commitment to the role of the nurse by academic class*

Academic class year	Percent highly committed
Entering freshmen	42.2
Freshmen	41.4
Sophomores	53.9
Juniors	64.1
Seniors	67.2

without loss. In the school of nursing program, this point of major non-transferable investments occurred in the junior year. During the first year of study or immediately after it, a student could change to a different major subject with little loss of academic credit and little or no delay in the probable time of obtaining a college degree; this loss would become moderate by the end of the sophomore year. The first two years in the program were devoted mainly to liberal arts courses required for the bachelor's degree, with only six semester hours of nursing in the freshman year and sixteen semester hours in the sophomore year. But beginning in the junior year the curriculum was devoted to nursing except for two courses. To transfer out of nursing would be increasingly costly after the beginning of the junior year.

Our measure of commitment was a Guttman-type scale borrowed from the Cornell Nursing Study, composed of six items and having a coefficient of reproducibility of .94. The questions asked about the intention of the student to actually work as a nurse, thus relating future intent to present activity. Examples of the questions composing the scale are: "How likely do you think you are to change your mind about going into nursing?" "How often do you find yourself thinking of going into some other type of work instead of nursing?" Scale scores were dichotomized at the median of all classes, with scores of 4, 5, and 6 classed as high commitment.

The pattern of development of commitment was less continuous than the development of status identification. About 40 percent of entering freshmen were highly committed to nursing (Table 10-3). This figure changed very little during the freshman year. But the sophomore and junior years brought a substantial net change. Commitment continued to develop during the senior year but at a somewhat slower rate, so that at the end of the senior year about two-thirds of the class were

Table 10-4. *Yearly change in commitment to the role of the nurse (in percent)*

Year-to-year commitment	Entering freshmen-freshmen	Freshmen-sophomores	Sophomores-juniors	Juniors-seniors
Stable low	77.0	65.3	52.5	63.0
Low to high	23.0	34.7	47.5	37.0
(Total low)	(74)	(75)	(59)	(46)
Stable high	66.7	81.1	78.3	84.1
High to low	33.3	18.9	21.7	15.9
(Total high)	(54)	(53)	(69)	(82)

about to graduate with high commitment to nursing. The pattern of development of commitment paralleled the increasing closure of opportunities to transfer out of the program without major costs. The main attrition from the program occurred before the start of the junior year, the point in the curriculum beyond which any student who left it incurred serious losses of nontransferable academic credit and specialized training.

Examination of individual shifts (Table 10-4) shows the course of the development. The program was not able to produce a consistent pattern of development of occupational commitment until the end of the sophomore year. The freshman year was more likely to support low than high commitment. For every six students whose initially high commitment the freshman year retained, it also left unchanged an initially low commitment of seven students; and for every seven students who shifted from low to high commitment, roughly ten freshman students shifted from high to low commitment. The sophomore year brought an increase over the freshman year in the program's ability to support commitment. This increase was sufficient to overcome the freshman pattern of more students shifting to low than to high commitment. The junior year was not only able to retain the high commitment of more students than stayed low in commitment during that year, it was also more than twice as likely to shift a student to high commitment as to shift one to low commitment. The junior year's support of commitment continued at about the same strength in the senior year.

In considering the critical period when the program exerted its most decisive influence on commitment, the method of aggregating respondents makes some difference in the findings. (See Appendix B.) Among the panel groups of graduating seniors and alumnae, the sophomore year appears to have been decisive in retaining already high commitment and shifting about twice as many students from low to high as from high to low. So decisive an influence did not appear until the junior year in the year-to-year individually matched population of students. We see two possible reasons for this difference. One is that the clinical experiences of the sophomore year were not only nontransferable to other lines of study, but were also enjoyable, so they built a value of investment in nursing. This interpretation seems unlikely, because attraction to nursing did not grow concurrently with commitment among the panel groups. The other interpretation is that the students in the panel groups had relatively low thresholds for tolerating the losses they would have incurred in abandoning their plans to be nurses; the sophomore year adds sixteen hours of nontransferable course work beyond the freshman year, and to transfer to a different major at the beginning of the junior year is usually difficult. Students conscious of such costs of a transfer from nursing could not easily abide a year such as the junior year in the nursing program, with its almost total absorption in nursing courses and long hours of clinical training in the hospital.

Attraction

Unlike commitment, which is preconditioned by structural arrangments connected with the line of activity, attraction arises from intrinsic values of the activities or of the status to which the activities are attached. Any value identified with or expressed through the activities of an occupational role or its status adds to its attractiveness. The values may be general societal ones brought in from outside the occupation or they may be learned from within the occupation or from groups that perform or are situationally related to the activities (Mills, 1953:215).

We have seen that student nurses identified nurturant values with nursing, considering them important in their decisions to go into nursing. We do not see these nurturant values brought from lay society as sufficient to sustain occupational attraction or to further its development if they are not built into the total context of the work role, including other subprocesses of occupational socialization. Attraction grows from sentiments that arise from interaction and common experience, clearly perceived as occupational in nature, in the accomplishment of occupational tasks. The interactions establish feelings of belonging to an occupational group.

Students in the school were introduced to an insider's view of the occupation through hospital experience in which they learned core skills and applied them in work with patients. The patterning of the curriculum around the role of the nurse in the hospital nursing service beginning with the clinical training of the sophomore year provided a basis for intrinsic evaluation of the actual work of a nurse, as distinct from an ideal lay-society image of nursing. Previous research has found that when students learn actual work roles within group settings that define them as members of a group engaged in occupational tasks, and the occupational group positively values the activities, the students learn the excitement of the work (Becker and Carper, 1956). The activities are endowed with meaning and significance, reflecting the group's high evaluation of its work, so that as students learn the tasks they also learn the group values that define them as intrinsically attractive. The effect is to establish a personal relation of the student to the occupation.

Thus, if the teaching of core nursing tasks in the hospital gave evidence of high evaluation of the tasks by the clinical teaching staff and hospital nurses and integrated students into hospital work groups, the sophomore year should have produced an increase over the freshman year in attraction to nursing. Attraction should have continued to rise in the junior and senior years with the increased involvement of students in actual nursing situations. Until students were experientially related to nursing in the sophomore year, we would expect their attraction to nursing to be unchanging or erratic, reflecting only the lay values they had used to validate their choice of nursing. This hypothesis on the development of attraction assumes that the faculty and hospital nurses found hospital nursing tasks interesting and satisfying and communicated these sentiments in interactions with students.

Our measure of attraction is a five-item Guttman-type scale with a reproducibility coefficient of .96. The items were developed by the Cornell Nursing Study. Examples are: "How much do you like to talk to other people about nursing and subjects related to nursing?" "Are you looking forward to working in the field of nursing?" "When you think of the kind of life that most women in nursing lead, how attractive does it seem to you?" Scale scores were dichotomized at the overall

Table 10-5. *Attraction to nursing by academic class*

Academic class year	Percent highly attracted
Entering freshmen	43.0
Freshmen	39.1
Sophomores	35.9
Juniors	36.7
Seniors	30.5

Table 10-6. *Yearly change in attraction to nursing (in percent)*

Year-to-year attraction	Entering Freshmen-freshmen	Freshmen-sophomores	Sophomores-juniors	Juniors-seniors
Stable low	69.9	76.9	76.8	81.5
Low to high	30.1	23.1	23.2	18.5
(Total low)	(73)	(78)	(82)	(81)
Stable high	50.9	56.0	60.9	51.1
High to low	49.1	44.0	39.1	48.9
(Total high)	(55)	(50)	(46)	(47)

median for all academic classes combined, with scores of 4 and 5 classed as high attraction.

Attraction to nursing declined fairly steadily though only slightly from the beginning to the end of the program (Table 10-5). The junior year temporarily arrested a slow but fairly steady annual decline, but the declines resumed in the senior year at almost double the previous rate. Thus, contrary to our expectation, the effect of four years in the nursing program was to reduce rather than to increase attraction to nursing, despite the sharp increases in status identification and commitment.

Table 10-6 shows that at no time did the school's program support a pattern of individual shifts toward attraction to nursing. The patterns for all four years were very similar. About two-fifths of the students who began a given year highly attracted shifted during the year to low attraction, but only about a fourth of the students who began a year with low attraction shifted to high attraction during the year. A freshman student who entered highly attracted was more than one and one-half times as likely to change to low attraction as an initially less attracted student was to become highly attracted; this adverse pattern became increasingly pronounced so that the corresponding ratio of probabilities of shifting attraction – high to low divided by low to high – had become almost 3 to 1 by the senior year. Clearly, the program did more to lessen than to enhance the attractiveness of nursing to its students.

The fact that the erosion of attraction was gradual rather than showing sharp annual changes suggests that its weakening did not result from anything specific in the program that made nursing unattractive, but from a lack of positive support. Core nursing skills were taught as isolated activities unrelated to any guiding conception of nursing during the early clinical experience of the sophomore year; and in the junior and senior years, when specialty training integrated discrete skills into larger patterns, the focus was on fitting students' work into the hospital's bureaucratic routines rather than on helping individual patients. The teaching of nursing skills was incongruent with students' predisposing values and did not reinforce them. Hospital nurses did not accept student nurses as occupational colleagues but treated them with tolerant disdain. Thus two of the conditions that developed occupational attraction among the physiology students by Becker and Carper (1956) – strong goal direction as the focus of skills being learned and a highly solidary collegial group engaged in common occupational tasks – were missing from the student nursing curriculum. The unintentionally bureaucratic and nonoccupational emphasis of the curriculum seems to have undercut the development of enthusiasm for nursing and its work. We had expected it to be kindled by the teaching of core skills and their incorporation into specialty nursing work.

What happened? We saw in the previous chapter that freshman students tended to shift from a patient-centered toward a bureaucratic view of the role of the nurse; they learned a compliant orientation that emphasized following doctors' orders and hospital routines. The bureaucratic orientation contrasts sharply with an active orientation such as the one toward research whose development Becker and Carper (1956) observed among physiology students in laboratory groups. The new physiology students saw physiological research tasks as interesting and stimulating because that is how their faculty and advanced fellow students saw them. We do not know the evaluative climate the nursing faculty communicated in teaching the skills of nursing, or the one that was present in the hospital wards and other settings of student nurses' clinical experiences. The very acceptance of a bureaucratic view of nursing that stresses compliance would seem, however, to lessen the likelihood of students' developing a feeling of excitement and interest in the tasks they are to perform. A bureaucratic perspective orients the person to see the occupation from its position within an organization and away from an autonomous view of an occupational group whose primary concern is its own reactions to its work. The bureaucratic conception of nursing work locates it within the framework of the hospital status system, focusing attention on rank in the work organization rather than on task performance as an end in itself or on occupationally judged task performance as the basis of rank. It is thus likely, though we cannot demonstrate it, that students did not become more attracted to nursing because the faculty's method of teaching, which unintentionally played up bureaucratic orientations, coupled with the status system of the hospital undermined the expression of interest in nursing tasks. In the bureaucratic view, hospital nurses were oriented to the hospital as a system, not to nursing as an occupation extending beyond the hospital. Students learned this bureaucratic view and it did not appear to foster intrinsic attraction to nursing.

Our findings on development of personal relatedness to the occupation fit in general the explanation that the processes of status identification and commitment develop from controls inherent in status and role options. Skills and behaviors of an occupation may be learned, but we cannot infer from this fact that the role has been invested with meaning. The investment of meaning derives less from the content of the role than from the closing out of alternative roles. "The structural characteristics of institutions and organizations provide the framework of the situations in which experience dictates the expediency of change" (Becker, 1964:52). It was not primarily students' values and learnings that involved them in nursing but mainly the arrangement of the curriculum, which identified students as nurses and provided the side-bets that linked them to nursing, without, however, making the occupation intrinsically attractive to them.

Persistence of relatedness to nursing among alumnae

What did nursing work do to graduates' personal relatedness to the occupation? When they graduated they identified themselves as nurses and were highly committed to the occupation, but most were not highly attracted to it. We do not have data on status identification among alumnae, but their intentions to work as nurses declined from 70.8 percent highly committed to 28.1 percent, and their already low percentage of 32.6 percent highly attracted to nursing fell to 10.1 percent. A massive erosion of relatedness to nursing occurred among the alumnae of the program.

Why did personal involvement in nursing decline despite the persistence of cognitive occupational orientations? We have identified shifts in status and role options as the conditions underlying personal relatedness to the occupation. These shifts occur within the total role configurations of the person. The people we studied were all women, and nearly all of them looked to marriage and family life as the scene of their central life roles. A year or more after completing their education and beginning their work as nurses, 73 percent had married or were engaged; slightly more than one-fourth of those who had married already had children, and an additional one-fifth expected to have children within a year. These fundamental status and role changes provided alternatives to nursing that, at least in the short run, may have been related to the sharp reversal of commitment and also to the continued decline in attraction because of the high value placed on family life. Only 28.9 percent of the alumnae, whether married or engaged or neither, did not plan to leave the labor force altogether for at least three years to devote themselves fully to having and rearing children. (Interestingly, this percentage was only 12.0 percent among graduating seniors who had not yet worked.)

Tables 10-7 and 10-8 show, however, that marital and parental status of alumnae were less related to commitment and attraction than might have been expected. The alumnae groupings who had children and who planned to have them within a year had been very similar in commitment to nursing as seniors, but those with no immediate parental plans had been slightly less likely to be committed as seniors. Those who had children were somewhat more likely to remain highly committed than were those who were not yet parents. Perhaps alumnae who were already parents but were continuing to work either found it necessary to work for financial reasons or chose to work in order to add variety to their lives as mothers. There is little evidence that they wanted to work because of love of nursing, as is seen in the findings on attraction.

Alumnae with children had been more highly attracted as seniors than alumnae who did not have children but expected their first child

Table 10-7. *Marital status of alumnae and stability of relatedness to nursing since graduation (in percent)*

	Married or engaged (N = 73)	Unattached (N = 27)
Commitment		
Stable low	27.4	37.0
Low to high	4.1	0.0
High to low	45.2	40.7
Stable high	23.3	22.2
Percent highly committed as alumnae	27.4	22.2
Attraction		
Stable low	67.1	63.0
Low to high	2.7	3.7
High to low	24.7	18.5
Stable high	5.5	14.8
Percent highly attracted as alumnae	8.2	18.5

within the year, or who had no immediate plans for child bearing (52.6 percent vs. 23.1 percent and 24.3 percent). The major change in attraction was away from it, occurring among those alumnae who graduated highly attracted; their attraction faded considerably, so that they came to resemble the alumnae who had graduated with low attraction.

We must remember that these women virtually all looked forward to marriage and family life as their primary source of gratification, and that nearly all of the alumnae not yet married or engaged were involved in dating relationships tht might lead to marriage. There may have been even less variation in expectation of importance of marriage and family life than in current family status. Work as nurses commanded little of the persons of these alumnae; it was a job that gave them what they had looked for as freshmen – work compatible with feminine values and family life. Interest in the tasks of nursing care had yielded to interest in good jobs defined by market criteria, a change evident in their increased endorsement of administrative and supervisory activities. Those who planned to work at some time after or while having a family showed a slightly greater tendency than others to be highly committed and to have remained so. (See Table 10-9.)

Table 10.8. *Family status and plans of married alumnae and stability of relatedness to nursing*

	Have children (N = 19)	Child expected within the year (N = 13)	No immediate plans (N = 37)
Commitment			
Stable low	15.8	23.1	29.7
Low to high	5.3	0.0	5.4
High to low	42.1	53.8	45.9
Stable high	36.8	23.1	18.9
Percent alumnae high	42.1	23.1	24.3
Attraction			
Stable low	47.4	76.9	70.3
Low to high	0.0	0.0	5.4
High to low	36.8	23.1	21.6
Stable high	15.8	0.0	2.7
Percent alumnae high	15.8	0.0	8.1

Thus, students' initial views of nursing's compatibility with family life may help to sustain intentions of intermittent employment interrupted by temporary retreats to the home; such intentions would be manifested in our data as declines in commitment. Attraction is unnecessary for the kinds of lives beginning nurses anticipate; were they strongly attracted to nursing work, their flexibility to alternate between major commitment to different roles within their total role configurations might be impaired. Lack of high attraction to nursing eases the move out of the labor force at times of heaviest family life cycle demands and need not prevent a later return to work. The labor market of nursing is organized in a way more accommodated to intermittent careers than some other occupations. Nursing has a wide market. Its training is of a kind that loses little market value from disuse, and experience adds little to its market value (Oppenheimer, 1970). The marketplace of nursing work appears to fit very well the aspirations of the women who enter it. Our data show that the alumnae wanted much from their jobs but had little emotional investment in their occupation. They reserved that investment for their families. They were Rossi's (1965) traditional women.

Table 10-9. *Marriage and family plans and change in commitment and attraction (in percent)*

	Not work at all or only if necessary (N = 21)	Work after youngest at least 8 (N = 23)	Work before youngest 8 (N = 25)	Work full-or part-time (N = 28)
Commitment				
Stable low	47.6	21.7	28.0	21.4
Low to high	0.0	0.0	8.0	3.6
High to low	38.1	52.2	44.0	46.4
Stable high	14.3	26.1	20.0	28.6
Percent alumnae high	14.3	26.1	28.0	32.1
Attraction				
Stable low	85.7	52.2	64.0	60.7
Low to high	0.0	0.0	8.0	3.6
High to low	14.3	34.8	20.0	25.0
Stable high	0.0	13.0	8.0	10.7
Percent alumnae high	0.0	13.0	16.0	14.3

Table 10-10. *Years when processes developed, stabilized, and reversed*

	Freshmen	Sophomores	Juniors	Seniors	Alumnae
Orientations to the role of the nurse					
Holistic views toward patients	D[a]		S[b]	S	NA
Individualized patient care		D	D	D	D
Orientations to a place in the occupation					
Collegialism				D	S
Administration and supervision				D	D
Relatedness to the occupation					
Status identification	D	D	S	S	NA
Commitment		D	D	S	R[c]
Attraction					D

Note: NA signifies "not asked."
[a] Development is designated with the letter "D."
[b] Stabilization is designated with the letter "S."
[c] Reversal is designated with the letter "R."

Summary of development of socialization process

A summary of findings on development, stabilization, and reversal of the seven processes of socialization discussed in this chapter and the preceding one is given in Table 10-10. It shows the years when each orientation or aspect of relatedness to the occupation was developed, stabilized, or reversed; blank cells indicate years when none of these things took place. Development is defined as either the first substantial net shift, regardless of its direction – that is, toward or away from the orientation or aspect of relatedness – or a later large net shift in the same direction as the initial one. Stabilization is defined as the absence of large net shift in any year after development had occurred, so that the previous development was not reversed. Reversal is defined as large net shift in the opposite direction from the earlier development. We define a large net shift as a change of at least 10 percent. The observations are based on Tables 9-1, 9-3, 9-5, 10-1, 10-3, and 10-5. Looking at commitment, for example, we see no development in the freshman year, development in the sophomore and junior years, stabilization at the same level in the senior year, and reversal of the development among alumnae.

Our interpretation of patterns of development and stabilization of orientations and relatedness to nursing is supported by correlations of each dependent variable with itself for all pairs of academic class years. (See Appendix A.) They agree with our analysis from the turnover tables, that once development of an orientation or a process of relatedness got under way, subsequent experiences reinforced it. The correlation coefficients are the highest for the year-by-year academic class pairs composed of the year of initiation of a development and the year immediately following it. These correlations also show no evidence of lagged effects of any kind on development.

11. Synthesis and differentiation of socialization processes

So far our analysis has looked at the development of seven separate processes classified under three dimensions of socialization. If socialization is a set of interrelated processes and not a mere sum of disparate developments, an essential aspect of the overall process is the combining of the processes into identifiable dimensions. Coherence of the processes helps to stabilize the direction of development of each. Were each process unrelated to the others, persistence of a kind of behavior across situations would be impaired, and consequently the predictability of occupational behavior would be limited. For example, an individual may identify with an occupation and claim membership in it, but such an identification may not predict working in the occupation unless it is coupled with occupational commitment. Although the integration of processes helps to stabilize each of them, an integration that mixed the dimensions into a single overall cluster might tend to produce workers whose life organization would be completely tied to a rigid and unchanging set of views of the occupation. So tight a configuration of aspects of socialization would impede changes in the nature of the occupation and labor mobility within it.

The markets of different professions are not alike. As we have discussed in Chapter 2, professional control of recruitment, including socialization, has adaptive value because it provides some degree of control over the market. Differentiation of dimensions of socialization is likely to vary from one occupation to another. We see the extent of their differentiation as influenced by the nature of recruitment, including the degree of the occupation's control of training and whether a practicum is a major training resource, and by the market. Inclusion of a practicum in the education of students introduces them to the marketing of the occupation's service through the use of its skills. As a practitioner, one must sell in an organized labor market what one has learned. To do this, one must adapt to whatever system for marketing the skills is prevalent. Some occupations organize their own markets; others do not, or only partially do. For example, physicians and lawyers in the traditional systems of individual client practice have organized their markets, but increasingly the members of these professions work in markets organized for them through big hospitals and law firms. The changes have cost individual practitioners a considerable loss of autonomy. The market for nurses is organized primarily and increasingly by large hospitals, not by the occupation.

The development of dimensions

If members of an occupation are to adapt to its market, especially at a time when the market is changing rapidly, and if they are to coordinate their work roles satisfactorily with their nonwork roles, the dimensions of socialization cannot be inflexibly tied to a particular work setting, a particular work function, or a particular work technique. All of these things change when there is a change in the occupation's market. Work in an occupation rests first and foremost on commitment and status identification, for these create enduring ties to the occupation, motivating persons to take jobs in the occupation and to seek others' identification of them with the occupation. The detachment of commitment and status identification, if not attraction, from cognitive orientations to the occupational role and to a place in the occupation allows flexibility of action, both within market situations and in the everyday performance of work. In a market that is organized by organizations, jobs are separate from persons; persons choose jobs and the choices are confirmed through employment. Work thus requires choice and choice is facilitated by the differentiation of motivation from cognitive orientations. One may evaluate a job from the standpoint of its fit with one's orientations to the work role, to a place in the occupation, and to nonwork roles. For example, a job may provide exactly the kind of work role one wants, but one may reject the job if it is not conducive to attaining one's desired place in the occupation or if it interferes unduly with one's nonwork roles. Rarely can people choose between jobs offering all and none of the opportunities and conditions they want. Differentiation of the dimensions of socialization eases job choice and maintains motivation to work by making it likely that some available job will meet the criteria established by one or another dimension.

Our research deals with only one occupation and one educational program, so we cannot observe how occupations that are differently organized or have different kinds of educational programs influence the differentiation of dimensions of socialization. In the case of nursing, we expect the dimensions to become differentiated during the educational program because of the centrality of the hospital practicum in the curriculum, and we expect the differentiation that occurs during education to persist among alumnae. Nursing markets are organized mainly by hospitals, so that the strong influence of the hospital practicum on the development and differentiation of dimensions of socialization fits the marketplace of this occupation very well.

This chapter will examine the synthesis and differentiation of processes of socialization by addressing two main kinds of questions. (1) Do the processes that are conceptually classified as a dimension interrelate to form a coherent dimension differentiated from other dimensions? Analysis of data bearing on this question will enable us to see whether experiences within the school resocialized students – and if so, the nature of the resocialization – or further developed or had no effect on their anticipatory socialization. (2) What is the overall pattern of development of the components and dimensions in relation to each other? Do they develop simultaneously as is implied in a cultural view of socialization, or in sequence, or in some other way?

If our conceptually defined dimensions of socialization are in fact empirical dimensions, the component processes of each should come to cohere during the recruitment process if they do not cohere from the time of matriculation. Several kinds of coherence are possible. If the processes form discernible dimensions at the time of entrance into school, persistence of the dimensions through the education of students and into their work as nurses will indicate that the pattern of socialization was set in lay society and that education merely furthered the development of anticipatory socialization along lines established in lay society. If the processes show no initial intercorrelation, socialization might integrate the disparate processes along with developing them. Or the processes might be initially integrated, but experiences during education might realign them to form new clusters. In either of these last two patterns, not only will the processes have been developed but their relations to one another will have changed. In the last-discussed pattern, resocialization will have taken place.

To investigate the development of dimensions of professional socialization we shall look for a clustering of processes. Our technique for this investigation is principal component analysis using varimax rotation. An eigenvalue of 1.00 is used as the criterion for inclusion of a component. The analysis is done separately for each academic class status from entering freshmen through alumnae, except in a few instances where some of the data on alumnae are missing. The analysis uses the panel data. (Cross-sectional data yield essentially the same findings.)

Before turning to this principal component analysis, we look first at the correlation matrix of the twenty-one zero-order correlations of the seven processes with each other for the freshman through alumna status groups. These are presented in Table 11-1. Processes conceptualized as belonging to the same dimensions, except individualized patient care and holistic view of patients, correlated more highly with each other than with those classified under different dimensions for every academic status except entering freshman. Patterns of correlation between pairs of processes were not the same for all academic statuses. All pairs correlated more highly among seniors than among entering freshmen, but the extent of this increase was not uniform, and not all correlations rose during every year of the educational program. The pair of processes showing the greatest increase and also the highest correlation over the course of students' education was attraction and commitment; but the correlation dropped considerably from the senior to alumna status, though the drop was less than the increase from entering freshman to junior status had been.

Principal component analysis shows the dimensions cohering in the senior year in a way that fits the conceptualization. Table 11-2 presents for each academic status the components yielded by the varimax rotation and the loadings of the processes on each component. In the senior year, each component included the processes of one of the conceptualized dimensions and no other subprocess. The senior-year pattern was repeated among the alumnae with respect to the processes for which we have data, a finding that suggests persistence of a dimension across a major status transition once it has come into being.

Although the three dimensions were evident by the end of the senior year, the growth of their coherence during earlier years was not gradual or consistent. Their somewhat erratic patterns of integration were attributable especially to the volatile character of individualized patient care and, to a lesser extent, of status identification and holistic views of patients. Individualized patient care changed its heaviest loading from one component to another each year, vacillating with respect to the other processes with which it shared its heaviest loading; not until the

Table 11-1. *Correlation matrices of socialization processes of the academic classes, graduation, and alumnae panels*

	IPC	HV	Col	A&S	A	Com	SI
Entering freshmen (N = 128)							
Individualized patient care		.089	.142	.203	.253	.075	.068
Holistic view			−.020	.010	−.048	−.005	.065
Collegialism				.301	.054	.013	−.026
Administration and supervision					.092	−.101	−.116
Attraction						.233	.161
Commitment							.164
Status identification							
Freshmen (N = 128)							
Individualized patient care		.088	−.118	−.004	.276	.227	.096
Holistic view			−.056	−.016	.032	.022	−.026
Collegialism				.475	−.137	−.151	.008
Administration and supervision					−.089	−.133	−.041
Attraction						.322	.188
Commitment							.127
Status identification							
Sophomores (N = 128)							
Individualized patient care		−.119	.104	.126	.109	.088	−.031
Holistic view			−.174	−.196	.029	−.024	−.116
Collegialism				.441	−.105	−.081	−.013
Administration and supervision					−.037	−.140	.053
Attraction						.326	.160
Commitment							.171
Status identification							

Table 11-1 (*cont.*)

	IPC	HV	Col	A&S	A	Com	SI
Juniors (N = 128)							
Individualized patient care		−.088	.090	.096	.327	.301	.065
Holistic view			−.074	−.010	−.079	−.100	−.123
Collegialism				.442	.033	−.027	−.003
Administration and supervision					.085	.054	−.042
Attraction						.578	.404
Commitment							.417
Status identification							
Seniors (N = 128)							
Individualized patient care		.032	.158	.149	.147	.193	.160
Holistic view			−.088	−.076	−.108	−.140	−.097
Collegialism				.401	.108	.109	−.011
Administration and supervision					.054	.100	.075
Attraction						.621	.307
Commitment							.391
Status identification							
Alumnae (N = 89)							
Individualized patient care		NA[b]	−.005	.085	.012	.047	NA
Collegialism				.194	−.018	−.053	NA
Administration and supervision					−.009	.009	NA
Attraction						.420	NA
Commitment							NA

[a] Column headings are the initials of row headings. [b] We have no data on holistic views and status identification for alumnae.

Table 11-2. *Component matrices for the academic classes, graduation, and alumnae panels*

	Component 1	Component 2	Component 3
Entering freshmen			
Individualized patient care	.541	.369	.292
Holistic view	−.001	−.061	.931
Collegialism	.679	−.014	−.092
Administration and supervision	.782	−.142	.003
Attraction	.272	.700	−.107
Commitment	−.106	.689	−.101
Status identification	−.199	.574	.276
Percent of variance explained	21.1	20.7	14.7
Freshmen			
Individualized patient care	.657	.037	.270
Holistic view	.121	−.006	.865
Collegialism	−.129	.836	−.091
Administration and supervision	−.025	.863	.056
Attraction	.738	−.082	−.053
Commitment	.654	−.175	−.048
Status identification	.464	.056	−.449
Percent of variance explained	25.5	20.9	14.7
Sophomores			
Individualized patient care	.287	.389	.698
Holistic view	−.577	−.116	.160
Collegialism	.734	−.168	.130
Administration and supervision	.776	−.123	.068
Attraction	−.064	.747	.028
Commitment	−.092	.750	−.056
Status identification	.240	.404	−.709
Percent of variance explained	29.0	21.1	13.4
Juniors			
Individualized patient care	.505	.223	

Table 11-2 *(cont.)*

	Component 1	Component 2	Component 3
Holistic view	−.237	−.101	
Collegialism	.016	.835	
Administration and supervision	.063	.829	
Attraction	.826	.033	
Commitment	.829	−.044	
Status identification	.665	−.157	
Percent of variance explained	30.1	19.4	
Seniors			
Individualzed patient care	.312	.338	.584
Holistic view	−.203	−.194	.827
Collegialism	.020	.822	−.020
Administration and supervision	.025	.807	.004
Attraction	.810	.048	−.035
Commitment	.852	.089	−.029
Status identification	.675	−.029	.039
Percent of variance explained	28.6	24.2	20.0
Alumnae			
Individualized patient care	−.106	.321	
Collegialism	.162	.697	
Administration and supervision	.052	.781	
Attraction	−.829	.071	
Commitment	−.839	.072	
Percent of variance explained	28.6	24.2	

senior year did it load most heavily on the same component as holistic views. The holistic view pattern also vacillated, but in a different way. It began by standing alone as a component, then loaded most heavily on the same component as orientations to a place in the occupation; eventually, in the senior year, it found its conceptually proper place in the same component as individualized care. The pattern of loadings of status identification was less erratic than that of either set of orientations to the occupational role. Its first heaviest loading was shared with other processes of relatedness to the occupation, and it resumed and retained this conceptually predicted place after a temporary aberration of sharing high loadings with orientations to the role of the nurse.

The other four processes were consistent year after year in sharing high loadings with their conceptual companion processes. From entering freshman through alumna status, attraction and commitment combined to define a component, as did collegialism and orientations to supervision and administration. The differentiation of these two pairs consisted of their separation from individualized patient care and holistic views of patients, and of disentangling status identification from other processes so that it came to share its highest loading with attraction and commitment. The coherence of the dimensions that involved these two pairs seems to have been less problematic than the coherence of orientations to the role of the nurse; no realignment of any of the four from its conceptually defined dimension occurred.

The variation in differentiation of dimensions is highlighted if for each academic status we assign each subprocess to the component on which it loaded most highly, then rank the subprocesses assigned to each component from highest to lowest strength of loading. Table 11-3 does this. (It omits alumnae because some data on them are missing.) This procedure shows that of the fourteen components that attained eigenvalues of 1.00 or more during students' education, five included conceptually misplaced processes. Individualized patient care was involved in four of these five components with misplaced processes. It is clear that the progressive differentiation of dimensions depended heavily on the realignment of orientations to individualized care. Equally clear is the fact that the progress of its realignment was far from smooth.

Table 11-3 indicates also the most problematic years of socialization. The sophomore year began clinical experiences. Two of the components that were unstable as students moved through the program attained eigenvalues of 1.00 or more in that year. The junior year began specialty nursing, with students assuming actual nursing roles whose work was charted as a part of hospital care; yet no component defined mainly by measures related to the role of the nurse first reached an eigenvalue of 1.00 in the junior year.

Taken as a whole, the findings of our principal component analysis

Table 11-3. *Assignments of processes to components of their highest loadings, in order of loadings on each component, for academic classes, graduation and alumnae panels*

	Component 1	Component 2	Component 3
Entering freshmen (N = 128)	A&S:.782 Col:.679 IPC:.541	A:.700 Com:.689 SI:.574	HV:.931
Freshmen (N = 128)	A:.738 IPC:.657 Com:.654 SI:.464	A&S:.863 Col:.836	HV:.865
Sophomores (N = 128)	A&S:.776 Col:.734 HV:−.577	Com:.750 A:.747	SI:−.709 IPC:.698
Juniors (N = 128)	Com:.829 A:.826 SI:.665 IPC:.505 HV:−.237	Col:.835 A&S:.829	
Seniors (N = 128)	Com:.852 A:.810 SI:.675	Col:.822 A&S:.807	HV:.827 IPC:.584
Alumnae (N = 89)[a]	Com:−.839 A:−.829	A&S:.781 Col:.697 IPC:.321	

[a]We have no data on holistic views and status identification for alumnae.

indicate a mixture of two kinds of differentiation of socialization processes. Some processes already cohered in the anticipatory socialization brought to the school by entering freshmen, and the program supported and further developed their coherence in the dimensions of socialization we have identified. The coherence of attraction and commitment, and of collegialism and orientations to supervision and administration, fitted this reinforcement pattern. Other processes – orientations to individualized patient care, holistic views of patients, and status identification – underwent redirection or realignment with erratic and annual changes. The erratic patterns of these three appear to have involved the separation of nurturance from the image of the self as a nurse. The sophomore year opposed the two views and, as a result, disentangled them. Once freed from nurturance, status identification shifted toward its eventual coherence with other processes of relatedness of the self to the occupation; it is a component distinct from orientations to the role of the nurse (cf. Habenstein and Christ, 1963).

It is not surprising that individualized patient care and holistic views of patients became differentiated from the other processes when one considers the bureaucratic nature of hospital work, which was the setting of students' training in the practicum. These personalized nurturant orientations are inconsistent with the bureaucratic demands of hospital roles. Their separation from other processes adapted the other dimensions of socialization to the work settings of most graduates. The growth and differentiation of dimensions that fit bureaucratic settings run directly counter to the ideal objectives of the program but equip students for the kind of work most of them will do.

Persistence of differentiation of dimensions among alumnae

We have alumnae data on only four of the seven processes. Orientations to a place in the occupation remained intact as a dimension of socialization, with collegialism and orientations to supervision and administration loading highly on a single component but not loading highly on any other component. Commitment and attraction continued to load most heavily on a separate component, but they loaded on it negatively, whereas they had loaded on it positively among seniors. This sharp reversal suggests that the alumnae were disaffected from nursing and regarded it as nothing but a job. Nevertheless, the component of orientations to a place in the occupation kept its strength among the graduates who had worked as nurses; alumnae appear to have been oriented to elite nursing positions and more oriented to elite jobs than to collegial activity, whose loading on the component was lower than among seniors.

These findings and conclusions are consistent with our earlier ones that most seniors and alumnae saw work as a secondary complement to family roles, even if they had not yet married; they wanted elite jobs, but they were not "career women" with heavy investments of self in their work. The forces that make a nurse see her work as simply a job and rob her of personal relatedness to the occupation seem to lie not only in family roles, which are the primary sources of her life satisfaction, but also in the occupation of nursing itself, with its dominant work setting in the routinized bureaucratic hospital of today.

Professional work is often a matter of applying standard procedures to rationally defined categories of problems. The honeymoon period of work in a profession may be brief, whether or not professional training includes a practicum. Disaffection may grow as the worker settles into a round of activities that come to be experienced as repetitive routines, many of them not requiring the exercise of skill and judgment commensurate with professional training. The conditions for reality shock of this kind are present not only in nursing and other occupations with similar structures of socialization, but also in a broad range of professions with varying types of training programs.

Pattern of differentiation of socialization processes

The data yielded by the principal component solution suggest some general observations about the pattern of differentiation of professional socialization processes. The data clearly show that socialization is multidimensional as we have indicated. Processes cohere in dimensions, and dimensions become differentiated from one another. Moreover, the multidimensionality and accompanying developments extend throughout the entire period of recruitment.

Socialization does not evolve from a simple to a complex state by adding on later learnings to earlier ones. The initial structure of the relations of processes to each other among entering freshmen was as complex as the structure among graduating seniors. (Because data are incomplete on alumnae we cannot comment on them in this regard, but we have no reason to think data on alumnae would alter this conclusion.) Three principal components were evident among freshmen and also among seniors, though the compositions of two differed. It is possible, of course, that the situation would differ in a less traditional and institutionalized occupation where anticipatory socialization would be less likely to have produced clearly delineated views among beginning students.

In fact, among the student nurses, the components that appeared among entering freshmen and seniors resembled each other more closely than those of any other pair of academic classes. They were alike with one exception, the theoretically misplaced location of individualized patient care among entering freshmen. This exception is, however, far from trivial; it indicates a critical difference in views of the two classes and a need for resocialization to produce the final structure consistent with the actual role of the nurse after graduation. The initial structure had to be rearranged. Cumulative cultural transmissions that merely added complexity to an initial structure developed through anticipatory socialization could not be the pattern of professional socialization of nurses.

The beginning misplacement of individualized patient care also meant that its position was to be shifted so that it might eventually cohere with holistic views of patients as a dimension that persisted across a status transition. A stable positioning of individualized patient care did not occur until educational experiences had separated the initial effect from it. Its erratic movements during the educational program call to mind what is generally referred to as the cynicism of professional students and may have represented temporary adaptations to exigencies of the curriculum. Its eventual proper theoretical alignment with holistic views suggests the possibility that even such temporary adaptations may be parts of emergent permanent transformations of occupationally relevant behavior. They appear as a phase in which service and other orientations are neutralized as aspects of one's personal relatedness to the occupation.

These findings argue that a view of socialization that defines it as a matter of learning or motivation is overly simple. Processes do not only develop individually; their development may require separation from other processes, or, conversely, integration with other processes. Failure to take account of the shifting relations among processes obscures the complexity of the overall process of socialization.

Summary

Principal component analysis shows that the professional socialization of student nurses consisted of three distinct dimensions corresponding to our conceptual distinctions. The processes that composed the dimensions of orientations to the occupation of nursing and relatedness to the role of the nurse cohered well from matriculation through work as alumnae. But the two sets of orientations to the role of the nurse did not cohere until after the program developed orientations to individualized patient care during the junior year. Once developed, they came together with holistic views as a component. The orientations that formed this dimension were the only ones the program resocialized: Holistic views with which students entered the program were changed to bureaucratic ones, and students' endorsement of individualized patient care was reversed. All the dimensions cohered among graduating seniors. The coherence persisted among alumnae, even though commitment and attraction shifted from positive to negative loading on the dimension of relatedness to the role of the nurse.

Part III

Individual influence sources and socialization processes

12. Lateral relations and socialization

In Chapter 3 we discussed how the educational program of the school, in bringing students together, exposed them to various definitions of occupational orientations and involved them in role settings that laid out status and role options. Some of the options and definitions were developed within the program; others were not. The ranges of socially supported definitions and options were sufficiently limited and structured to produce prevailing patterns of choice, some of which we have identified as program influences on socialization; but not all students responded identically to the ranges of choice that were open to them. For example, the program brought all students who stayed in it beyond the freshman year into contact with occupational groups in the hospital, but students varied in their ways of relating to hospital groups.

In Part III we shall examine students' perceptions of and relations to three potential influence sources other than the educational program to see if they were associated with their socialization. The influence sources consisted of students' lateral relations (Olesen and Whittaker, 1970) and their relationship to the program, the faculty, and the hospital.

The lateral relations we shall study are associations with the student-nurse group and nonnursing women students and expectations concerning the accommodation of marriage and family roles with work. The student-nurse group was highly self-suffecnt. Student nurses were socially and psychologically insulated from other students in the university. Their group life approximated a total institution, built in part from their close personal relations and common objectives. Under such conditions of completeness and insularity, do students' relations act as conduits transmitting definitions of the role of the nurse and of places in nursing?

Students varied in their expectations concerning the accommodation of marriage and family roles with work. At the same time when data for this study were gathered, there were no institutionalized, routine ways to integrate work and family life. A woman's societal status and identity were determined in large measure by her husband's. As we have seen in Chapter 6, student nurses expected to work and some wanted to be working twenty years after graduation. Virtually all expected to marry, and the majority looked to family life for their main life satisfactions. Nursing is a feminine occupation and its work opportunities are widely distributed. These occupational characteristics should ease integration of work and family life but not remove all difficulties. Scheduling work, finding child care, and other objective problems would inevitably occur. Added to them might be subjective concerns. High investment of self in family and marital relations could undermine work motivation. How students expected to mesh their family and work roles would seem to influence their work motivations. At the least, time given to one could not be given to the other.

The second potential influence on socialization that we shall examine is students' relations with the faculty and their orientations to the program. Had the values and objectives of the program been built into students' roles as guides to their learning, one would expect a simple relationship in which students most oriented to the program and those having the most contacts with the faculty would be the most influenced by the ideology of the faculty. We have seen, however, that what the program actually imparted was different from the faculty's ideal objectives. In such a situation, what influence can we expect among students with strong ties to the faculty and favorable views of the faculty and program? When faculty members interacted informally with students, did they uphold in conversation the ideology and conscious objectives of the program? Frequent contacts with the faculty might have helped to sustain its ideal objectives so as to reduce the program's unintentional support of orientations contrary to the school's ideology.

A third category of influences consists of students' associations with occupational groups in the hospital and their views of these groups. Student nurses' concern with their relations to hospital groups differed from their concern with their relations to each other and to other students. Some but not all student nurses wanted their clinical-training roles functionally integrated into the hospital division of labor among doctors and nurses. They varied in the attitudes they brought to their hospital training. The division of labor in the hospital projected an image of nursing that was consistent with the way in which nursing actually was taught but was not consistent with the ideology of the educational program. Students who most wanted their education to include contacts with hospital nurses and doctors would seem open to hospital influences on their socialization.

Chapters 9, 10, and 11 have shown that the development of socialization processes paralleled the school program, with different processes developing during different academic class years. No process developed cumulatively and undirectionally from time of entry to graduation. Instead, development of the processes occurred in different academic years. This pattern of development is an important consideration for our analysis in Part III. Ideally, we would like to sort out yearly the program's influence from that of individual involvements, but we cannot, because we studied only one school. We can compensate for this sample limitation, however. We can control the program's influence, because it was organized by academic classes. We will take account of the overall socialization pattern by doing our analysis *within* each academic class year. We will be attentive to the fit of the findings on individual involvements to those of the program. If individual involvements influenced socialization, at what times in the program did these influences occur? Did they precede, follow, or coincide with the program's influence? By doing our analysis within academic classes, we can fit the timing of the individual patterns with the timing of the program patterns. In this way we hope to show how the school created or allowed conditions for systematic modes of individual departure from its program's predominant structuring of students' socialization.

Our analysis techniques will be Pearsonian correlations and differences in means for categorical variables. We violate assumptions in using them. They assume independent observations, but we repeated measurements on the same individuals. Nonetheless, we are confident that repeated measurements have not distorted our findings, as we discussed in Chapter 4. We will use the panel data for this section. The findings based on them agree almost perfectly with those of the cross-sectional aggregations. The panel size varies for a few of the analyses. Two questions were not asked the pilot class in its freshman year, and in other instances a few students failed to answer questions used as independent variables. Drops in panel size will be noted in footnotes to tables.

The student-nurse group

The student-nurse group was embedded in the organization of the school's program, which systematically structured and limited students' opportunities for various forms of social participation. Student nurses lived within a context of substantial but not total attachment to the student-nurse group. How did participation in the student-nurse group and perspectives toward it support or modify the impact of the program on professional development?

Participation in the student-nurse group

The student-nurse group was organized around both the total student-nurse body and each academic class, as well as around personal interests out of which friendships developed. The school had its own Student Government Association, to which every student nurse belonged. The association's governing body was composed of elected officers of the student body, mainly seniors, and representatives elected by each class. These student officials made and enforced rules to govern students' social and academic lives; for example, they adopted an honor system long before the entire university had one. Besides its regulatory activities, the Student Government Association handled matters related to the study of nursing, ranging from a "big sister" counseling service for freshmen to assisting with capping ceremonies to acting as sponsor for representative participation by students in campus activities and in local, state, and national nursing affairs. The association was formally chartered to relate students instrumentally and expressively to the school's program and to the profession of nursing in accord with its goal "to cooperate with the faculty in creating and maintaining high ideals for the Duke University School of Nursing." In so doing, it encouraged interaction across academic class lines but within the context of the school's program.

Relations between students of different classes were also facilitated by their living arrangements. All students lived apart from other female students. Sophomores, juniors, and seniors were housed together in floors above the administrative offices, freshmen in an annex to the main school of nursing building. Students of each class tended to segregate themselves in clusters of dormitory rooms, but the dormitory offered opportunity for substantial contact. All student nurses usually ate in a cafeteria across from their residences. The big sister arrangement encouraged interaction of freshmen with more advanced students and inclined each class to look to those above it in learning the ropes and coping with problems. Although the total student-nurse body formed a group, each academic class formed a subgroup within it. Students went through the program as cohorts, responding to shared problems as they took classes and clinical training together. Participation within one's academic class would seem likely to have related students to the world of nursing as experienced and defined by the class as a whole; such experiences and definitions changed as students advanced from one academic year to the next.

The effects of participation in a student group should depend on the relation of the group and its perspectives to the orientations emphasized in the program. If the group we studied held perspectives in accord with those of the program, then participation in it should have reinforced the program's influence. If, however, the student group grew up around student interests not expressed in the program, then participation in the student group should have lessened the program's influence or had no systematic effect on it.

Five indexes were constructed to gauge lateral social participation inside and outside the student-nurse group. They measured contact with nonnursing female students, participation in the Student Government Association, instrumental and "social" relations with student nurses across academic class lines, and mutual aid within one's student-nurse academic class. The index of contact with nonnursing female students comprised seven items on such things as the number of nonnursing female friends and the frequency of visiting them in the dormitories. The three-item index of Student Government Association participation included questions on participation and interest in student government and visiting other students to talk about student government affairs. Interclass instrumental relations were measured by three items indicating whether as many as half of one's contacts with student nurses to study together, learn the ropes, and get information about the faculty were with students in academic classes other than one's own. The measure of interclass social relations was similar and involved dormitory visiting, double dating, and social outings. Intraclass student-nurse mutual aid was indexed with three items on sharing information about the faculty, helping one another with assignments, and arriving at common views and solutions of problems encountered in education. Each index was constructed by scoring responses to each item and then totaling the item scores for each student.

Table 12-1 shows the participation patterns of the four academic classes. Freshmen and seniors stood out as distinctive, each being substantially highest or lowest of the classes on four of five measures of lateral participation. On three measures, there was an annual progression from high to low or vice versa. Seniors were extreme on one of the remaining two, and the classes hardly differed on the other. Sophomores and juniors were more similar to each other than to freshmen or seniors. From these facts it seems clear that the patterns of different classes reflected conditions specific to each year of the program and were not simply manifestations of growing experience or rising status.

Freshmen's participation in student government was lower than that of other classes. Their separate housing in the annex limited their interclass "social" participation, which was lower than that of sophomores and juniors. The freshman curriculum consisted of academic classes and did not provide the opportunity for mutual aid in the hospital, where other classes' assignments brought them together on the same wards. Despite the heavy concentration in nonnursing academic courses during the freshman year, which freshmen took with nonnursing female students, freshmen had the lowest rates of "social" interpersonal contacts with them. Classroom contacts did not eventuate in further contacts. Sophomores and juniors were the classes most similar in lateral participation. Sophomores stood out, however, in having the highest rate of interclass instrumental relations, perhaps occasioned by concern over the beginning of clinical activities in the sophomore year. Seniors were lower than juniors in all forms of participation except mutual aid and interpersonal relations with nonnursing female students; they were the highest class in rates of contact with nonnursing female students. This may reflect the growth of friendships over the four years and changes in patterns of double dating. Seniors were lowest in both kinds of nursing interclass contacts, perhaps because their curriculum included public-health nursing, which took them off campus for clinical experience.

From these findings it is evident that the academic classes differed markedly in lateral participation. They indicate the need to look within academic classes to see if participations correlate with the socialization processes, and if so, how they correspond to the program's overall pattern of development of students' orientations to nursing. After introducing another aspect of lateral relations, perspectives toward the student-nurse group, we shall look at data showing the correlation of involvement with professional development within each academic year.

Table 12-1. *Patterns of participation among student nurses by academic class (mean scores and standard deviations)*

Participations	Freshmen		Sophomores		Juniors		Seniors	
	M	SD	M	SD	M	SD	M	SD
Student Government Association	11.6	3.5	12.5	3.7	12.7	3.8	12.8	4.1
"Social relations within and across academic classes	13.1	3.2	13.6	3.2	13.4	3.3	11.4	3.4
Instrumental relations within and across academic classes	10.6	2.3	10.4	2.2	9.7	2.6	8.1	3.0
Mutual aid within academic class	3.4	1.0	3.7	1.1	3.7	1.1	3.8	1.0
Contacts with nonnursing female students	7.5	2.4	9.2	2.6	9.3	2.8	10.2	2.9

Note: The number of cases ranged from 115 to 126.

Perspectives toward the student group

Perspectives orient students to common ways of seeing their roles. The perspectives we shall discuss focused on the student-nurse role and would seem likely conduits for conveying definitions of nursing. Definitions transmitted by the student group might have supported or opposed the definitions stressed in the educational program, depending on whether the student group evolved norms to define a student image of nursing – consistent or not with that of the program – depending also on the extent of subjective insulation of students imposed by a belief that student nurses were different from other students. When one defines one's role in a social setting as distinct from the roles of others laterally placed, this perceived distinctiveness opens one to influences from those who are seen as establishing or legitimizing the distinctiveness.

Measures of perspectives toward the student-nurse group were constructed in the same way as were the indexes of participation. They were based on questions asking if respondents thought that student nurses as a group had their own special ways of viewing their experiences. Items on group views of college, classroom learning, and intellectual interests were scored together to provide a general measure of perspectives toward college. Items on group views of extracurricular activities, dating, and religious interests were scored together for a general measure of perspectives toward nonnursing roles. A measure of the perceived separation and distinctiveness of student nurses on campus was constructed from responses to a question that asked how the respondent thought other students saw student nurses.

Table 12-2 shows the patterning of perspectives by academic class. These data should be seen in the light of the observation made in Chapter 6 that student nurses entered the school seeing their status as distinctive and the finding in Chapter 8 that this view of themselves as distinct was carried throughout their education though it diminished somewhat. (The measure used here, unlike those in Chapters 6 and 8, is an index constructed from several questions.)

Table 12-2 shows that the perceived distinctiveness of the student nurse and her roles was not a function of sheer contact with nonnursing students. The freshman year, with its heavy concentration of academic study, provided the greatest opportunity for educationally related contact with other students; such opportunity was less in the sophomore year

Table 12-2. *Perspectives toward the student-nurse group by academic class (mean scores and standard deviations)*

Perspectives	Freshmen		Sophomores		Juniors		Seniors	
	M	SD	M	SD	M	SD	M	SD
Distinctive expectations of college	3.3	1.9	2.8	1.7	2.7	1.8	2.3	1.9
Distinctive expectations of societal roles	.8	.9	.7	.9	.6	.9	.6	1.0
Perceived social separation of student nurses	3.4	1.6	3.0	1.5	2.8	1.6	2.8	1.7

Note: Number of cases ranged from 115 to 126.

and largely absent in the junior and senior years. Yet the student nurses were more internally oriented in the freshman year than in any other year, and their internal orientations declined steadily throughout their education on one of the three perspectives and stabilized at a reduced level from the junior year onward on the others. These shifts in perspectives toward the student group were sharpest between the freshman and sophomore classes on two of the three measures. Clinical experience in actual nursing, begun in the sophomore year, seems to have lessened the perceived distinctiveness of the student-nurse group. Particularly in the freshman year, perceived distinctiveness may well have reflected relatedness to nursing. If so, it would seemingly promote socialization.

The student-nurse group and processes of socialization

Our expectation that participation in the student group would influence orientations to the role of the nurse finds little support in the data (see Table 12-3). Virtually all nursing education dealt directly in one way or another with the role of the nurse; students were taught nursing skills and trained in the hospital to learn the role. Yet the student group appears to have had no norms favoring either a holistic, patient-centered, or a bureaucratic conception of the role. For holistic views, only two of twenty correlations are statistically significant at a .05 level of probability: one among freshmen and one among seniors. For individualized patient care, four of twenty are significant at a .05 probability level. Although the ratio of actual to possible associations is slight, the facts that two are among seniors and two among freshmen may not be coincidental, particularly when we consider that different categories of involvement are significant for the two classes. Seniors who participated highly in the student-nurse group also endorsed individualized patient care, but there is no evidence to suggest a student group norm extolling individualized care. Had the student-nurse group carried a norm of individualized patient care, all academic classes should have been influenced by it. Instead, a kind of ideological selectivity appears to have occurred. Seniors took public-health nursing off campus, and they were at the end of their training when their thoughts turned outward to what they would do following graduation. Their situation was less conducive to participating in the student group than the situations of freshmen, sophomore, and juniors. What seniors would participate? One would expect them to be the most ideologically oriented. Similarly, we also

Table 12-3. *Participation in and perspectives toward the student-nurse group and orientations to the role of the nurse (Pearsonian correlations)*

	Holistic views				Individualized patient care			
	Fresh-men	Sopho-mores	Juniors	Seniors	Fresh-men	Sopho-mores	Juniors	Seniors
Participation in student-nurse group								
Student Government Association	.03	−.10	−.04	−.11	−.13	−.00	.02	.19[a]
"Social" relations within and across academic classes	.13	.02	.04	−.04	−.04	−.11	−.05	.18[a]
Instrumental relations within and across academic classes	.20[a]	.10	.05	−.10	−.05	.14	−.10	.07
Mutual aid within class	.05	.04	.12	−.01	.09	.01	.00	.11
Contacts with nonnursing female students	−.02	−.08	−.04	.08	−.09	−.08	.00	−.04
Perspectives toward the student-nurse group								
Distinctive expectation of college	−.06	−.12	.03	−.17[a]	.21[a]	−.13	−.13	−.01
Distinctive expectations of societal roles	.10	.07	.05	−.01	−.02	−.03	−.08	.06
Perceived social separation	−.02	.06	.04	.01	.15[a]	−.07	−.12	−.03

[a] Significance level ≤.05.

see no evidence that group norms affected freshmen. As you will recall, socialization moved attitudes away from, not toward, individualized patient care, and it was the most volatile of any process. Entering freshmen wanted to serve individual patients. The freshman year began to uproot holistic views of that service. Insular perspectives toward the student-nurse group appear to have supported retention of an individualized view of patient care through the freshman year. But once hospital experiences were begun, the support dissipated.

Table 12-4 presents data on the relation of participation in the student group and perspectives toward it to orientations to a place in the occupation. Its logic of presentation and manner of interpretation are the same as those of Table 12-3.

We have seen that the program did not develop orientations to a place in the occupation until the senior year. Before that year, little attention to a place in the occupation was evident in the program. Perhaps because of the relative lack of program emphasis, participation in the student group made a difference in orientations to collegialism. The difference was most marked for freshmen. All correlations for the freshman year were significant at the .05 probability level. Participation patterns associated with collegial orientations were high participation in student government, low participation with nonnursing female students, high interclass instrumental and social relations, and low in-class mutual aid. These last three may have prevented encapsulation within in-class cliques, particularly among freshmen who lived in an annex apart from upperclassmen. The dispersion of differences among the four academic classes suggests that no norms supporting collegialism developed, but that students whose participation directed their attention to the student-nurse body as a group were disposed also to collegialism. Low contact with non-nursing students fixed boundaries between student nurses and outsiders.

The influence of participation in the student-nurse group on collegialism did not carry over fully to orientations toward supervision and administration. Only six of twenty correlations reached a significance level of .05. These six instances were disproportionately in the freshman and senior classes: three among freshmen and two among seniors. Freshmen were generally disinclined to administration and supervision, and seniors inclined. Very likely, those freshmen who were favorable toward administration and supervision acquired their favorable views from high involvement with upperclassmen in the Student Government

Table 12-4. *Participations in and perspectives toward the student-nurse group and orientations to a place in the occupation (Pearsonian correlations)*

	Collegialism				Supervision and administration			
	Fresh-men	Sopho-mores	Juniors	Seniors	Fresh-men	Sopho-mores	Juniors	Seniors
Participations in student-nurse group								
Student Government Association	.17[a]	.08	.16[a]	.19[a]	.19[a]	.12	.27[a]	.15[a]
"Social" relations across academic classes	.24[a]	−.04	.02	.12	.17[a]	.09	.10	.06
Instrumental relations within and across academic classes	.16[a]	−.07	.17[a]	.15[a]	.24[a]	−.06	.12	.01
Mutual aid within class	−.18[a]	−.15[a]	−.02	.08	.09	.05	.03	−.03
Contacts with nonnursing female students	−.16[a]	−.08	−.12	−.26[a]	−.08	−.02	−.05	−.15[a]
Perspectives toward the student-nurse group								
Distinctive expectation of college	.17[a]	−.05	−.12	.23[a]	.06	−.08	−.10	.14
Distinctive expectations of societal roles	.03	−.07	−.21[a]	.17[a]	−.05	.02	−.05	.00
Perceived social separation	−.01	.04	−.09	−.03	−.02	.05	.13	.06

Association and from between-class instrumental and social relations. Many of these contacts were with seniors who were "big sisters" to freshmen. The nature of contacts between the academic classes probably changed in the sophomore year; clinical nursing started and students moved from the annex to the main nursing dormitory. Sophomores, juniors, and seniors shared experiences that stood freshmen apart from them. Wide contacts with the student group as a whole seem to have directed freshmen toward views typical of seniors.

Table 12-5 parallels the preceding two tables. Its variables are status identification, commitment, and attraction. The correlations that reach a significance level of .05 are hardly more than can be expected on a chance basis: Of thirty-two for each, only one reaches significance for attraction, three for status identification, and seven for commitment. The only pattern pertains to commitment. Not one of the seven significant correlations occurs in the junior year. Remember, the junior year curriculum consisted only of nursing courses. Specialization of the curriculum developed commitment, according to our argument. In the years immediately preceding and following the junior year, when the program had its main effect, involvements in the student group as a whole appear to have built slight investments in nursing. Or, alternatively and as conceivably, high commitment may have inclined students to participate in the student group.

Family life and work expectations

Chapter 6 has shown that even though entering students wanted to be nurses, they were considerably more oriented to home-centered female roles than to nursing work. Nursing degrees would prepare them to work when they wanted or in case they had to. Because female roles link individuals to the family rather than to work, a simple causal model would see orientations to female roles affecting professional development substantially and negatively. Such an effect, however, might well be reduced in amount or reversed in direction among nursing students because nursing is feminine in tradition (Strauss, 1966) and sex composition. It is the most female of all professions, with less than 3 percent of its employees male in 1960, during the period of this study (U.S. Bureau of the Census, 1963).

Nursing's feminine tradition and sex composition might conceivably help to accommodate the social definitions of the occupation to non-

Table 12-5. *Participations in and perspectives toward the student-nurse group and relatedness to nursing (Pearsonian correlations)*

	Status identification				Commitment				Attraction			
	Freshmen	Sophomores	Juniors	Seniors	Freshmen	Sophomores	Juniors	Seniors	Freshmen	Sophomores	Juniors	Seniors
Participations in student-nurse group												
Student Government Association	.06	.03	.06	.24[a]	−.01	.21[a]	.04	.21[a]	.09	.08	.03	.14
"Social" relations within and across academic classes	.09	.11	.06	.01	−.00	.05	−.05	.05	.09	−.11	.05	.04
Instrumental relations within and between academic classes	.14	.04	.00	.02	.02	.26[a]	−.08	.08	.08	.09	.05	.11
Mutual aid within class	.15[a]	−.02	−.07	−.01	.11	−.01	.09	.18[a]	.07	.04	.12	.22[a]
Contacts with non-nursing female students	.01	.11	.14	.07	.15[a]	.03	.13	.04	.09	.14	.01	.02
Perspectives toward the student-nurse group												
Distinctive expectation of college	.01	.03	.09	.03	.18[a]	−.11	−.01	.01	.08	.03	−.02	.12
Distinctive expectations of societal roles	−.05	−.09	.09	.01	.13	.05	.09	.15[a]	.12	−.02	−.00	.14
Perceived social separation	.15[a]	−.09	−.07	.07	−.02	−.13	−.04	.05	−.06	−.05	−.04	−.03

[a] Significance level ⩽.05.

work female roles so as to reduce subjective disparity of the sex identifications of work and family roles (cf. Epstein, 1970). Both predispositions to home-centered roles and the feminine tradition of nursing are embodied in a complex of domestic values, expressed in the occupation as in family relations along a nurturance dimension. Intentions to subordinate one's work to family life, or to accommodate them in other ways that keep family life as a central life value, might help sustain a nurturant view of the nursing role, thereby countering the program's development of bureaucratic orientations to nursing. Value compatibility of nursing and family roles cannot eliminate the objective difficulties of simultaneously enacting both roles, such as competing time demands (cf. Simpson and Simpson, 1969); but we have seen in Chapter 6 that student nurses chose the occupation partly because they considered it comparatively easy to combine it with family life. They did not see a nurse's work as overly demanding in time and commitments or emotional investments, and they saw its widely dispersed job market as an advantage.

Any way of accommodating family and work roles involves an arrangement of one's total configuration of roles. Therefore, commitment to nursing would seem likely to be related to the expected place of work and female roles in students' lives, especially among the extreme respondents who indicated the intentions of continuous full-time work or never working again after the birth of children. A predisposition toward family roles over work roles, by definition, involves a choice that sees the rewards of family life as overshadowing the rewards of work. A perfect negative correlation between predispositions toward work and toward family roles might be undercut, however, by the fact that most women not only expect to work before their families are begun, but also realize that they might have to work later whether or not they would prefer to return to work. To put aside completely as objectively valueless a work role for which one has been extensively trained seems unlikely. Even those students who intended not to work after the birth of children were likely to have put at least some psychological investment in nursing, as a resource upon which they might have to fall back in the future or which would provide knowledge and skills to benefit their performance in family-centered female roles.

We used two measures of orientations to work and female roles. These assessed students' anticipated accommodation of work and family roles, and the kinds of activities from which they expected to

Table 12-6. *Expected life satisfaction and family and work goals by academic class (in percent)*

	Entering Freshmen	Freshmen	Sophomores	Juniors	Seniors[a]
Anticipated work plans					
Not to work at all or stop at birth of first child	28.9	18.0	20.3	21.1	22.7
Work until first child return when youngest is over 8 years of age	42.2	48.4	50.8	39.1	29.7
Work until first child, return before youngest is 8 years of age	21.9	22.7	24.2	35.9	39.1
Continuous work, full or parttime or with minimal interruptions	7.0	10.9	4.7	3.9	7.8
Expected life satisfaction					
Work and career	18.8	9.4	7.0	5.5	3.1
Family life	65.6	82.8	87.5	89.1	88.3
Community and other participations	15.6	7.8	5.5	5.5	7.8

[a]N was 127 for seniors but 128 for all other classes.

realize their greatest satisfactions (work and career, family, and community and other participations). Table 12-6 presents data on accommodation of work and family roles as expressed in varying degrees of anticipated continuity of work, and data on expected life satisfaction, by academic year. (The question on continuity of work did not distinguish work in nursing from work in other occupations.)

A little less than a fifth of the entering freshmen looked to work and career for their main life satisfactions, but this figure fell rapidly during the freshman year and continued to drop in each succeeding year, along with a parallel rise in looking to family life for main life satisfaction. Although career as the expected principal source of satisfaction gave ground rapidly to family life early in students' education, anticipated patterns of accommodation of work and family roles changed little until the end of the junior year. The change involved mainly a shortening of the expected period of interruption of work by motherhood. Thus, during the course of their education, and especially in the freshman year, the minority of students who initially looked to careers or community participation for their chief satisfations came to rely more heavily on family life as a source of satisfaction.

Family life expectations and processes of socialization

As students went through their education, their family life expectations increasingly evidenced a fairly consistent relationship to each orientation (see Table 12-7), but the patterns unfolded in different years. By the end of the sophomore year a pattern had begun to form relating anticipated work plans to holistic views. The pattern was clearly evident at the end of the senior year: Students most extreme in expecting to subordinate work roles to family life were the most likely to have holistic views of patients, and those expecting to work continuously even when they had young children were the least holistic in their views of patients. Anticipated work patterns showed less overall association with orientations to individualized patient care, but one relation started to emerge at the end of the junior year: The students least oriented to work were the least oriented to individualized care, and the other three categories of students, all of whom intended to work, were very similar to each other.

To understand why these two patterns differed, it is helpful to recall that the individualized patient care scale measured how much the student would like to do special things for patients, most of which were over and above the required daily routine: tidying patients's rooms, making purchases for them, bringing them water, and other personal services, which provided contexts for understanding their needs. Holistic views of patients were measured with a scale of agreement or disagreement with statements about taking account of the total person in giving patient care and believing one had the authority to do so. A student might think the judgments mentioned in the holistic views index desirable but be unsure of her authority to make them; her primary and inescapable responsibility was to follow the instructions on patients' charts. Individualized patient care, in contrast, consisted of doing things the student definitely was authorized to do; the only impediment to these activities was lack of time.

Table 12-7. *Family life orientations and orientations to the role of the nurse by academic class (mean scores)*

Family life orientations	Holistic views					Individualized patient care				
	Entering Fresh-men	Fresh-men	Sopho-mores	Juniors	Seniors	Entering Fresh-men	Fresh-men	Sopho-mores	Juniors	Seniors
Anticipated work plans										
Not work at all or stop at birth of first child	5.03	4.35	2.89	3.00	2.70	4.46	4.13	3.85	2.93	2.10
Work until first child, return when youngest is over 8 years of age	4.78	3.17	2.80	2.52	2.48	4.15	3.95	3.75	3.24	3.15
Work until first child, return before youngest is 8 years of age	4.68	3.72	1.65	2.50	2.46	4.93	4.03	4.29	3.43	2.86
Continuous work, full- or part-time or with minimal interruptions	5.11	3.36	2.17	2.20	2.00	3.89	3.50	3.16	3.10	3.20
Expected life satisfaction										
Work and career	5.08	3.83	3.22	2.85	2.75	4.20	4.17	3.33	3.71	3.50
Family life	4.68	3.47	2.45	2.59	2.54	4.39	3.94	3.93	3.24	2.80
Community and other participations	4.85	3.80	2.43	2.57	1.90	4.60	3.80	3.71	2.57	2.50

The consistent findings concerning these orientations suggest that atypical plans modified slightly the program's influences on holistic views and orientations to individualized care, though in different ways. Students not intending to work, or not intending to work once they had married or had children, were relatively high in their endorsement of holistic views throughout their education; and in the senior year their average score on holistic views exceeded the norm of all seniors, and seniors who wanted to work continuously fell far below the class norm. The two categories of seniors who anticipated stopping work to rear children but resuming work later were very close to the class norm in their endorsement of holistic views. This pattern was almost reversed in the relation of work anticipations to individualized care: Students least oriented to work fell below the senior class norm and all other categories were very close to this norm.

What do these findings mean? If a student did not really expect a career as a nurse, she had a defense against the program's erosion of a view that gives the nurse the authority to make nursing decisions taking account of the whole patient. This approach to the role would seem particularly significant in the junior and senior years, when students had to comply with hospital routines and obey doctors' orders. The expectation that she would not have a career as a nurse allowed a student to react uninhibitedly to doing individualized services for patients. If she disliked such services, her lack of intention to work in nursing may have enabled her to feel no compunction in admitting her distaste for them.

The decline in expectation of deriving one's major life satisfaction from work was so sharp that only a handful of seniors held this expectation. As a result, we cannot confidently compare students who looked to family life with those who looked to careers for their chief satisfactions. The differences that did occur between them, however, tended to correspond by the senior year to differences associated with anticipated work patterns. On each orientation to the role of the nurse, seniors who looked to the family for their major life satisfaction fitted the modal pattern.

Table 12-8 gives data on how anticipated work plans and expected life satisfactions related to orientations to collegialism and to administration and supervision. Students who did not intend to work consistently over the four years averaged the lowest scores on collegialism. The same general pattern was evident with respect to orientations to ad-

Table 12-8. *Family life expectations and orientations to a place in nursing (mean scores)*

Family life expectations	Collegialism					Administration and supervision				
	Entering Fresh-men	Fresh-men	Sopho-mores	Juniors	Seniors	Entering Fresh-men	Fresh-men	Sopho-mores	Juniors	Seniors
Anticipated work plans										
Not work at all or stop at birth of first child	2.05	1.96	2.00	2.07	2.69	2.75	2.13	2.57	2.55	2.89
Work until first child, return when youngest is over 8 years of age	2.50	2.00	2.36	2.46	2.78	2.68	2.30	2.58	2.60	3.08
Work until first child, return before youngest is 8 years of age	2.96	2.03	2.35	2.41	3.14	3.11	2.41	2.67	2.72	3.34
Continuous work, full- or part-time or with minimal interruptions	2.89	1.57	3.16	2.40	3.20	2.11	2.50	2.83	2.40	3.30
Expected life satisfactions										
Work and career	2.79	1.83	3.00	1.71	3.00	3.12	1.83	2.11	3.14	3.25
Family life	2.30	1.96	2.27	2.39	2.94	2.59	2.37	2.68	2.57	3.14
Community and other participations	3.00	2.00	2.42	2.57	2.90	3.00	2.20	2.14	3.14	3.40

ministration and supervision. Students who did not intend to work were the least favorable toward administration and supervision. Expected life satisfaction was associated with orientations to collegialism in the same way as anticipated work patterns, but it was not related to supervision and administration. On both orientations, the intermediate categories consisting of students who expected to take time out for rearing children were split around the senior class average: 2.93 for collegialism and 3.16 for administration and supervision. (See Appendix C.) Orientations of students who expected to return to the labor force before their youngest child was eight corresponded closely to the orientations of their classmates who wanted to work continuously, whereas students who wanted to devote substantial time to motherhood were closer in orientations to their classmates who did not want to work at all. Anticipation of continuous work or a relatively short period out of the labor force for child rearing seemingly inclined students to collegialism and to administration and supervision. But the causal chain could have been in the other direction; if so, the anticipated accommodation would reflect socialization to collegialism and administration and supervision.

Whatever the causal chain, work plans were consistently related to orientations to the role of the nurse and to a place in nursing. Accommodations that emphasized family at the expense of work went with low orientations to collegialism and to supervision and administration. These are orientations that relate the student to the occupation of nursing as a collectivity, and the data suggest that women who devote themselves fully to the family separate themselves from occupational collectivities and commitments that might compete with involvement in the home. The next set of findings, on personal relatedness to the occupation, adds general support to this interpretation.

The sheer amount of work a student intended to do does not fully explain the relation of anticipated work patterns to processes of relatedness to nursing (Table 12-9). To be sure, the amount of work correlated with identification as a nurse, but the correlations were not uniform over the stages of education. The relations shifted from negative among entering freshmen, to positive among freshmen, to curvilinear among sophomores, and virtually disappeared among juniors and seniors. Students who wanted to devote their lives fully to family roles averaged the lowest status identification in their junior and senior years, as they had from the end of their freshman year, but students in

Table 12-9. Family life expectations and orientations to a place in nursing (mean scores)

Family life expectations	Status identification					Commitment					Attraction				
	Entering Fresh-men	Fresh-men	Sopho-mores	Juniors	Seniors	Entering Fresh-men	Fresh-men	Sopho-mores	Juniors	Seniors	Entering Fresh-men	Fresh-men	Sopho-mores	Juniors	Seniors
Anticipated work plans															
Not to work at all or stop at birth of first child	.22	.48	.80	.81	.79	3.27	2.26	3.54	2.81	3.14	3.16	3.22	3.31	1.96	2.27
Work until first child, return when youngest is over 8 years	.22	.53	.92	.98	1.00	3.35	3.38	3.77	3.98	4.10	3.54	3.42	3.09	3.12	2.95
Work until first child, return before youngest is 8 years	.17	.62	.94	.97	.96	2.64	3.55	3.74	4.06	4.76	3.78	3.37	3.48	3.28	3.06
Continuous work, full- or part-time or with minimal interruptions	.11	.64	.83	1.00	1.00	3.44	3.14	4.17	4.00	2.50	3.78	3.28	3.66	3.60	2.40
Expected life satisfactions															
Work and career	.20	.67	.78	.71	1.00	3.50	3.83	4.44	2.43	3.75	3.83	3.83	3.67	2.57	2.25
Family life	.24	.53	.90	.95	.94	3.16	3.03	3.67	3.82	4.06	3.35	3.25	3.22	2.98	2.78
Community and other participations	.05	.70	1.00	1.00	.90	2.85	4.10	3.71	4.14	3.20	3.70	3.90	3.29	2.85	2.70

the other work-expectation categories did not differ; all identified themselves as nurses.

Neither did anticipated work plans correlate uniformly or directly with commitment over the five stages of academic study. Had commitment simply reflected accommodation of family roles to work, then anticipated work plans should have correlated directly with commitment, and the correlations should have been uniform over the academic stages. They were not. Instead, seniors who intended to work continuously or not at all were lower in commitment than the intermediate categories of students who expected to take time out for motherhood. Students who did not want to work ranked lowest in commitment from the freshman year onward, but the average commitment of students who planned to work continuously fluctuated considerably for the five stages of education: Their commitment was highest among entering freshmen and lowest among seniors.

Essentially the same curvilinear pattern is also observed with respect to attraction. Consistently over the four-year period, students who did not want to work were the least attracted. There were no systematic patterns of difference in attraction among the three other categories of student nurses until the senior year, when the average attraction of seniors who wanted to work continuously dropped below that of the intermediate categories.

There was no consistent pattern of relationship between expected life satisfaction and any process of relatedness to nursing. This absence of pattern probably reflects the very mixed views regarding the accommodation of work and family roles among those students who looked to family life for their main satisfactions. Anticipated work patterns would seem likely to have much more to do with processes of personal relatedness to nursing than would expected life satisfaction, as is seen in the findings.

Taken together, the findings indicate two ways in which anticipated work plans modified the program's development of processes of personal relatedness to the occupation. The modal patterns were represented by the intermediate categories of students, who wanted to stop working when their children were young but return later; modifications of the modal pattern were among the extreme categories of students, who did not want to work or who wanted to work continuously. Those not intending to work appeared relatively immune to the program's influence on orientations and aspects of relatedness to the occupation, so that they could follow other dispositions more easily than if they had intended to work as nurses. They far exceeded the norm in holistic views of patients up through the senior year, yet they fell considerably below the norm in favorableness to individualized care. They had little desire for collegial involvement or taste for administrative and supervisory activities. Their relatedness to the occupation was less than that of other students. In all respects they changed the least of any work-anticipation category from entry into the school through completion of the senior year.

Wanting to work continuously also modified the modal pattern, in some ways similarly to not wanting to work and in other ways differently. Anticipation of continuous work strongly reinforced the program's influence in developing orientations that favored a bureaucratic role of the nurse and an elite administrative place in nursing, but it also increased enthusiasm for direct-patient care. Unlike the patterns of these two orientations among other categories of students, they went in opposite directions among students who wanted continuous work. These students saw the nurse as having little authority, but they endorsed individualized patient care. Perhaps this contradiction directed them away from nursing to other occupations for the kinds of careers they wanted.

Summary

Lateral relations differ from hierarchical ones in being equalitarian, personal, and ready transmitters of information and sentiment. These characteristics make them potential influences on socialization. But of the three we studied, two were not. These were participation in the tightly bonded student-nurse group and holding distinctive perspectives. The student-nurse group organized student nurses' participations, but participation in it was unrelated to their socialization. Distinctive perspectives toward college life and societal roles for nurses expressed in-group solidarity of the student-nurse group but had little effect on the socialization of students. Expectations regarding the accommodation of family life and work were the other lateral influence studied. They increasingly related to socialization processes as students moved through the program. Not wanting to work at all or wanting to work continuously modified the modal pattern of developing socialization typical of each academic class. We will comment further on these findings after we have reported on the influence of relations to the faculty and hospital groups.

13. Students' relations to the program, faculty, and hospital and their socialization

This chapter will continue the kind of analysis begun in the preceding one, looking this time at students' relations to the program and the faculty and to occupational groups in the hospital. Our objective, again, is to see if involvements with influence sources modified the aggregate patterns of socialization developed by the program. We shall first examine students' relations to the program and the faculty, describing our measures of these and then seeing if they were associated with socialization processes.

Relations to the program and the faculty

Chapters 9 and 10 have shown that processes of socialization developed in conjunction with shifts in the nature of the curriculum. The curriculum was rigidly structured with little opportunity for choice. All students were subject to the same objective constraints, yet not all of them perceived the curriculum identically or related to its objectives and the faculty with the same interest or affect. When the same mechanisms of socialization are built into the curriculum for all students, do socialization processes nevertheless differ in accordance with individual involvement with the program and the faculty? In other words, do personal feelings and interactions modify the structural impact of the program?

A student who strongly favors the objectives of a program is likely to seek out faculty members to discuss educational matters, over and above the required student-faculty contact. Faculty members presumably are glad to talk informally with this kind of student. Such eagerness would seem likely to sensitize the student to the orientations purveyed in the program's teachings and in its training situations. From this it might seem to follow that high approval of the program and involvement with the faculty should enhance the program's influence. We have seen, however, that training situations did not express the program's ideals, nor did the orientations generated by the curriculum's

196

educational experiences. These disparities would lessen the likelihood that involvements with the program and the faculty would develop only one kind of orientation. To expect students' attitudes to relate in only one way to orientations would ignore the divergence of ideology and role orientations.

Strong and favorable involvement with the program and the faculty would seem likely to support orientations to an integral place in the occupation. A subjective stance of eager compliance fits a person psychologically into an educational program in a way that is self-perpetuating. In so doing, it should direct the student to consider collective perspectives and to perceive the occupation as a salient entity, including its characteristic division of labor. Students strongly and favorably involved with the program and the faculty should also be highly oriented to collective occupational perspectives.

Similar reasoning leads to the expectation that involvement with the program and the faculty should enhance occupational status identification and commitment. Such involvements socially and psychologically encase students in the status of nurse. They produce heavy investments of time, energy, and emotion in becoming a nurse and may reduce sensitivity to the possibilities of other occupations. The rewards of high attraction to the program and the faculty might also support attraction to nursing as an occupation, something the program was unable to do for most students.

We constructed five indexes of involvement with the program and the faculty. They measured perceived importance of nursing curriculum activities for a nursing education, educational orientation mainly to nursing, use of the nursing faculty as an evaluative reference group, amount of contact with nursing faculty, and perceived academic standing within one's class in the university (i.e., not just in the nursing school class). These indexes, except class standing, were scored similarly to the ones pertaining to the student-nurse group. A low score on the index of educational orientation mainly to nursing indicated high regard for nonnursing academic study. The scoring of faculty as an evaluative reference group is described later in this chapter.

Table 13-1 shows the mean scores of students at the end of each academic year on the five indexes. Yearly mean changes tended to parallel changes in the structure and sequence of the program. In the junior year students became more oriented to nursing (as distinct from being oriented to both academic and nursing faculty and courses), whereas in

Table 13-1. *Faculty and program involvement by academic class (mean scores and standard deviations)*

Orientations and relations	Freshmen		Sophomores		Juniors		Seniors	
	M	SD	M	SD	M	SD	M	SD
Nursing faculty as evaluative reference group	4.0[a]	.0	3.8	.9	3.6	1.0	3.6	.9
Contact with nursing faculty	2.4	1.4	4.5	1.5	4.6	1.5	5.0	1.5
Educationally oriented mainly to nursing	6.0	1.6	6.8	1.6	7.3	1.8	7.4	1.5
Perceived importance of nursing curriculum	3.5	1.7	3.6	1.5	3.8	1.7	3.8	1.5
Perceived class standing	3.4	2.5	3.5	3.0	4.1	2.8	4.8	2.8

[a]The N for this variable was 78, because pilot class freshmen were not asked the questions used to construct the index in their freshmen year. Other N's ranged from 112 to 127.

the freshman and sophomore years, with their heavier concentration on the academic part of students' education, students were less likely to be oriented only to nursing. Similarly, the junior year produced a slight increase in favorableness to the nursing curriculum. It also reduced students' appreciation of the nursing faculty as an evaluative reference group concurrently with the introduction of specialty nursing, which greatly increased the resemblance of the student-nurse role to the professional-nurse role. With the beginning of clinical experience in the hospital under nursing faculty supervision in the sophomore year, students' contacts with the nursing faculty increased sharply over the freshman year; such contacts continued to increase, though the rate of increase was less, during the junior and senior years. Perceived class standing rose annually and considerably after the sophomore year, either because student nurses' academic competition with nonnursing students vanished or because clinical and specialty nursing gave them added self-confidence.

Program and faculty involvement and socialization processes.

Table 13-2 shows little relationship between involvements with the program and faculty and orientations to the role of the nurse, although there were some relationships that seem worthy of comment. Only three of twenty correlations of involvements with the program and faculty with holistic views toward patients were significant at the .05 level. The facts that two of the three involved perceived academic class standing, that it correlated negatively with holistic views, and that the two were for the freshman and junior classes may be noteworthy. Remember that the program began to uproot holistic views in the freshman year, and we think it did so principally through its nursing course in interpersonal relations. Students who saw their academic class rank as low may have failed to learn the lessons of the nursing course. Their low academic rank may have helped sustain their holistic views when their classmates were turning away from theirs. A similar situation may have happened again in the junior year. Specialty nursing was started; students were expected to give nursing care to the *whole* patient, but their training roles were geared to bureaucratic specialty nursing. Perhaps the students who perceived their academic standing as relatively low tried to compensate for their low rank by holding on to nurturant conceptions of patients.

Table 13-2. *Program and faculty involvements and orientations to the role of the nurse (Pearsonian correlations)*

Program and faculty involvements	Holistic views				Individualized patient care			
	Freshmen	Sophomores	Juniors	Seniors	Freshmen	Sophomores	Juniors	Seniors
Nursing faculty as evaluative reference group	b	−.04	.08	−.16[a]	b	−.11	.02	−.02
Contact with nursing faculty	.02	−.04	.04	−.05	.11	.06	.02	.06
Educationally oriented to nursing	−.02	.01	.11	−.04	.03	.01	.18[a]	.06
Perceived importance of nursing curriculum	−.02	.01	.01	−.01	.00	.08	.19[a]	.13
Perceived class standing	−.19[a]	−.14	−.16[a]	−.06	−.12	−.15[a]	−.06	−.12

[a] Significance level ≤.05.
[b] Correlations could not be computed for freshmen for the variable, nursing faculty as an evaluative group, because there was no variation in students' scores. All the freshmen gave the same answers to the questions that composed the index.

No aspect of program and faculty involvement was consistently related to orientations to individualized patient care. Only three of the twenty correlations were significant at the .05 level. Two of these occurred in the junior year, the year when the program began to redirect orientations consistently away from individualized care despite its contrary ideology. The perceived importance of the nursing curriculum and the educational orientation mainly to nursing may have helped students withstand resocialization away from individualized care, but only in the junior year.

Favorable attitudes toward the curriculum and high class standing were associated consistently with high collegialism from the beginning to the end of the educational program, and high evaluation of academic study and contact with faculty were correlated with collegialism in two of the four years (Table 13-3). Though fewer and less consistent, the significant correlations with administration and supervision generally correspond to those with collegialism. Altogether, these findings suggest that involvement with the program and faculty helped to develop orientations that embody nursing as a collective entity.

Table 13-4 presents data on faculty and program involvement and processes of relatedness to nursing. Involvements correlated more often with attraction than with commitment or status identification: Correlations that reached .05 significance levels were nine, five, and six respectively with these processes, of a possible twenty apiece. The numerous correlations of involvements with attraction probably resulted from the program's failure to develop attraction, whereas it did develop commitment and status identification. Six of the significant correlations showed two variables' continuing relationships to attraction from the sophomore year through the senior year. These variables were the use of the faculty as an evaluative reference group and an educational orientation mainly to nursing. Both of these persistent correlations support our theory of how occupational attraction develops. An educational orientation mainly to nursing sets it psychologically apart from other pursuits. Using the faculty as an evaluative reference group opens students to its sentiments directed to nursing.

Though only about a fourth of the correlations with commitment and with status identification were statistically significant, all the involvements entering into these correlations supported the two processes in ways consistent with our theory. Especially noteworthy are the correlations of perceived high class standing with commitment in the soph-

Table 13-3. *Program and faculty involvements and orientations to a place in nursing (Pearsonian correlations)*

Program and faculty involvements	Collegialism				Administration and supervision			
	Freshmen	Sophomores	Juniors	Seniors	Freshmen	Sophomores	Juniors	Seniors
Nursing faculty as evaluative reference group	b	.10	-.10	-.02	b	.17[a]	.04	-.07
Contact with nursing faculty	.00	.17[a]	.05	.16[a]	.13	.17[a]	.08	.09
Educationally oriented mainly to nursing	-.28[a]	-.19[a]	-.07	-.02	-.01	-.18[a]	-.02	.06
Perceived importance of nursing curriculum	.34[a]	.18[a]	.20[a]	.16[a]	.10	.05	.16[a]	.16[a]
Perceived class standing	.23[a]	.22[a]	.30[a]	.17[a]	.01	.08	.08	.09

[a] Significance level ≤.05.
[b] Correlations could not be computed because of lack of variance in the independent variable.

Table 13-4. *Program and faculty involvements and relatedness to nursing (Pearsonian correlations)*

Program and faculty involvements	Status identification				Commitment				Attraction			
	Fresh-men	Sopho-mores	Juniors	Seniors	Fresh-men	Sopho-mores	Juniors	Seniors	Fresh-men	Sopho-mores	Juniors	Seniors
Nursing faculty as evaluative reference group	b	-.06	.11	.16[a]	b	.05	.11	-.09	b	.15[a]	.15[a]	.15[a]
Contact with nursing faculty	.01	.16[a]	.07	.09	.17[a]	.04	-.02	.07	.08	-.03	-.00	.13
Educationally oriented mainly to nursing	.17[a]	.08	.12	.19[a]	.10	.06	.23[a]	.10	.06	.24[a]	.16[a]	.21[a]
Perceived importance of nursing curriculum	-.07	.03	.11	.14	-.06	-.00	.11	.22[a]	.12	.03	.13	.25[a]
Perceived class standing	.15[a]	.08	.17[a]	.01	.01	.15[a]	-.02	.15[a]	-.15[a]	-.28[a]	-.04	.05

[a] Significance level ≤.05.
[b] Correlations could not be computed because there was no variance in the independent variable.

omore and senior years – years that preceded and followed the aggregate rise of commitment in the junior year. High academic standing almost certainly reflected an investment in nursing beyond that which arose from the curriculum's concentration on nursing courses. In the junior year, the program's impact was undoubtedly reinforced by an educational orientation mainly to nursing; such an orientation added subjective value to the junior year's almost total specialization in nursing.

Orientations to groups in the hospital

Hospital training brought students together with three important groups: patients, doctors, and nurses. We have seen in Chapter 6 that entering students' conceptions of nursing rested on strong orientations to patients and physicians. Students wanted to help patients and work with physicians; doing these things was nursing to them. When they began clinical training as sophomores, they encountered the scalar and functional divisions of health personnel. The personnel did not work together as people united in a common endeavor but through formalized occupational roles and modes of communication. The nurse–doctor relationship was organized more by the patient's chart than as a person-to-person handmaiden relationship. But this was not all the students saw or experienced. More important was their status vis-à-vis the hospital groups. As student nurses, they were fitted into the complex organization that included nurses, doctors, and patients. They were subclassified within nursing by their student status. Their access to nurses and doctors was kept to a minimum or made formal and distant by the fact that their performances in the student-nurse hospital role were under the supervision and authority of their faculty. It was through this status and authority maze that they perceived nurses and physicians.

Their access to the role of the nurse increased as they moved out of the sophomore year, having learned core skills; the functional difference between student nurses and hospital nurses was much less in the junior and senior years than in the sophomore year. But a complex status difference remained. Student nurses lacked the full status that hospital nurses enjoyed; they were merely students. Yet their student status was in a collegiate program, and its being collegiate gave them a prestige gain over most of the hospital nurses because they would receive bachelor's degrees. Although student nurses were not yet able to claim objectively the status of nurse, they were being educated for elite positions within nursing; moreover, the fact that their education was in an expensive private university embellished their student status with social class privilege that most of the hospital nurses had never had and would never have.

The duality in student nurses' status in the hospital vis-à-vis hospital nurses was matched by a similar duality in patients' positions vis-à-vis the student nurses' role. The genuineness of the roles of patients legitimized student nurses' clinical training as real-life experience; but at the same time, student nurses were supposed to view the patients as educational resources – that is, as providers of opportunities to practice nursing skills. As students gained increased access to the duties of the nursing role, the configurations of their activities changed and brought corresponding changes in the nature of their attention to patients. Sophomore students were taught core nursing skills piecemeal; their assignments focused on particular skills and procedures. In such a situation, the patient looms very centrally as the object of nursing activities. A skill is practiced on a patient, and it is the patient's presence that makes the exercise authentic. As students' access to the role increases to include more coordination of activities and more conscious linking of one's activities with those of other persons' roles, one's view of the patient seems likely to undergo a subtle but fundamental change. The focus shifts from the individual patient to the organization of routines to care for many patients simultaneously. The student adapts her performance to hospital routine, which gains primacy over the individual patient.

Students' clinical experiences were in the hospital and they were functionally a part of its division of labor, but they were not of the hospital. They drew on ward routines in learning nursing care, and their work was fitted into the organization of the nursing service; but the faculty wanted to protect them from being corrupted by the poor nursing practices they might encounter. At the same time, the faculty wanted them to learn to work with the hospital's occupational groups, including its nurses. To this latter end, faculty members talked about the importance of students' being a part of a nursing team; but the team idea was an abstract slogan and did not correspond to a functional grouping that might serve as an educational setting, let alone a system to give meaning and context to students' experience. Students' activities were supervised on the spot by their faculty, who were not a part of the hospital nursing service. (An exception was in public-health nursing, which did not occur in the hospital.) The patient's chart was the medium of regularized communication between the students and the hospital nurses and doctors; it was also the method of coordinating students' assignments with the hospital nursing service. The complexity of functional and status relations in the hospital created tensions for both hospital nurses and students.

In so complex a situation, how did students perceive the hospital groups? Students might perceive the groups in many ways, but two seem particularly pertinent to their socialization. Even though students did not have regularized interactions with these groups, they nevertheless were in physical proximity if not social contact with them. Students also knew that these were the groups that got the work of the hospital done, and that their own experiences were set within the work context of these groups. It seems highly likely that under such conditions students would orient to hospital groups as evaluative reference groups, desiring their members' approval of their activities in the role of the nurse and fearing their reprimands. Knowing that these groups were the objects or performers of the core functions of the hospital, students undoubtedly had views regarding the educational importance of contacts with them.

Our remaining examination of findings will look at students' perceptions of the importance of contacts with physicians and hospital nurses for their education, and at their use of physicians, hospital nurses, and patients as evaluative reference groups in judging how well they were performing.

When we ask about the importance of hospital groups as evaluative reference groups, we are inquiring about an expansion of the seeking of approval to extend beyond the school and its authority system. Does expansion of the number and variety of groups one wants to please invite uncertainty about the quality of one's work (cf. Merton and Kitt, 1950)? It seems reasonable to think it might, especially when the sum of the added reference groups is superior to students in status, knowledge, and experience. Does the use of such evaluative reference groups relate differently to socialization processes among students at different stages of an educational program, who differ in knowledge and experience?

The other attitude we shall examine pertains to the importance of contacts with hospital physicians and hospital nurses for nursing education. Does a belief that relations with these groups are important in her education lead a student to take the occupational world of nursing as a context for judging her progress toward being a nurse and as a context for evaluating places in the occupation? Does it further her orientations to the occupation of nursing as a collegial entity, her self-identification as a nurse, her commitment and attraction to nursing?

The evaluative reference group index was made up of two questions: From whom would the students most appreciate receiving praise if they had done something good on the ward, and from whom would they be most bothered by receiving blame if they had done something wrong. Six possible evaluative reference groups were listed: patients, nursing instructor, attending physician, staff nurse, another student nurse, and oneself. The respondent was asked to rank these six on appreciation for doing something good on a ward and on the meaning of blame for making a mistake on a ward. The two scores were combined to form a single index.

We constructed separate measures of relatedness to hospital nurses and doctors. The relatedness indexes for doctors and nurses were composed of questions asking students the importance of contacts with each group for their education and the desire for contact with them.

Table 13-5 presents the mean scores of students by academic class for use of doctors, nurses, and patients as evaluative reference groups and for perceived educational importance of contacts with doctors and nurses. It shows that doctors and patients, followed by nurses, were highly significant evaluative groups for freshmen but that with hospital experience in the sophomore year the uses of all three groups as evaluative reference groups dropped markedly; the drop was especially pronounced for doctors and nurses. The extent of use of these three groups as evaluative reference groups changed little from the sophomore through the senior year. In contrast, perceived educational importance of contacts with nurses and doctors was affected little by increasing access to the role of nurse. In the junior year, when specialty nursing began, the perceived importance of contacts rose slightly, but it dropped somewhat in the senior year.

Orientations to groups in the hospital and socialization processes

Students' perceptions of the importance of contacts with hospital groups were essentially unrelated to their orientations. (See Table 13-6

Table 13-5. *Orientations to groups in the hospital by academic class (mean scores and standard deviations)*

Orientations to groups in the hospital	Freshmen		Sophomores		Juniors		Seniors	
	M	SD	M	SD	M	SD	M	SD
Physicians as evaluative group	5.8	1.0	1.9	2.0	2.3	1.8	2.1	1.9
Educational benefit of contact with physicians	5.2	1.4	5.1	1.5	6.2	1.4	5.8	1.5
Nurses as evaluative group	3.9	.5	2.5	1.0	2.6	1.1	2.8	1.1
Educational benefit of contact with nurses	5.5	1.3	5.2	1.5	5.9	1.6	5.6	1.6
Patients as evaluative group	5.8	1.0	3.1	2.0	3.1	2.1	2.8	2.1

Note: N's for freshmen ranged from 69 to 82 because the pilot class was not asked the questions used to construct the indices in their freshman year. In the other classes, N's ranged from 117 to 127.

Table 13-6. *Orientations to hospital groups and to the role of the nurse (Pearsonian correlations)*

Orientations to groups in the hospital	Holistic views				Individualized patient care			
	Fresh-men	Sopho-mores	Juniors	Seniors	Fresh-men	Sopho-mores	Juniors	Seniors
Physicians as evaluative group	−.09	.04	.07	.16[a]	.13	−.06	−.11	−.09
Educational benefit of contact with physicians	.12	.08	.17[a]	.09	.11	.15[a]	.01	.10
Nurses as evaluative group	−.08	−.01	.10	−.10	.01	−.10	−.06	.08
Educational benefit of contact with nurses	.09	.01	.06	.10	.18[a]	.15[a]	.27[a]	.11
Patients as evaluative group	−.03	.00	.12	.12	−.03	.12	.03	.14

[a]Significance level ≤.05.

and Table 13-7.) There is only one consistent pattern among the eighty correlations. Students who thought contacts with hospital nurses benefited their education tended also to endorse individualized patient care through their junior year, but the relationship faded in the senior year. We conclude from the overall pattern that hospital groups did not transmit opinions to student nurses about the role of the nurse or the occupation of nursing. Groups in the hospital did not directly support or compete with the program in developing orientations.

The findings on perceived educational value of contacts with hospital nurses might appear to contradict our analysis in Part II. We reasoned there that training in the hospital, with its stress on specific skills and routine procedures, moved students away from an individualized care orientation toward a bureaucratic view that fitted the hospital's authority lines and formalized division of labor. We shall comment later on this apparent discrepancy when we discuss findings that show orientations to hospital nurses and doctors were associated with personal relatedness to the occupation in ways similar to the association with individualized care we have just reported.

Although students' perceptions of hospital groups had little influence on orientations, they did influence relatedness to nursing. Table 13-8 shows fairly consistent patterns: The use of hospital nurses and doctors as evaluative reference groups, but not the use of patients, went with low relatedness to the occupation. The relationship involving patients as a reference group was very different from this: Using them as an evaluative reference group correlated with commitment and attraction in the junior and senior years but not in the earlier years. In the junior and senior years, the use of patients as a reference group was associated with relatedness to the occupation in the opposite direction from the use of doctors and, especially, nurses. Once specialty nursing had begun, students highly oriented to patients as an evaluative reference group exceeded their class norms in commitment and attraction, whereas students highly oriented to hospital nurses and doctors fell below class norms in status identification, commitment, and attraction.

Our other main variable concerning students' orientations to hospital groups is the perceived educational benefit of contacts with physicians and nurses. Table 13-8 shows that seeing high educational benefit in contacts with nurses was consistently associated with commitment to the occupation and to attraction from the sophomore year onward. These relationships appear offhand to run counter to the ones concern-

Table 13-7. *Orientations to hospital groups and to a place in nursing (Pearsonian correlations)*

Orientations to hospital groups	Collegialism				Administration and supervision			
	Fresh-men	Sopho-mores	Juniors	Seniors	Fresh-men	Sopho-mores	Juniors	Seniors
Physicians as evaluative group	.21[a]	−.03	−.16[a]	−.12	.08	−.02	.11	−.20[a]
Educational benefit of contact with physicians	−.10	.15[a]	−.06	.09	−.15[a]	.05	.11	.02
Nurses as evaluative group	.12	−.09	−.09	−.02	.04	−.04	−.06	.12
Educational benefit of contact with nurses	−.27[a]	−.03	−.08	.06	−.15[a]	.00	.09	.06
Patients as evaluative group	.08	.02	−.17[a]	.11	.05	.02	−.07	.11

[a]Significance level ≤.05.

Table 13-8. Orientations to hospital groups and relatedness to nursing (Pearsonian correlations)

Orientations to hospital groups	Status identification				Commitment				Attraction			
	Freshmen	Sophomores	Juniors	Seniors	Freshmen	Sophomores	Juniors	Seniors	Freshmen	Sophomores	Juniors	Seniors
Physicians as evaluative group	-.18[a]	-.10	.04	-.10	-.07	-.13	-.10	-.02	.07	.10	-.20[a]	-.09
Educational benefit of contact with physicians	.04	-.16[a]	.13	.03	.13	-.05	.06	.22[a]	.03	.03	.03	.24[a]
Nurses as evaluative group	-.21[a]	.02	-.06	.03	.03	.12	-.12	-.15[a]	.12	-.07	-.17[a]	-.17[a]
Educational benefit of contact with nurses	.01	-.02	.12	.16[a]	.28[a]	.21[a]	.23[a]	.23[a]	.09	.18[a]	.23[a]	.27[a]
Patients as evaluative group	-.18[a]	-.02	.08	.21[a]	.03	-.13	.16[a]	.15[a]	.06	-.09	.23[a]	.17[a]

[a]Significance level ⩽.05.

ing use of doctors and nurses as evaluative reference groups, in which the relationships between orientations to hospital occupational groups and relatedness to nursing were negative rather than positive. The key to the puzzle seems to be the very different nature of the different orientations to the occupational groups. As we have described, students' position in the hospital was complex, involving more than one system and principle of status ordering and authority. Their structurally complex situation may help to explain the divergent influences of orientations to hospital groups on personal relatedness to nursing. Let us see how this might have been so.

To want contact with an occupational group, and to see educational benefit in such contact, allow the perception of oneself from the viewpoint of the occupation's work context. For a student nurse, a perceptual vantage point of this kind should enhance identification with the status of nurse, help create conditions conducive to occupational commitment, and link her status to the hospital groups so as to build the perceptually solidary division of labor we identified in Chapter 3 as facilitating occupational attraction. (Equally plausible, of course, is the possibility that a student already identifying as a nurse, committed to nursing, and attracted to it is predisposed to want contact with hospital occupational groups.) On the other hand, to look to these groups for evaluation of one's performance suggests a lack of self-confidence, which might logically be reflected in undeveloped identification as a nurse, low occupational commitment, and low occupational attraction. When student nurses entered the junior year and started carrying out an integrated set of patient care activities, their use of patients as an evaluative reference group began to show a positive relation to commitment and attraction. Not until students' training roles permitted them to fit the care of patients into an organized framework of hospital work were evaluations by patients fitted perceptually into a functional context of nursing.

The fitting of patients' evaluations into the context of the training role appears to have been facilitated by the nature of the patient–student-nurse relationship. The use of a doctor or a nurse as an evaluative referee subjected the student to judgment by an expert. The patient, however, had less basis for evaluating nursing techniques than the student had. Patients' conditions and feelings, not an understanding they might have of the nursing role, were what underlay their judgments of student performance. In using themselves – the alter of the student role – as the basis for judgments, the patients may have helped the student modify her behavior to take their judgments into account. The definition of specialty nursing roles begun in the junior year was sufficiently flexible to enable the student to adapt her behavior to patients' expectations. Because she could act confidently in incorporating patients' judgments into her decisions, the use of patients as an evaluative reference group did not call forth the feelings of uncertainty about her performance that seem to have been evoked by use of occupational experts as reference groups. With patients, she was the expert.

Summary

This chapter and the preceding one have examined involvements with potential influence sources that were connected with the study of nursing at Duke but were not built directly into the curriculum. These included students' lateral relations and expectations of family life, their involvements and attitudes pertaining to the faculty and the program, and their orientations to groups in the hospital (though not their actual interactions with hospital groups).

Our analyses in these chapters point to three general conclusions. First, varying involvement with potential influence sources did not substantially alter the overall pattern of socialization shaped by the school's curriculum and its experiences. But within this overall pattern, some of the variations in involvement with potential influence sources were associated with deviations from aggregate norms; some of them reinforced the program's influence on socialization processes, others reduced it. Deviations generally did not survive beyond the academic year of their occurrence. Data not reported here fail to show any consistent relation between individual involvements and change in students' orientations or relatedness to nursing from one year to the next.

A second conclusion is that the influence sources were related to different socialization processes. Involvements in the student group showed few consistent relationships to socialization, except for orientations to collegialism. Orientations to hospital groups and expectations of family life were related fairly consistently to processes of occupational relatedness, but less so to occupational orientations. Involvements with the faculty and program related more consistently to orientations and to occupational relatedness than did involvement with any other potential influence source.

Third, the processes of socialization differed with respect to the influence sources that were most related to them.

All of these general conclusions are what we expected. Patterns shaped by the educational program were not sharply changed by varying patterns of involvement with nonprogram influence sources. Potential influence sources were not alike in their relationships with socialization processes, because different processes were developed by different conditions.

It may be helpful to summarize these two chapters' analyses in tabular form, shifting from a main focus on the influence sources to a focus on the socialization processes. Table 13-9 summarizes the data from these chapters that bear on orientations to the role of the nurse, Table 13-10 concerns orientations to a place in the occupation, and Table 13-11 treats processes of personal relatedness to the occupational role. In these summaries the reader should keep in mind that we used differences in means of categories to infer associations for family life expectations but correlations for all other variables.

Table 13-9. *Summary of associations between students' involvements with potential influence sources and orientations to the role of the nurse*

	Freshmen		Sophomores		Juniors		Seniors	
	Holistic views	Individualized patient care	Holistic views	Individualized patient care	Holistic views	Individualized patient care	Holistic views	Individualized patient care
Participation in student-nurse group								
Student Government Association								+
"Social" relations mainly between classes								+
Instrumental relations mainly between classes	+							
Within class mutual aid								
Low nonnursing coed contact								
Perspectives toward student nurse group								
Distinctive expectations of college		+						
Distinctive expectations of societal roles								
Perceived social separation		+	−				−	
Orientations to the future								
Career as a main life satisfaction	+	+				+		+
Goal of continuous work		−	−		−		−	+
Program and faculty involvements								
Nursing faculty as evaluative group						+	−	
High contact with faculty						+		
Weak academic orientation						+		
Nursing curriculum highly important					−			
Above average class standing	−			−				

Table 13-9 (*cont.*)

	Freshmen		Sophomores		Juniors		Seniors	
	Holistic views	Individualized patient care	Holistic views	Individualized patient care	Holistic views	Individualized patient care	Holistic views	Individualized patient care
Groups in the hospital								
Physicians as evaluative group							+	
Educational benefit of physician contact				+	+			
Nurses as evaluative group								
Educational benefit of nurse contact				+		+		
Patients as evaluative group		+						

217

Table 13-10. *Summary of associations between students' involvements with potential influence sources and orientations to a place in the occupation*

	Freshmen		Sophomores		Juniors		Seniors	
	Colle-gialism	Adminis-tration and super-vision	Colle-gialism	Adminis-tration and super-vision	Colle-gialism	Adminis-tration and super-vision	Colle-gialism	Adminis-tration and super-vision
Participations in the student group								
Student Government Association	+	+					+	+
Social relations mainly between classes	+	+			+	+	+	+
Instrumental relations mainly between classes	+	+			+			
Within class mutual aid	−		−		+		+	
Low nonnursing coed contact	+						+	+
Perspectives toward student-nurse group								
Distinctive expectations of college	+						+	
Distinctive expectations of societal roles					−		+	
Perceived social separation							+	
Orientations to the future								
Career as a main life satisfaction	−		+	−	−	+	+	
Goal of continuous work	+		+	+	+		+	+

Table 13-10 (*cont.*)

	Freshmen		Sophomores		Juniors		Seniors	
	Colle-gialism	Adminis-tration and super-vision	Colle-gialism	Adminis-tration and super-vision	Colle-gialism	Adminis-tration and super-vision	Colle-gialism	Adminis-tration and super-vision
Program and faculty involvements								
Nursing faculty as evaluative group								
High contact with faculty			+	+			+	
Weak academic orientation	–		–	–				
Nursing curriculum highly important	+		+	+	+	+	+	+
Above average class standing	+		+		+		+	
Groups in the hospital								
Physicians as evaluative group	+				–			–
Educational benefit of physician contact		–						
Nurses as evaluative group			+					
Educational benefit of nurse contact		–						
Patients as evaluative group	–				–			

Table 13-11. *Summary of associations between students' involvements with potential influence sources and processes of personal relatedness to nursing*

	Freshmen			Sophomores			Juniors			Seniors		
	Status identification	Commitment	Attraction	Status identification	Commitment	Attraction	Status identification	Commitment	Attraction	Status identification	Commitment	Attraction
Participation in student-nurse group												
Student Government Association												
"Social" relations mainly between classes					+					+	+	
Instrumental relations mainly between classes					+							
Within class mutual aid	+										+	+
Low nonnursing coed contact		+										
Perspectives toward student-nurse group												
Distinctive expectations of college		+										
Distinctive expectations of societal roles												
Perceived social separation	+										+	
Orientation toward the future												
Career as a main life satisfaction	+	+	+	+	+	+	+	+	−	+	−	
Goal of continuous work	+	+		+	+			+	+	+	−	−

Table 13-11 (*cont.*)

	Freshmen			Sophomores			Juniors			Seniors		
	Status identification	Commitment	Attraction	Status identification	Commitment	Attraction	Status identification	Commitment	Attraction	Status identification	Commitment	Attraction
Program and faculty involvements												
Nursing faculty as evaluative group												
High contact with faculty		+		+		+			+	+		+
Weak academic orientation	+					+		+	+	+		+
Nursing curriculum highly important											+	+
Above average class standing	+		−		+	−	+				+	
Groups in the hospital												
Physicians as evaluative group	−								−			
Educational benefit of physician contact				−					−		+	+
Nurses as evaluative group	−										−	−
Educational benefit of nurse contact		+			+	+		+	+	+	+	+
Patients as evaluative group	−							+	+	+	+	+

221

PART IV
Implications: Basic Patterns of Socialization

14. Some reconsiderations of occupational socialization

Our main effort in this study has been to develop a synthetic model of socialization to deal with issues in the field and to explore its utility in a case study of a collegiate school of nursing. In this concluding chapter we assess the usefulness of our model and findings for the study of occupational socialization and suggest implications for professional schools and for the occupation of nursing.

Studying occupational socialization

As we discussed in Chapter 1, two fundamentally different views of socialization have divided studies of the phenomenon; the research in each tradition has not benefited from the other's insights. The division of research into separate traditions is not, however, the only or even the major reason for lack of cumulativeness of research. Studies within each tradition have built very little on one another. We think the essential impediments to cumulative research have been the loose use of the notion of socialization and the failure to perceive the variety of implicit meanings sometimes attached to it. Studies have used the concept globally, not recognizing its multidimensional nature.

Our study has attempted to clarify the concept of occupational socialization by specifying its multidimensionality. We have shown that it involves learning skills and knowledge of the occupation, developing orientations to occupational roles and to a place in the occupation, and relating the person to the occupation. Each dimension consists of distinct processes, and these were developed by different conditions. The timing and stability of their development appeared to depend on the program's timing of students' experiences. The interrelations of processes to form coherent dimensions also varied. In some cases they cohered from the start and their coherence was strengthened with the development of each process, but in other instances, especially that of orientations to the occupational role, the eventual coherence of dimen-

225

sions required the disentanglement of some processes from others along with the development of each. These findings argue that a multidimensional view of occupational socialization should be used and that it should be a dynamic and processual view.

Studies that focus only on a limited range of aspects of socialization, studied at one or two points in time, may capture only temporary reactions to immediate situations, which future events may replace with more stable behaviors and orientations. Studies that use before-and-after designs to indicate amounts of socialization by observing the differences may distort its essential nature; they impose a conception of simple growth on processes whose development may entail displacement of earlier states, realignment of processes, or other developmental processes not captured in a model of unidimensional cumulation. Designs that specify predetermined behaviors or orientations as indicators of the direction and extent of socialization may obscure its very directionality; they narrow the field of vision to exclude behaviors and orientations not foreseen by the researcher or by the socializing agents. Thus, a researcher may conclude that socialization has failed to occur when, in fact, extensive socialization has occurred in directions other than those anticipated by the sociologist or the designers of the educational program. As we have seen in the instance of the nursing students we studied, the direction of development, particularly the development of orientations to the occupational role, may diverge from the official ideology of the occupation and also from the original expectations of its students. Our research has shown the importance of avoiding a static, unidimensional or unidirectional conception of a complex processual phenomenon composed of interrelated processes.

Nature of socialization processes

Socialization is commonly conceived as learning the behaviors, skills, and outlooks that prepare one to perform in a role. Such a conception makes the individual the significant unit in the process, with the outcome seen as evidence of how well the learning has succeeded. Our findings suggest the value of looking at socialization not as individual learning but as occupational recruitment. Arrangements of role options attached student nurses to the occupation.

Orientations were learned, but to say they were learned tells little about the process. Students learned many expectations of behavior.

They used some of these to inform their behavior toward the occupation and its roles but ignored or put aside others. Therefore, the significant questions are why and how students incorporated into their behavior some of the things they learned and rejected others, so that only a portion of their learnings persisted as enduring patterns. Moreover, the set of learnings they used may have involved the redirection of orientations they had learned earlier, and the learning of ways to manage disparities between other sets of learnings. In instances such as these, the development of orientations requires selection among orientations learned from different socialization agents.

Our study further suggests that the selection of orientations is regulated by students' progress through the program as groups. For example, the program we studied filtered the development of orientations to the occupation through its methods of teaching skills and knowledge and its provision of a practicum whose effect was to regulate which set of learnings the students actually would use. Orientations to a place in the occupation were dependent on students' progress through the program, which enabled them to visualize places in the occupation with some degree of realism. Our findings support a view of development of orientations through the school's equipping students for the occupational role.

To see socialization as equipping persons for roles suggests a need to reexamine the idea that socialization is chiefly a matter of individuals' modeling their behavior on that of significant others. Role models may not always serve as major influences in the way that is sometimes attributed to them. Students do much more than simply imitate role models. When one sees imitation as the central socialization process, the student is implicitly regarded as the main determinant of the outcome: A good imitation produces a good outcome. Our findings indicated that controls within the program but outside the student regulated the nature and degree of acceptance of orientations and behaviors observed in potential role models. Individual students' relations to their faculty and program made them more likely to accept what was urged upon them but it did not appear independent of the program's overall influences, including its unintended ones.

Not only do our findings argue for rethinking the nature of the processes of socialization, they also suggest that conditions associated primarily with individual students will not enter significantly into the general pattern of equipping novices for occupational roles. The only individual relationships and attitudes that showed any systematic influence were to faculty and hospital training agents and to anticipated marriage and family roles. Contrary to some other studies, ours did not find that involvement in the student group or perceptual separation from other (nonnursing) students affected socialization except in collegial orientation. This being the case, the encasing of novices in a "total institution" to remove them from competing influences may be unnecessary. The role of professional student may coexist with a variety of other roles, such as coed in a university, without the other roles' interfering with professional development by the school's program. Homogeneity of entering students and cohesive student groups may provide opportunities for intense interaction and feelings, but we found no evidence that the student group or individuals' relations to it served as conduits for definitions of roles, evolved their own definitions, or sanctioned their own or anyone else's definitions. Nor did the roles of students as students provide long-run status options in the profession once they no longer would be students.

At the same time, anticipated future roles such as wife and mother influenced the development of orientations, often independently of current roles, and with no apparent possibility of regulation by the school. Students' anticipated commitment to family roles altered their orientations to places in nursing and their nursing career motivations.

Our findings suggest that if roles are temporary and not expected to be carried through life, they are not likely to have a lasting influence. Marital and family statuses endure. An educational program can have enduring effects because it controls access to occupational goals. But youthful friendships are transitory and appear to have little or no influence on orientations to work or the relation of the self to work.

Persistence of socialization across status transitions

A major question in the study of occupational socialization is whether behaviors, orientations, and motivations acquired in one situation persist when the individual moves to a new situation. Studies using the induction approach, as we have indicated in Chapter 1, see the continuity of the occupation and the normative obedience of its practitioners as resting largely on the persistence in practice of orientations and behaviors acquired during professional schooling. Reaction studies cast doubt on this assumption and emphasize that change in the individual's status from student to professional necessarily entails new adaptations. Our study, in contrast to most, followed students at least one year after their graduation and our findings may help to clarify issues involved in the continuity of behavior and orientations from schooling to work. We found that orientations persisted across the status transition from student to practitioner, but personal relatedness to nursing declined. This difference in persistence indicates again the multidimensionality of socialization and the need to distinguish its dimensions in analysis. The literature on continuity has addressed primarily orientations, apparently assuming that motivation persists.

In examining the transition from student to practitioner status, we found that students' orientations to activities of the nursing role and to a place in the occupation persisted unchanged or continued to develop in the directions initiated during education. The persistence was unrelated to type of work organization. These findings urge us to rethink the basis of continuity of socialization from one situation to another. Induction studies see the continuity as based on the internalization of norms and on the organization of the occupation in a way that ensures their persistence. Given this viewpoint, if continuity were observed it might simply be assumed to have resulted from internalized norms, with the continuity taken as a surrogate variable for the internalization that had supposedly caused it and no real evidence adduced to show the assumed causation. Neither have induction studies demonstrated the kind of collegial system that would be needed to guarantee the persistence of normatively prescribed orientations and behaviors; and what we found was that collegialism, an orientation to the occupational collectivity, was at no time sufficiently related to orientations to the occupational role to explain its persistence.

The view of the reaction studies, that orientations are adaptations to current situations, cannot explain the persistence of socialization when the situation had changed from that of student to that of professional nurse at work. Granted, this status transition may have brought less change in role options and power than occurs in occupations whose graduates move into positions with more authority than nurses have. But it is noteworthy that role options of the alumnae varied with the kinds of organizations in which they worked, yet type of organization was not related to the orientations of alumnae or to the persistence of orientations. Clearly, continuity of socialization did not rest on similarity of work settings or role alters to those the almunae had encountered in nursing school.

If continuity is not explained by peer pressures or by continuing types of relations with role alters, and has not been shown to result from internalization of norms, what then were its sources? It appears that it depended on the skills and knowledge the alumnae had learned as students. The students' education, particularly the hospital practicum, shifted their attention away from alters of the occupational role toward the self as initiator of behavior in the role. This shift effectively insulated a student from the person of the role alter; the alter became essentially an object of her action and an element of the situation in which she acted. Once this view of the self as the initiator of behavior has developed, we should not expect it to change with the transition from school to work or with any other status change. Ego, not alter, determines ego's actions. Alters may or may not approve of ego's actions with respect to them, but it is ego who has the license to act on the occupation's mandate. The license is derived from the skills and knowledge of the occupation. Our findings thus suggest that knowledge and skills, as the basis of the occupation's authority, are the essential conditions for the persistence of orientations to the occupational role.

This interpretation is consistent with the often-observed continuance of individuals' work habits even in rapidly changing occupations. People become attached to specific skills and types of knowledge, define them as giving the authority to choose appropriate behaviors and initiate action rather than react to others' expectations, and therefore keep doing things in accustomed ways even if the nature of the occupation – that is, the prevailing role expectations of alters – may have changed. The occupation changes primarily through the learning of new skills and knowledge, and the habituation to new behaviors, by successive generations of practitioners. The persistence of socialization in individuals may create problems for the occupation, and perhaps for its clients and other role alters, from aging practitioners' continued use of obsolete knowledge and skills.

Not only orientations to the occupational role, but also orientations to a place in the occupation persisted among the alumnae we studied. Variation in type of work organization did not alter the continuance of these orientations. The absence of a relationship of type of employing organization to orientations to a place in the occupation undoubtedly reflects an overarching, universally perceived mobility ladder within the field of nursing as a whole, which facilitates movement across kinds of work organizations in pursuit of the best job one can get. For the occupation, it increases labor mobility by preventing segregation of rigidly differentiated kinds of nurses in different kinds of organizations.

Unlike orientations, motivational processes of socialization were not continuous across the status transition from student to nurse. Occupational commitment reversed in direction, and attraction to nursing fell precipitously among alumnae. These findings point again to the separateness of the dimensions of socialization. Orientations are not sources of motivation to stay in the occupation, nor does the desire to remain in the occupation support the continuance of orientations. The dissipation of motivation during the first few years of work reminds us that work does not require strong attraction or commitment to its future pursuit; most kinds of work are day-to-day affairs and do not call for long-range plans or commitments.

Nevertheless, the decline in motivation bears on the general question of conditions that sustain work motivation. The decline seems to have had two sources, the erosion of initial enthusiasm and the shifting configurations of roles. Reality shock among beginning workers has been identified as the sudden realization that the actual work situation departs radically from students' preexisting images, and therefore as something that can be cushioned or eliminated by including a practicum in the educational program. In addition, there may be a more common process that accompanies entry into new statuses. In graduating from a professional school and attaining certification, students reach a goal they have worked long and hard to achieve. The event is exhilarating, not only because it is the capstone of years of effort, but perhaps even more because it celebrates the beginning of a new and long anticipated stage of life. The exhilaration reflects eagerness to undertake full-time work in the occupation. But the zest of attaining a status and embarking on its activities is worn away as one settles into the daily routines of the job, most of which soon come to seem rather ordinary and unexciting.

The humdrum routine of work seems insufficient, however, to explain the full extent of dissipation of work motivation we observed among alumnae nurses, who already had been prepared for some of it in the program's hospital practicum. The total life situation of these women seems to have changed after they graduated. It must be remembered that they graduated in the early 1960s, when the expectation of continuous full-time work by middle-class married women was less prevalent than it now is. Their move from school to work seems to have involved much more than a change of scene. It ended the regulation of their lives by the school's program and presented them with a variety of choices. Roles other than work, mainly marriage and family roles, were likely to provide the essential organizing scheme of their total configuration of roles. It is not surprising that a sharp decline in commitment to work accompanied their shift of attention to nonwork roles. The work of the young middle-class wife in the 1960s was widely regarded as only temporary, something to be done until children came along or the husband was able to provide the family's whole financial support; but by that time it was already the normal expectation that the wife would return to work when her children had begun school or grown up. The orientations of the women we studied equipped them well for such an expectation. Although their commitment to work declined, their orientations to work remained stable, so that they would be able to leave and reenter the labor force and adjust their work motivations to the succeeding stages of their life cycles.

These findings argue that any study of occupational socialization must take into account the relations of work roles to nonwork roles.

Implications for professional schools

Our findings hold a message for professional schools. They show that a professional school is more than a gateway to occupational practice. As Goode (1957) wrote, a professional school socializes its students in common occupational perspectives. It does so through its program and the experiences it organizes. Failure to socialize, like success in doing so, rests with the school and its program. Foremost among what students learn are the occupation's knowledge, skills, and approaches to work. If students are taught through practicums in real-life work organizations, they can learn to apply their education in work roles. In the practicums, students' orientations are developed around the technical skills and knowledge they apply in the work role. These orientations tell students how to conduct themselves in carrying out role responsibilities. Orientations are embedded in the work organization's routines and procedures, and students habituate themselves to them by following the routines. The focus of the orientations students develop through those experiences is on the use of the knowledge and skills. If practicums are restricted to homogeneous work organizations, little diversity in graduates' orientations should be expected.

Our findings on the acquisition of orientations suggest an adage: Lessons are retained if they are used to solve problems. Teachers influence their students by giving them problems to solve together with the technical knowledge to solve them. If students are only lectured to, they are likely to forget what they hear; but if they apply their lessons in work situations, they develop orientations toward the occupation. Once the orientations are learned, their endurance does not require continued work or the expectation of it. This is true because the orientations are adaptations to the use of knowledge and skills to do the occupation's work. They are cognitive guides carried by the certified professional. This conclusion goes beyond the view that work orientations relate workers to clients or co-workers. Very often they do, but the view fails to specify the base of the orientations. We see orientations not in workers' expectations of how to deal with alters' expectations, but in workers' relations to their knowledge and skills. The persistence of orientations need not depend on continuing interaction with role alters.

Our findings also underscore some observations in the reaction tradition, pertaining to motivation and problems related to it. Student motivation is typically seen as an individual problem: The good student works hard, is committed, and follows the advice of mentors. If a student is good, achievement results. The school treats motivation as an individual affair and seeks typically to ensure that students are motivated through selective recruiting of only those who are. A school carefully weighs its applicants to select only those properly motivated. Selective recruiting reduces heterogeneity of a student body and controls external sources of influence on students. All this is true and important in professional education but insufficient to explain motivation. Students' motivation is much affected by the program design: What options does the program permit? Is withdrawal costly and continuance profitable? Programs with few hurdles and wide options cannot expect to retain high percentages of their students. They are like sieves: Students can easily pour through them because they fail to direct the efforts of students toward concentrated lines of study and eventual use of what they are taught. If a school loses many of its students, the school's program, not its students, should be indicted.

A school can effectively commit its students to its occupation but fail to attract them. But to do so imperils the occupation. The occupation means little to unattracted workers. However well the workers may perform – and conceivably they could do better at rigidly defined jobs than attracted workers – they perform in their own names, or the name of the employing organization, not of the occupation. The pride of identity is lacking, robbing the occupation of a vital resource.

Implications for nursing

Our effort in this monograph has been to develop a synthetic model of socialization and to apply it in a case study of a school of nursing. It has not been to understand the socialization of nursing students as such, but to test the efficacy of our model. Nonetheless, our findings do suggests implications for nursing. They pertain to the organization of the occupation and to its labor force. Chapter 7 discussed discrepancies and tensions between collegiate nursing education and nursing service. Collegiate nursing education has led in the movement to professionalize nursing; it has gained control over nursing education, devised a curriculum intended to teach individualized patient care as a professional ideal, and stressed acquisition of a knowledge base for nursing work. This movement took place to counteract a contradictory trend occurring in nursing service. Nursing work has increasingly been bureaucratized in large hospitals. Its work roles emphasize tasks and the work of the hospital, not patients. Collegiate education sought to redirect attention from tasks to patients to accord with nursing ideals. An outcome, according to some writers, was a schism between nursing service and nursing education.

Our findings do not show a schism between nursing service and nursing education in the socialization of the Duke students. On paper the Duke program endorsed the ideology of professional nursing consisting of a holistic view of patients and individualized patient care, but students acquired orientations that were consistent with nursing roles in which they were trained in the hospital. The orientations they acquired prepared them to work in hospitals. Additionally, they learned to look with favor upon positions in nursing administration. The contradiction between the professional ideals of their school and the bureaucratic realities of hospital nursing, if faced by the students, was resolved in favor of the hospital.

The basis of the schism appears not to have lain in what students learned but between the educators and the hospital service. Its roots are in the movement of nursing education from hospital-controlled diploma programs to autonomous baccalaureate and associate degree programs. Interests of educators and practitioners differ in some ways but have some common elements. The common elements are likely to grow as more and more nursing supervisors and administrators are products of collegiate schools. Collegiate ties will bind educators and nursing administrators. These ties may become barriers that block mobility of diploma and associate degree program graduates into nursing administration. Nursing will become even more stratified, with baccalaureate nurses its elite.

Of the Duke graduates, 82.5 percent worked in hospitals during their first year after graduation. This percentage exceeded the percentage of a national sample of baccalaureate nurses who began their nursing education in 1962. In the national sample, 73.6 percent worked in hospitals (Knopf, 1975;16). The Duke graduates were mostly employed as staff nurses, but their work, as described by 67.4 percent, entailed mainly administrative, clerical, and supervisory duties. The departure from direct patient care, the ideal of the baccalaureate program, was not disparaged by Duke graduates; 64.6 percent selected administrative assignments as the most satisfying nursing assignments.

A second main implication of our findings for nursing pertains to the retention of baccalaureate graduates. The graduates' first jobs and their stated job preferences seemed destined to move them rapidly up the nursing administrative ladder. If their lives had involved only jobs, the jobs would undoubtedly have committed them to continous work. But that was not their desire. They expected to leave nursing to bear and rear children. This was true not only of Duke nurses but of baccalaureate nurses generally. Knopf (1975:21) found that five years after graduation only 49.3 percent of baccalaureate graduates who were full-time workers had had no interruptions, compared with 53.3 percent of associate degree and 58.0 percent of diploma graduates. Judging from these figures and the expectations of Duke graduates, the baccalaureate programs contribute proportionately the fewest graduates to the nursing labor force. This failure of baccalaureate nurses to work full time continuously should less likely be charged to their education than to the options the graduates have. As college graduates they marry husbands with higher earnings and are less financially restrained to stay in the labor force when their children are small. Nonetheless, the conclusion is inescapable that many resources used to educate baccalaureate nurses have not been returned in productive labor. With the increased participation of women in the labor force, it is of course possible that the dropout pattern of baccalaureate graduates, which exceeds that of other graduates, may be changing.

Epilogue

Twelve to fifteen years have passed since our panel classes graduated from Duke in 1963, 1964, and 1965. The alumnae now average between thirty-five and thirty-seven years of age. They are in the age bracket when the average woman has completed childbearing and has sent her youngest child to school. It is also the period in the life cycle when many women who left the labor force to have families reenter it. What are the Duke graduates doing? We were able to get some information on them from the Duke Alumni Office. The alumna membership card lists employment status and mailing address in addition to degree and year of graduation. Records were updated in 1976, so the information on the alumnae is fairly current.

The graduates from our panel classes numbered 160. Of these graduates, 91.3 percent are active alumnae. (An active alumna status means the office has a correct mailing address.) Their employment status is given in Table E-1. As we see, large numbers have not returned to work. As many are housewives as are employed full time in nursing and in other work – 39.0 percent. But significantly more are employed full time than hoped to be when they were freshmen. Whereas 48.3 percent wanted to work part time, in fact only 6.8 percent work part time. This low percentage is not due to lesser opportunities for part-time work, judging from Knopf's data. She found 14.6 percent of baccalaureate graduates working part time five years after graduation (Knopf, 1974: 12). The low percentage of Duke alumnae employed part time probably reflects their wishes; if they work, they are inclined toward full-time employment, and if not, they are housewives. Their aspirations as freshmen to divide their time between home and work have changed toward full-time work. In fact, this change was the biggest one between their earlier aspirations and their actual statuses.

Despite the fact that more are working full time than said they aspired to, their participation in the labor force, including part time, is below the average for their age bracket in 1970, when 51.0 percent of

Table E-1. *Employment status of alumnae and aspirations of freshmen twenty years after graduation (in percent)*

Statuses	Employment status of alumnae	Aspirations of freshmen[a]
Housewife	39.0	54.7
Part-time work	6.8	48.3
Work in nursing	36.3	–
Nonnursing work	2.7	–
No information	15.1	–

[a]Percentages do not add to 100 because responses are from separate questions. See Table 6-3 for the entire list of aspirations.

thirty-five- to forty-four-year-old women were in the labor force. Although more alumnae are working full time than aspired to be when they were freshmen, a larger percentage are housewives than anticipated being housewives when they were seniors. Only 28.9 percent of the seniors indicated they did not want to work after they had children (see Table 12-6), but 39.0 percent of the alumnae are housewives. Only five of the alumnae had mailing addresses in their own given names; we interpret this to mean that these were the only alumnae who were not married. Three of these five use the title Mrs. – probably they are divorced or separated – and one each uses the titles Miss and Ms. The familistic interests of the students seem to have directed their lives as alumnae. Some who are now housewives may reenter the labor force, but in all likelihood large numbers will remain housewives.

Of the alumnae who are working, most have remained in nursing. This fact is not surprising, but the extent of loyalty to nursing is. Most seniors who anticipated full-time work were not committed to nursing, and the already low level of commitment fell sharply among most graduates during the first year after graduation. Twelve to fifteen years later, only 2.7 percent had deserted nursing for other work. Family life seems to have been nursing's only serious competitor.

Appendix A. Correlation matrices of dependent variables for all pairs of academic classes, graduation panel

	Entering freshmen	Freshmen	Sopho-mores	Juniors	Seniors
Holistic view					
Entering freshmen	1.00	.31	.06	.06	.05
Freshmen		1.00	.28	.23	.23
Sophomores			1.00	.43	.38
Juniors				1.00	.37
Seniors					1.00
Individualized patient care					
Entering freshmen	1.00	.45	.47	.35	.25
Freshmen		1.00	.22	.32	.23
Sophomores			1.00	.27	.32
Juniors				1.00	.52
Seniors					1.00
Collegialism					
Entering freshmen	1.00	.43	.34	.25	.19
Freshmen		1.00	.51	.37	.29
Sophomores			1.00	.57	.42
Juniors				1.00	.50
Seniors					1.00
Administration and supervision					
Entering freshmen	1.00	.41	.32	.27	.12
Freshmen		1.00	.42	.21	.22
Sophomores			1.00	.48	.35
Juniors				1.00	.35
Seniors					1.00

239

	Entering freshmen	Freshmen	Sopho-mores	Juniors	Seniors
Status identi-fication					
Entering freshmen	1.00	.26	.17	−.03	−.03
Freshmen		1.00	.22	.16	.09
Sophomores			1.00	.34	.23
Juniors				1.00	.47
Seniors					1.00
Commitment					
Entering freshmen	1.00	.48	.18	.05	.16
Freshmen		1.00	.48	.25	.12
Sophomores			1.00	.40	.27
Juniors				1.00	.60
Seniors					1.00
Attraction					
Entering freshmen	1.00	.20	.20	.14	.10
Freshmen		1.00	.39	.29	.30
Sophomores			1.00	.28	.37
Juniors				1.00	.54
Seniors					1.00

Appendix B. Tables using three different samples

Appendix B gives tables on three samples of students based on the different aggregations described in Chapter 4. They correspond to the tables in Chapters 9 and 10, and include data from the tables in those chapters for easy comparison.

Table B-1. *Student orientations toward holistic view of the role of the nurse and toward individualized patient care, and faculty orientations toward holistic view of the role of the nurse (in percent)*

Nursing orientations	Faculty		Entering freshmen		Freshmen		Sophomores		Juniors		Seniors		Alumnae	
	%	(N)	%	(N)	%	(N)	%	(N)	%	(N)	%	(N)	%	(N)
Holistic view														
Cross-sectional sample	60.6	(33)	78.8	(511)	40.4	(451)	26.4	(329)	25.9	(251)	24.2	(236)		
Year-to-year individual cases[a]			79.0	(461)	39.4	(325)	27.4	(201)	26.0	(177)	24.3	(177)		
Graduation panel			80.5	(128)	50.0	(128)	27.3	(128)	21.9	(128)	23.4	(128)		
High individualized patient care														
Cross-sectional sample			66.0	(515)	60.7	(450)	60.8	(329)	46.5	(241)	34.0	(241)		
Year-to-year individual cases[a]			66.0	(462)	66.4	(324)	64.7	(201)	44.0	(175)	36.0	(175)		
Graduation panel			75.8	(128)	66.4	(128)	65.6	(128)	46.1	(128)	37.5	(128)		
Alumnae panel			76.4	(89)	69.7	(89)	64.0	(89)	44.9	(89)	38.2	(89)	25.8	(89)

[a] Individual cases, in this and other tables, are those who completed the academic year following the one in which the data shown were obtained. The cross-sectional sample includes all who were in the class and responded to the questionnaire at the time that it was administered. The graduation panel includes students who moved through the program and were observed in each academic year from entrance until shortly before graduation. The alumnae panel includes only students observed from entrance until at least one year after graduation. No data on holistic view are available for the alumnae panel.

Table B-2. *Yearly change in students' orientations toward holistic view of the role of the nurse for three samples (in percent)*

Holistic view orientations	Entering freshmen- freshmen	Freshmen- sophomores	Sophomores- juniors	Juniors- seniors
Year-by-year individual cases				
Stable holistic	45.9	40.6	38.2	45.7
Holistic to bureaucratic	54.1	59.4	61.8	54.4
(Total holistic)	(364)	(128)	(55)	(46)
Stable bureaucratic	80.4	82.2	81.5	83.2
Bureaucratic to holistic	19.6	17.8	18.5	16.8
(Total bureaucratic)	(97)	(197)	(146)	(131)
Graduation panel				
Stable holistic	54.4	40.6	42.9	53.6
Holistic to bureaucratic	45.6	59.4	57.1	46.4
(Total holistic)	(103)	(64)	(35)	(28)
Stable bureaucratic	68.0	85.9	86.0	83.0
Bureaucratic to holistic	32.0	14.1	14.0	17.0
(Total bureaucratic)	(25)	(64)	(93)	(100)
Alumnae panel				
Stable holistic	51.4	37.2	43.5	45.0
Holistic to bureaucratic	48.6	62.8	56.5	55.0
(Total holistic)	(70)	(43)	(23)	(20)
Stable bureaucratic	63.2	84.8	84.8	87.0
Bureaucratic to holistic	36.8	15.2	5.2	13.0
(Total bureaucratic)	(19)	(46)	(66)	(69)

Note: The base N's for percentages, in this table and in others, are the numbers who were high and who were low at the first of the two times.

Table B-3. *Yearly changes in students' orientations toward individualized patient care for three samples (in percent)*

Individualized patient care	Entering freshmen-freshmen	Freshmen-sophomores	Sophomores-juniors	Juniors-seniors
Year-by-year individual cases				
Stable low	63.7	55.0	71.8	82.7
Low to high	36.3	45.0	28.2	17.3
(Total low)	(157)	(109)	(71)	(98)
Stable high	73.4	68.8	58.5	59.7
High to low	26.6	31.2	41.5	40.3
(Total high)	(305)	(215)	(130)	(77)
Graduation panel				
Stable low	67.7	41.9	68.2	84.1
Low to high	32.3	58.1	31.8	15.9
(Total low)	(31)	(43)	(44)	(69)
Stable high	77.3	69.4	46.4	62.7
High to low	22.7	30.6	53.6	37.3
(Total high)	(97)	(85)	(84)	(59)
Alumnae panel				
Stable low	61.9	37.0	62.5	81.6
Low to high	38.1	63.0	37.5	18.4
(Total low)	(21)	(27)	(32)	(49)
Stable high	79.4	64.5	49.1	62.5
High to low	20.6	35.5	50.9	37.5
(Total high)	(68)	(62)	(57)	(40)

Table B-4. Percent highly favorable toward collegialism and toward administration and supervision by academic class, three samples

	Entering freshmen		Freshmen		Sophomores		Juniors		Seniors		Alumnae	
	%	(N)	%	(N)	%	(N)	%	(N)	%	(N)	%	(N)
Collegialism												
Cross-sectional sample	48.9	(515)	40.0	(450)	50.9	(332)	50.4	(236)	65.6	(241)		
Year-to-year individual cases	48.9	(462)	40.4	(324)	52.2	(201)	49.7	(175)	64.6	(175)		
Graduation panel	52.3	(128)	36.7	(128)	50.0	(128)	46.9	(128)	64.8	(128)		
Alumnae panel	48.3	(89)	36.0	(89)	47.2	(89)	46.1	(89)	65.2	(89)	61.8	(89)
Administration and supervision												
Cross-sectional sample	61.6	(516)	51.2	(450)	60.3	(303)	56.4	(236)	76.0	(242)		
Year-to-year individual cases	60.0	(463)	52.9	(325)	59.4	(202)	54.3	(175)	75.4	(175)		
Graduation panel	64.8	(128)	50.0	(128)	58.6	(128)	51.6	(128)	71.1	(128)		
Alumnae panel	66.3	(89)	53.9	(89)	57.3	(89)	48.3	(89)	68.5	(89)	84.3	(89)

Table B-5. *Yearly change in orientation toward collegialism for three samples (in percent)*

Occupational collegialism orientations	Entering freshmen-freshmen	Freshmen-sophomores	Sophomores-juniors	Juniors-seniors
Year-by-year individual cases				
Stable low	81.8	69.4	77.1	58.0
Low to high	18.2	30.6	22.9	42.0
(Total low)	(236)	(193)	(96)	(88)
Stable high	64.2	80.9	71.4	87.4
High to low	35.8	19.1	28.6	12.6
(Total high)	(226)	(131)	(105)	(87)
Graduation panel				
Stable low	85.2	66.7	79.7	57.4
Low to high	14.8	33.3	20.3	42.6
(Total low)	(61)	(81)	(64)	(68)
Stable high	56.7	78.7	73.4	90.0
High to low	43.3	21.3	26.6	10.0
(Total high)	(67)	(47)	(64)	(60)
Alumae panel				
Stable low	82.6	70.2	83.0	60.4
Low to high	17.4	29.8	17.0	39.6
(Total low)	(46)	(57)	(47)	(48)
Stable high	55.8	78.1	78.6	95.1
High to low	44.2	21.9	21.4	4.9
(Total high)	(43)	(32)	(42)	(41)

Table B-6. *Yearly change in orientations toward administration and supervision for three samples (in percent)*

Administration and supervison	Entering freshmen-freshmen	Freshmen-sophomores	Sophomores-juniors	Juniors-seniors
Year-by-year individual cases				
Stable low	70.8	58.8	65.9	40.0
Low to high	29.2	41.2	34.1	60.0
(Total low)	(185)	(153)	(82)	(80)
Stable high	65.1	76.2	70.0	88.4
High to low	34.9	23.8	30.0	11.6
(Total high)	(278)	(172)	(120)	(95)
Graduation panel				
Stable low	75.6	60.9	68.5	43.5
Low to high	24.4	39.1	31.5	56.5
(Total low)	(45)	(64)	(54)	(62)
Stable high	63.9	76.6	66.2	84.8
High to low	36.1	23.4	33.8	15.2
(Total high)	(83)	(64)	(74)	(66)
Alumnae panel				
Stable low	73.3	70.7	71.1	47.8
Low to high	26.7	29.3	28.9	52.2
(Total low)	(30)	(41)	(38)	(46)
Stable high	67.8	81.3	62.7	86.0
High to low	32.2	18.8	37.3	14.0
(Total high)	(59)	(48)	(51)	(43)

Table B-7. Students' identification with the status of nurse by academic class for four samples (in percent)

Status identi-fication (high)	Entering freshmen		Freshmen		Sophomores		Juniors		Seniors	
	%	(N)	%	(N)	%	(N)	%	(N)	%	(N)
Cross-sectional sample	26.8	(508)	53.3	(473)	84.5	(336)	93.7	(254)	94.3	(246)
Year-to-year individual cases	27.3	(451)	57.2	(320)	90.0	(200)	93.7	(174)	94.8	(174)
Graduation panel	20.3	(128)	55.5	(128)	89.8	(128)	93.8	(128)	93.8	(128)
Alumnae panel	18.0	(89)	52.8	(89)	89.9	(89)	92.1	(89)	93.3	(89)

Table B-8. *Yearly change in identification with the status of nurse for three samples (in percent)*

	Entering freshmen-freshmen	Freshmen-sophomores	Sophomores-juniors	Juniors-seniors
Year-by-year individual cases				
Stable low	54.0	21.2	30.0	45.5
Low to high	46.0	78.8	70.0	54.5
(Total low)	(328)	(137)	(20)	(11)
Stable high	69.9	91.3	96.7	97.5
High to low	30.1	8.7	3.3	2.5
(Total high)	(123)	(183)	(180)	(163)
Graduation panel				
Stable low	51.0	17.5	30.8	50.0
Low to high	49.0	82.5	69.2	50.0
(Total low)	(102)	(57)	(13)	(8)
Stable high	80.8	95.8	96.5	96.7
High to low	19.2	4.2	3.5	3.3
(Total high)	(26)	(71)	(115)	(120)
Alumnae panel				
Stable low	50.7	16.7	44.4	57.1
Low to high	49.3	83.3	55.6	42.9
(Total low)	(73)	(42)	(9)	(7)
Stable high	68.8	95.7	96.3	97.6
High to low	31.3	4.3	3.8	2.4
(Total high)	(16)	(47)	(80)	(82)

Table B-9. *Percent high commitment to the role of the nurse by academic class for four samples (in percent)*

High commitment to the role of nurse	Entering freshmen %	(N)	Freshmen %	(N)	Sophomores %	(N)	Juniors %	(N)	Seniors %	(N)	Alumnae %	(N)
Cross-sectional sample	39.7	(516)	36.9	(450)	43.3	(330)	58.5	(236)	66.9	(242)		
Year-to-year individual cases	41.7	(463)	40.0	(325)	51.0	(202)	59.4	(175)	66.9	(175)		
Graduation panel	42.2	(128)	41.4	(128)	53.9	(128)	64.1	(128)	67.2	(128)		
Alumnae panel	42.7	(89)	40.4	(89)	60.7	(89)	65.2	(89)	70.8	(89)	28.1	(89)

Table B-10. *Yearly change in commitment to the role of nurse for three samples (in percent)*

	Entering freshmen-freshmen	Freshmen-sophomores	Sophomores-juniors	Juniors-seniors
Year-by-year individual cases				
Stable low	80.4	70.3	60.6	59.3
Low to high	19.6	29.7	39.4	40.8
(Total low)	(270)	(195)	(99)	(71)
Stable high	60.1	63.8	80.6	84.6
High to low	39.9	36.2	19.4	15.4
(Total high)	(193)	(130)	(103)	(104)
Graduation panel				
Stable low	77.0	65.3	52.5	63.0
Low to high	23.0	34.7	47.5	37.0
(Total low)	(74)	(75)	(59)	(46)
Stable high	66.7	81.1	78.3	84.1
High to low	33.3	18.9	21.7	15.9
(Total high)	(54)	(53)	(69)	(82)
Alumnae panel				
Stable low	72.5	56.6	54.3	61.3
Low to high	27.5	43.4	45.7	38.7
(Total low)	(51)	(53)	(35)	(31)
Stable high	57.9	86.1	77.8	87.9
High to low	42.1	13.9	22.2	12.1
(Total high)	(38)	(36)	(54)	(58)

Table B-11. Attraction to nursing by academic class for four samples (in percent)

High attraction to nursing	Entering freshmen		Freshmen		Sophomores		Juniors		Seniors		Alumnae	
	%	(N)	%	(N)	%	(N)	%	(N)	%	(N)	%	(N)
Cross-sectional sample	35.1	(516)	34.7	(450)	33.3	(330)	30.1	(236)	26.9	(242)		
Year-to-year individual cases	36.5	(463)	37.5	(325)	38.1	(202)	32.6	(175)	28.0	(175)		
Graduation panel	43.0	(128)	39.1	(128)	35.9	(128)	36.7	(128)	30.5	(128)		
Alumnae panel	44.9	(89)	41.6	(89)	39.3	(89)	39.3	(89)	32.6	(89)	10.1	(89)

Table B-12. *Yearly change in attraction to nursing for three samples (in percent)*

	Entering freshmen-freshmen	Freshmen-sophomores	Sophomores-juniors	Juniors-seniors
Year-by-year individual cases				
Stable low	78.2	77.8	79.2	83.1
Low to high	21.8	22.2	20.8	16.9
(Total low)	(294)	(203)	(125)	(118)
Stable high	56.8	53.3	53.2	50.9
High to low	43.2	46.7	46.8	49.1
(Total high)	(169)	(122)	(77)	(57)
Graduation panel				
Stable low	69.9	76.9	76.8	81.5
Low to high	30.1	23.1	23.2	18.5
(Total low)	(73)	(78)	(82)	(81)
Stable high	50.9	56.0	60.9	51.1
High to low	49.1	44.0	39.1	48.9
(Total high)	(55)	(50)	(46)	(47)
Alumnae panel				
Stable low	67.3	76.9	75.9	81.5
Low to high	32.7	23.1	24.1	18.5
(Total low)	(49)	(52)	(54)	(54)
Stable high	52.5	62.2	62.9	54.3
High to low	47.5	37.8	37.1	45.7
(Total high)	(40)	(37)	(35)	(35)

Appendix C. Mean scores and standard deviations
for all socialization processes, graduation panel

Table C-1. Mean scores and standard deviations for all socialization processes, graduation panel

	Entering freshmen		Freshmen		Sophomores		Juniors		Seniors	
	M	SD	M	SD	M	SD	M	SD	M	SD
Orientations										
Holistic views	4.9	1.4	3.5	1.6	2.5	1.6	2.6	1.4	2.3	1.4
Individualized patient care	4.4	1.4	4.0	1.5	3.9	1.3	3.2	1.4	2.8	1.5
Collegialism	2.5	1.5	2.0	1.4	2.3	1.4	2.3	1.2	2.9	1.3
Supervision and administration	2.7	1.3	2.3	1.4	2.6	1.5	2.6	1.5	3.1	1.4
Relatedness to nursing										
Status identification	.2	.4	.6	.5	.9	.3	.9	.2	.9	.2
Commitment	3.2	1.8	3.2	1.9	3.7	1.9	3.9	2.0	4.0	1.9
Attraction	3.5	1.1	3.4	1.1	3.3	1.1	3.0	1.4	2.8	1.3

References

Alutto, Joseph A., Lawrence G. Hrebiniak, and Ramon C. Alonso, 1973. "On Operationalizing the Concept of Commitment." *Social Forces* 51 (June): 448-54.

American Nurses' Association, 1965. "American Nurses' Association's First Position Paper on Education for Nursing." *American Journal of Nursing* 65 (December): 106-11.

——— 1966. *Facts About Nursing: A Statistical Summary.* New York: American Nurses' Association.

——— 1977. *Facts About Nursing, 1976-77.* Kansas City, Mo.: American Nurses' Association.

Banfield, Edward C., 1970. *The Unheavenly City.* Boston: Little, Brown.

Barnard, Chester I., 1938. *The Functions of the Executive.* Cambridge, Mass.: Harvard University Press.

Becker, Howard S., 1960. "Notes on the Concept of Commitment." *American Journal of Sociology* 66 (July): 32-40.

——— 1963. *Outsiders.* New York: Free Press.

——— 1964. "Personal Change in Adult Life." *Sociometry* 27 (March): 40-53.

Becker, Howard S., and James W. Carper, 1956. "The Development of Identification with an Occupation." *American Sociological Review* 61 (June): 289-98.

Becker, Howard S., and Blanche Geer, 1958. "The Fate of Idealism in Medical School." *American Sociological Review* 23 (February): 50-6.

Becker, Howard S., Blanche Geer, Everett C. Hughes, and Anselm L. Strauss, 1961. *Boys in White.* Chicago: University of Chicago Press.

Becker, Howard S., and Anselm L. Strauss, 1956. "Careers, Personality, and Adult Socialization." *American Journal of Sociology* 62 (November): 253-63.

Bloom, Samuel W., 1965. "The Sociology of Medical Education: Some Comments on the State of a Field." *Milbank Memorial Fund Quarterly* 43 (April): 143-84.

——— 1973. *Power and Dissent in the Medical School.* New York: Free Press.

Bressler, Marvin, and William M. Kephart, 1955. *Career Dynamics.* Harrisburg: Pennsylvania Nurses' Association.

Brim, Orville G., 1966. "Socialization through the Life Cycle." In Orville G. Brim and Stanton Wheeler, eds., *Socialization After Childhood,* 1-49. New York: Wiley.

Broom, Leonard, and Philip Selznick, 1973. *Sociology.* 5th ed. New York: Harper & Row.

Brown, Esther Lucile, 1966. "Nursing and Patient Care." In Fred Davis, ed., *The Nursing Profession: Five Sociological Essays,* 176-203. New York: Wiley.

Bucher, Rue, and Anselm L. Strauss, 1961. "Professions in Process." *American Journal of Sociology* 66 (January): 325-34.

Bureau of Health Professions Education and Manpower Training, Department of Health, Education and Welfare, Public Health Service, 1969. *Health Manpower Source Book, Section 2 - Nursing Personnel.* rev. ed. Public Health Service Publication No. 263. Washington, D.C.: U.S. Government Printing Office.

Carlin, Jerome E., 1962. *Lawyers on Their Own.* New Brunswick, N.J.: Rutgers University Press.

Davis, James A., 1964. *Great Aspirations.* Chicago: Aldine.

——— 1965. *Undergraduate Career Decisions.* Chicago: Aldine.

Davis, Fred, and Virginia L. Olesen, 1963. "Initiation into a Women's Profession: Identity Problems in the Transition of Coed to Student Nurse." *Sociometry* 26 (March):89-101.

Davis, Fred, Virginia L. Olesen, and Elvi Waik Whittaker, 1966. "Problems and Issues in Collegiate Nursing Education." In Fred Davis, ed., *The Nursing Profession: Five Sociological Essays*, 138-75. New York: Wiley.

Donovan, Frances R., 1920. *The Woman Who Waits*. Boston: R. G. Badger.

   1929. *The Saleslady*. Chicago: University of Chicago Press.

   1938. *The Schoolma'am*. New York: Frederick A. Stokes.

Dornbusch, Sanford M., 1955. "The Military Academy as an Assimilating Institution." *Social Forces* 33 (May): 316-21.

Duncan, Otis Dudley, 1961. "A Socio-Economic Index for all Occupations." In Albert J. Reiss, Jr., *Occupations and Social Status*, 109-138. New York: Free Press.

Durkheim, Emile, 1951. *Suicide*. 2d. ed. Trans. by John A. Spaulding and George E. Simpson. Glencoe, Ill.: Free Press. (Original 1897)

   1964. *The Division of Labor in Society*. 3d. ed. Trans. by George E. Simpson. Glencoe, Ill.: Free Press. (Original 1902)

Elliott, Philip, 1972. *The Sociology of the Professions*. New York: Herder and Herder.

Epstein, Cynthia Fuchs, 1970. *Woman's Place: Options and Limits in Professional Careers*. Berkeley: University of California Press.

Etzioni, Amitai, 1961. *A Comparative Analysis of Complex Organizations*. New York: Free Press.

   1964. *Modern Organizations*. Englewood Cliffs, N.J.: Prentice-Hall.

Fox, Renée C., 1957. "Training for Uncertainty." In Robert K. Merton, George G. Reader, M.D., and Patricia L. Kendall, eds., *The Student-Physician*, 207-41. Cambridge, Mass.: Harvard University Press.

Freidson, Eliot, 1970. *The Profession of Medicine*. New York: Dodd, Mead.

Glenn, Norval, 1977. *Cohort Analysis*. Beverly Hills, Calif.: Sage Publications.

Goffman, Erving, 1961. *Encounters*. Indianapolis: Bobbs-Merrill.

Goldsen, Rose K., Morris Rosenberg, Robin M. Williams, Jr., and Edward A. Suchman, 1960. *What College Students Think*. Princeton, N.J.: Van Nostrand.

Goode, William J., 1957. "Community Within a Community: The Professions." *American Sociological Review* 22 (April): 194-200.

   1969. "The Theoretical Limits of Professionalization." In Amitai Etzioni, ed., *The Semi-Professions and Their Organization*, 266-313. New York: Free Press.

Gouldner, Alvin W., 1962. "Anti-Minotaur: The Myth of a Value-Free Sociology." *Social Problems* 9 (Winter): 199-213.

Habenstein, Robert W., and Edwin A. Christ, 1963. *Professionalizer, Traditionalizer, and Utilizer*. Columbia, Mo.: Department of Sociology, University of Missouri.

Hall, Oswald W., 1949. "Types of Medical Careers." *American Journal of Sociology* 55 (November): 243-53.

Hilfer, Anthony Channell, 1969. *The Revolt from the Village*. Chapel Hill, N.C.: University of North Carolina Press.

Hirschi, Travis, 1969. *Causes of Delinquency*. Berkeley: University of California Press.

Holley, John W., 1971. "Professional Socialization in Graduate School." Paper presented at the annual meeting of the Southern Sociological Society.

Homans, George, C., 1950. *The Human Group*. New York: Harcourt, Brace.

Hughes, Everett C., 1945. "Dilemmas and Contradictions of Status." *American Journal of Sociology* 50 (March): 453-9.

   1955. "The Making of a Physician." *Human Organization* 14 (Winter): 21-5.

   1958. *Men and Their Work*. Glencoe, Ill.: Free Press.

   1961. "Education for a Profession." *The Library Quarterly* 31 (October): 336-43.

Hughes, Everett C., Helen McGill Hughes, and Irwin Deutscher, 1958. *Twenty Thousand Nurses Tell Their Story.* Philadelphia: Lippincott.

Huntington, Mary Jean, 1957. "The Development of a Professional Self-Image." In Robert K. Merton, George G. Reader, M.D., and Patricia L. Kendall, eds., *The Student-Physician,* 179–87. Cambridge, Mass.: Harvard University Press.

Kadushin, Charles, 1969. "The Professional Self-Concept of Music Students." *American Journal of Sociology* 75 (November): 389–404.

Kanter, Rosabeth Moss, 1972. *Community and Commitment.* Cambridge, Mass.: Harvard University Press.

Kendall, Patricia L., and Hanan C. Selvin, 1957. "Tendencies toward Specialization in Medical Training." In Robert K. Merton, George G. Reader, M.D., and Patricia L. Kendall, eds., *The Student-Physician,* 153–74. Cambridge, Mass.: Harvard Universtiy Press.

Knopf, Lucille, 1975. *RN's: One and Five Years After Graduation.* New York: National League for Nursing (Pub. No. 19-1535).

Levenson, Bernard, 1968. "Panel Studies." In David L. Sills, ed., *International Encyclopedia of the Social Sciences.* Vol. 11. New York: Macmillan and the Free Press.

Lortie, Dan C., 1959. "Laymen to Lawmen: Law School, Careers, and Professional Socialization." *Harvard Educational Review* 29 (Fall): 363–7.

McKinney, John C., and Thelma Ingles, 1959. "The Professionalization Process in Nursing." *Nursing Outlook* 7 (June): 365–8.

McPartland, Thomas S., 1957. "Formal Education and the Process of Professionalization: A Study of Student Nurses" (mimeographed). Kansas City, Mo.: Community Studies, Inc., Publication 107 (March).

Martin, Harry W., and Ida Harper Simpson, 1956. *Patterns of Psychiatric Nursing: A Study of Psychiatric Nursing in North Carolina.* Chapel Hill, N.C.: Institute for Research in Social Science, University of North Carolina.

Mauksch, Hans O., 1972. "Nursing: Churning for a Change?" In Howard E. Freeman, Sol Levine, and Leo G., Reeder, eds., *Handbook of Medical Sociology.* 2d. ed., 206–30. Englewood Cliffs, N.J.: Prentice-Hall.

Merton, Robert K., 1949. *Social Theory and Social Structure.* Glencoe, Ill.: Free Press.
    1957. *Social Theory and Social Structure.* Rev. ed. Glencoe, Ill.: Free Press.
    1957. "Some Preliminaries to a Sociology of Medical Education." In Robert K. Merton, George G. Reader, M.D., Patricia L. Kendall, eds., *The Student-Physician,* 3–79. Cambridge, Mass.: Harvard University Press.

Merton, Robert K., and Alice S. Kitt, 1950. "Contributions to the Theory of Reference Group Behavior." In Robert K. Merton and Paul F. Lazarsfeld, eds., *Continuities in Social Research: Studies in the Scope and Method of "The American Soldier,"* 40–105. New York: Free Press.

Merton, Robert K., George G. Reader, M.D., and Patricia Kendall, eds., 1957. *The Student-Physician.* Cambridge, Mass.: Harvard University Press.

Miller, Kenneth, 1967. "The Reluctant Professional," unpublished manuscript. Atlanta, Ga.: Emory University.

Mills, C. Wright, 1953. *White Collar.* New York: Oxford University Press.

Morris, Richard T., and Basil J. Sherlock, 1971. "Decline of Ethics and the Rise of Cynicism in Dental School." *Journal of Health and Social Behavior* 2 (December): 290–9.

Mumford, Emily, 1970. *Interns: From Students to Physicians.* Cambridge, Mass.: Harvard University Press.

National Committee for the Improvement of Nursing Service, 1950. *Nursing Schools at the Mid-Century.* New York: American Nurses' Association.

Olesen, Virginia L., and Elvi W. Whittaker, 1968. *The Silent Dialogue.* San Francisco: Jossey-Bass.
    1970. "Critical Notes on Sociological Studies of Professional Socialization." In J. A. Jack-

son, ed., *Professions and Professionalization*, 181–221. Cambridge, England: Cambridge University Press.

Oppenheimer, Valerie Kincade, 1970. *The Female Labor Force in the United States.* Population Monograph Series, No. 5. Berkeley: University of California.

Parsons, Talcott, 1939. "The Professions and Social Structure." *Social Forces* 17 (May): 457–67.

Rogers, David E., 1977. "The Challenge of Primary Care." *Daedalus*, Vol. 106 (Winter): 81–103.

Rosenberg, Morris, with the assistance of Edward A. Suchman and Rose K. Goldsen, 1957. *Occupations and Values.* Glencoe, Ill.: Free Press.

Rossi, Alice S., 1965. "Barriers to the Career Choice of Engineering, Medicine, or Science Among American Women." In Jacquelyn A. Mattfeld and Carol Van Aken, eds., *Women and the Scientific Professions*, 51–127. Cambridge, Mass.: M.I.T. Press.

Roth, Aleda V., and Alice R. Walden, 1974. *The Nation's Nurses: 1972 Inventory of Registered Nurses.* Kansas City, Mo.: American Nurses' Association.

Sherlock, Basil J., and Richard T. Morris, 1967. "The Evolution of the Professional: A Paradigm." *Sociological Inquiry* 37 (Winter): 27–46.

Simpson, Richard L., and Ida Harper Simpson, 1960. "Values, Personal Influence, and Occupational Choice." *Social Forces* 39 (December): 116–25.

1969. "Women and Bureaucracy in the Semi-Professions." In Amitai Etzioni, ed., *The Semi-Professions and Their Organization*, 196–265. New York: Free Press.

Smith, Harvey L., 1955. "Two Lines of Authority Are One Too Many." *Modern Hospital* 84 (March): 59–64.

Smuts, Robert W., 1959. *Women and Work in America.* New York: Columbia University Press.

Strauss, Anselm L., 1966. "Structure and Ideology of the Nursing Profession." In Fred Davis, ed., *The Nursing Profession: Five Sociological Essays*, 60–104. New York: Wiley.

Surgeon General's Consultant Group on Nursing, U.S. Public Health Service, 1963. *Toward Quality in Nursing: Needs and Goals.* U.S. Public Health Service Publication No. 992. Washington, D.C.: U.S. Government Printing Office.

Sutherland, Edwin H., 1937. *The Professional Thief.* Chicago: University of Chicago Press.

Thibaut, John W., and Harold H. Kelley, 1959. *The Social Psychology of Groups.* New York: Wiley.

U.S. Bureau of Census, 1963. *U.S. Census of the Population, 1960.* PC (2)-7E. Washington, D.C.: U.S. Government Printing Office.

U.S. Bureau of Health Resources Development, Division of Nursing, 1974. *Source Book: Nursing Personnel*, DHEW Publication No. (HRA) 75-43. Bethesda, Md.: U.S. Department of Health, Education and Welfare, Public Health Service, Health Resources Administration. December.

Warnecke, Richard B., 1966. *Drop-Outs from Collegiate Nursing: A Typological Study of Role Conflict.* Unpublished Ph.D. dissertation. Department of Sociology, Duke University, Durham, N.C.

Wheeler, Stanton, 1966. "The Structure of Formally Organized Socialization Settings." In Orville G. Brim and Stanton Wheeler, eds., *Socialization After Childhood*, 51–116. New York: Wiley.

Wilensky, Harold L., 1964. "The Professionalization of Everyone?" *American Journal of Sociology* 70 (September): 137–58.

Wright, Charles R., 1967. "Changes in the Occupational Commitment of Graduate Sociology Students: A Research Note." *Sociological Inquiry* 37 (Winter): 55–62.

Wrong, Dennis H., 1961. "The Oversocialized Conception of Man in Modern Sociology." *American Sociological Review* 26 (April): 183–93.

Zeisel, Hans, 1957. *Say It with Figures* (5th rev. ed.). New York: Harper.

Index